APOSTLE ISLANDS
WATER TRIPS

AN EXPLORER'S GUIDE
2ND EDITION

JOHN C. FRANK

trails books

AN IMPRINT OF BOWER HOUSE

DENVER

FRIENDS *of the*
APOSTLE ISLANDS
NATIONAL LAKESHORE

Apostle Islands Water Trips: An Explorer's Guide, 2nd Edition. Copyright © 2021 by John C. Frank. All rights reserved. No part of this book may be used or reproduced in any manner whatsoever without written permission except in the case of brief quotations embodied in critical articles and reviews. For information contact Bower House.

BowerHouseBooks.com

Cover design by Margaret McCullough
Interior design by D. Kari Luraas
Cover photograph © Don Hynek

Printed in Canada

Library of Congress Control Number: 2021934971
ISBN 978-1-934553-83-1

10 9 8 7 6 5 4 3 2 1

To my grandchildren
May they continue to enjoy air so clean and water so pure
when they reach my age.

And to Paul Matteoni, whose spirit and wit remain with us after his
passing.

Contents

Acknowledgments vii
Apostle Islands map viii
Introduction to the Apostle Islands National Lakeshore 1
Kayakers: Getting on the Water 10
Camping at the Apostles 22

The Islands

Basswood	36	Oak	108
Bear	43	Otter	116
Cat	50	Outer	121
Devils	55	Raspberry	131
Hermit	61	Rocky	140
Ironwood	69	Sand	147
Long	74	South Twin	156
Madeline	81	Stockton	161
Manitou	88	York	169
Michigan	94	Mawikwe Bay/Meyers Beach	
North Twin	103	(Mainland Unit)	174

Notes 180
Resources 181

Acknowledgments

This book was completed thanks to the help of my friends who have given me memories, photographs, and spiritual support.

My best friend and wife, Signe, had the courage to try a new sport at a time when others might have crawled into a protective cocoon, thereby introducing me to kayaking and the Apostle Islands National Lakeshore. Over the years her view of my competence at paddling and camping always seemed higher than my own, but she helped me build my level of confidence, especially for the solo trips.

Bob Mohelnitzky has always been ready for another adventure, whether on the Wisconsin River, in the Boundary Waters, at Isle Royale, or in the Apostle Islands. His irreverent sense of humor usually has me laughing uncontrollably even before we depart from the driveway on a trip.

Karen and Paul Matteoni have been doing the planning and logistics for group trips for over twenty-five years. Thanks for allowing me to be one of the many paddlers who have enjoyed your trips and planning skills. Paul has passed away since the first printing of this book, but his memory remains with us.

Don Hynek (book writer, ice climber, and paddler, among other things) first discussed writing an Apostle Islands guidebook with me about ten years ago. I regret that we never quite got around to doing it together, but I owe Don a great deal of thanks for the advice and his unending quest for another paddling adventure. Some of the best pictures in this book were taken by him and his wife, Joy Chen, on their summer and winter trips to the Apostles.

Robert Rolley brings the interesting and contemplative point of view of a wildlife ecologist with him on a kayak camping trip. One of my lasting memories of a trip with Robert and Don is observing a black bear working its way along a Lake Nipigon shoreline (toward our camp?). Pictures taken by him and of him are among my favorites.

Verification of flora species as well as a sharp wit on several trips was provided by James Busse. I trust his identifications because, after all, he is a doctor.

Thanks to Mark Weller for the pictures, the interest in the project, and the encouragement. His series of lighthouse pictures, given freely to the Friends of the Apostle Islands National Lakeshore, inspired my own donation of royalties.

Thanks to the National Park Service for the photographs and particularly to Neil Howk who helped choose pictures for this book, and who, with Justin Olsen, helped to keep the updated 2021 edition factually correct and current.

Bob Mackreth's blog, experience, and wisdom helped provide legitimacy and substance to some of the side stories related to my trip experiences in the Apostle Island National Lakeshore.

And finally, thanks to the original editor, Mira Perrizo, and her staff for their competent and friendly help on the first edition in 2015, and to the folks at Bower House, Derek Lawrence and Caleb Seeling, for their help in the production of this 2021 update.

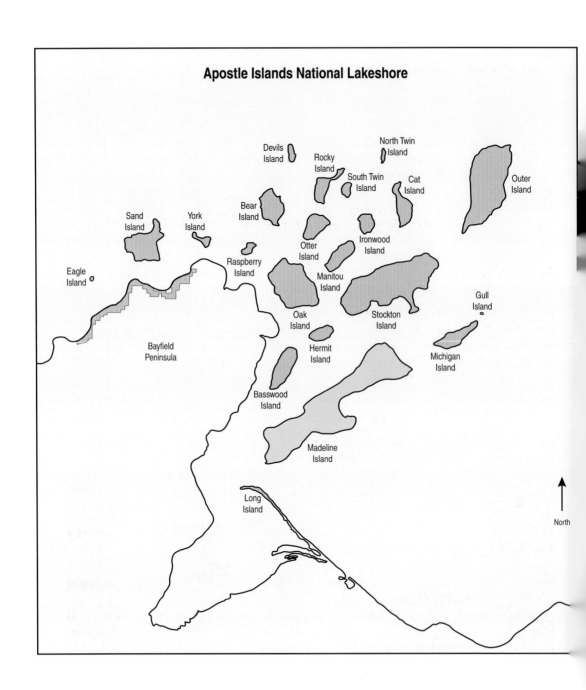

Apostle Islands National Lakeshore

Devils Island

North Twin Island

Rocky Island

South Twin Island

Cat Island

Outer Island

Sand Island

York Island

Bear Island

Eagle Island

Raspberry Island

Otter Island

Ironwood Island

Manitou Island

Gull Island

Bayfield Peninsula

Oak Island

Stockton Island

Hermit Island

Michigan Island

Basswood Island

Madeline Island

Long Island

North

Introduction

The Islands— Then and Now

The early twenty-first century visitor to the Apostle Islands National Lakeshore will find a near wilderness experience on most of the islands in the archipelago. Sure, there are campsites, hiking trails, ranger stations, docks, and lighthouses maintained by National Park Service (NPS) staff and volunteers. But away from the areas used by humans, the islands are increasingly reverting back to their physical condition of three hundred years ago.

Compared to the long-term history of the islands, the relatively short three hundred–year occupation by people of European descent has left numerous marks on the islands. Some of the landmark changes from the last three hundred years are being maintained and improved by the NPS. Nine light towers (including two on Long Island and two on Michigan), once tended by full time keepers,

lie within the National Lakeshore. Eight of them still send light from the shorelines of the islands to aid navigation. On the south shore of Manitou Island, a fishing camp, now on the National Register of Historic Places, has been restored by the NPS to look like it did in the 1940s.

However, other changes made by the Europeans are rusting away and decaying, allowing for wilderness reclamation by the forest and lake. On Sand Island, the trail between the East Bay campsites and the lighthouse passes the remains of two old cars, one of them, a 1930 Chevy Coupe, was owned by Gertrude Wellisch, a school teacher who rented the abandoned lighthouse from the federal government from 1925 to 1943. At the other end of the archipelago, decaying pieces of equipment and buildings are all that remain at the Lullabye Furniture logging camp, operated until the mid-1950s on the northeastern shore of Outer Island.

Original Michigan lighthouse, the first in the Apostles (photo by author).

Boat and net drying rack at Manitou Fish Camp (photo by Paul Matteoni).

Sand Island parking lot (photo by author).

Building at Lullabye Logging Camp on Outer Island (photo courtesy National Park Service).

Basswood Island quarry (photo courtesy National Park Service).

Some markers from the European period are slower to disappear. Sandstone quarries perch near the water's edge on Basswood, Hermit, and Stockton Islands, and underwater enthusiasts can explore shipwrecks, preserved by the cold waters of Lake Superior, at several locations along the mainland coast and off Sand, Outer, and Stockton Islands.

There are still some private land leases within the National Lakeshore on Sand Island and Rocky Island. The life estates were reserved at the time that the federal government acquired ownerhip in the 1970s. Eventually the private leases will expire and all of the properties will be under National Park Service management.

Prior to the European occupation of the islands, there is archeological evidence of archaic native people who may have followed the receding glacier north eleven thousand years ago, although artifacts from such early periods may be limited on the Apostle Islands themselves because of the fluctuating lake levels in Lake Superior and its predecessors. Carbon dating from an ancient campsite on Stockton Island indicated human occupation about five thousand years ago.[1]

More recently, oral tradition indicates that the Ojibwe migrated from the St. Lawrence River region to western Lake Superior around 1400 or perhaps as late as 1500.[2] The Chippewa occupation of the area was contested by the powerful Dakota and Fox tribes for several centuries, and during much of the late seventeenth and early eighteenth centuries these conflicts influenced the trade relationships with the encroaching Europeans.

As is so often the case, the human exploitation of resources for individual economic gain was the driving force behind the "development" of the islands. From the late-seventeenth century until the mid-nineteenth century the economics took the form of Native Americans trading furs for manufactured goods initially with the French, then with British and finally American companies through the trading post at La Pointe. As European tastes changed, fur trade changed to lumbering with the islands first supplying wood to burn in the steam engines of lake vessels, and later to provide wood for construction. For a few years, from about 1870 to 1900, sandstone quarried from the mainland and Basswood, Hermit, and Stockton Islands provided stone for buildings in Wisconsin and in the growing midwestern cities including Minneapolis, Milwaukee, and Chicago.[3] From the late-nineteenth century to the mid-twentieth century Norwegian fishermen immigrated to the Apostle Islands to find fishing similar to what they experienced in the waters of their birthplace. Commercial fishing nearly came to an end in the mid-1950s when the opening of the St. Lawrence Seaway allowed sea lampreys to invade the Great Lakes and prey upon the native lake trout and other fish.

Ribs of the *Fedora* in Buffalo Bay (photo by author).

New ranger station at Little Sand Bay (photo courtesy National Park Service).

Twilite Display at Little Sand Bay (photo courtesy National Park Service.)

Little Sand Bay in the afternoon sun (photo courtesy National Park Service).

Bayfield School volunteers working on Mainland Trail (photo courtesy National Park Service).

Now the prevailing economic interest is tourism, a result foreseen by President John F. Kennedy in a speech at the Ashland, Wisconsin, airport on September 24, 1963, after viewing the Apostle Islands with Wisconsin's then Senator Gaylord Nelson. Nelson's work in the U.S. Senate, together with the work of Martin Hanson and Harold C. "Bud" Jordahl and many others, resulted in the establishment of the National Lakeshore by Public Law 91-424, which was signed by President Nixon on September 26, 1970. Originally, the National Lakeshore included twenty islands and a 12-mile strip of mainland. Long Island, together with control over all of the lighthouses (previously under the Coast Guard) was added to the National Lakeshore in 1986. In 2004, Congress added The Gaylord Nelson Wilderness designation, and in December, 2014 the Ashland Breakwater light was added to the National Lakeshore.

So, what lies ahead in the usage of the Apostle Islands? The National Park Service has prepared a General Management Plan for the Lakeshore for the next fifteen to twenty years, and its Summary Document can be viewed online.[4] The Gaylord Nelson Wilderness map on page 53 of the Summary (see footnote) shows the areas within the park that are part of the designated wilderness as well as the areas outside the wilderness designation (parts of Stockton, Rocky, and Oak Islands, and all of Sand, Basswood, and Long Islands, and also the Mainland Unit). Not surprisingly, the General Management Plan calls for more intense maintenance and establishment of hiking trails, campsites, and other facilities in the non-wilderness areas, while leaving The Gaylord Nelson Wilderness more primitive with no planned increase in the total number of designated campsites.

Various repairs, restoration, and maintenance on the lighthouse sites are planned in the next few years, and additional lighthouse projects will be necessary in the future.

The NPS has completed a new ranger station together with new exhibits at Little Sand

Bay, and an improvement to the lake access at Meyers Beach may be coming in the future. But there are no plans to change the length or use of the Mainland Trail along the shoreline. Operating with an always-tight budget, the park service receives project assistance from organizations like the Friends of the Apostle Islands National Lakeshore (www.friendsoftheapostleislands.org), the National Park Foundation (www.nationalparks.org), and the National Parks of Lake Superior Foundation (www.nplsf.org). Public support through these and other organizations may well determine the future use of the Apostle Islands National Lakeshore.

About This Book

The purpose of this book is to provide a guidebook with paddling, boating, and camping information for one mainland site and twenty islands in the Apostle Islands archipelago, including each island's location relative to the mainland or its neighbors, its geography and history, its shoreline and landing sites for small watercraft, its camping and hiking facilities, and its possible integration into a multi-island kayak, motorboat, or sailboat trip. Each island (or mainland) location is described in a separate chapter and includes a map showing the island's shoreline features, landing sites, and other important information for kayakers and boaters.

In addition to the guidebook information, each chapter also includes a vignette or essay related to the chapter's location and based on the author's paddling and camping experiences on each island over a twenty-two-year period.

The book does not include two of the islands in the National Lakeshore—Gull Island and Eagle Island. Both of these small islands are bird sanctuaries from May 15 to September 1, and landing on them or even approaching them closer than 500 feet is prohibited. On the other hand, the book does include

Layered sandstone (photo by Mark Weller).

a chapter on Madeline Island, although it is not part of the National Lakeshore, and it also contains a chapter about the Mainland Unit of the National Lakeshore with a hiking trail, a remote campsite, and most of all, sea caves deserving of a normal summer visit, or a wonderful winter visit in years when Lake Superior freezes sufficiently to allow access.

A few words about the information in this book are in order.

Scale on Island Maps—Please realize that the maps accompanying each chapter in this book are not all drawn to the same scale. Each island map has its own scale and the smaller islands appear larger compared to the size shown on the maps of the larger islands.

Landings—The "landings" on the maps are identified primarily for kayakers who might be looking for a safe landing for emergencies or simply for a lunch break. However, in calm weather, temporary landings by kayak may be made in many more locations than are identified on the map. Similarly, some of the landing locations on the maps may not be usable when the lake level is high or when four-foot waves are battering the shoreline.

Hiking Trails—The level of maintenance of the trails located within the Apostle Island National Lakeshore varies greatly. For example, because of muddy and slippery conditions, the initial and most heavily used portion of the Mainland Trail near Meyers Beach was made into a boardwalk in 2014. In contrast the middle 5 to 6 miles of the trail from the Outer Island sandspit to the Outer Island Lighthouse is very difficult to follow even with a compass and a topographical map.

Docks—The docks shown on the maps vary considerably in size and usefulness for boaters. Information about the length and depth available on the docks is contained in an NPS brochure (www.nps.gov/apis/planyourvisit/upload/Boaters_guide.pdf), and the brochure's table of dock information is reprinted below.

Campsite information—As campsites suffer from heavy use, their locations and amenities can change. Current campsite information is summarized on page 35 and can also be found in a printed park service brochure or on line at http://www.nps.gov/apis/planyourvisit/upload/camping.pdf.

Paddling Distances—When planning a longer kayak trip it is important to know the distances between more than just neighboring islands. Some of the distances on the "Distance in Miles between Selected Points in the Apostle Islands" table are shown on page 8 (and available online at http://www.nps.gov/apis/parkmgmt/upload/mileage.pdf).

Current Information—Change is inevitable. Shoreline information will change over time due to normal lake action. Rock shelves and arches sometimes become eroded and collapse into the lake. After a decade of average or lower water levels, the higher lake levels since 2014 have caused the immersion and possibly even the disappearance of some narrow sand beaches along the shorelines of the islands. As the conditions at certain campsites deteriorate with use, the park service may change the location of the site or close the site completely. It is wise to check with the park service office for current information regarding changes and closings when venturing out on the islands. For information updates, go to http://www.nps.gov/apis.

Lake levels—The maps and shoreline information in this book are based on a "normal" lake level of 601 feet above sea level. Lower lake levels will expose more rocks and shoreline and higher levels will reduce the width of sandy shorelines and the size of sandspits.

Temperatures—References to temperatures in this book are in degrees Fahrenheit.

Public Docks at Apostle Islands National Lakeshore		
Location	**Description**	**Depth***
Basswood, West	Concrete/Steel Bin	2–4′
Devils, South Landing	Wood, Small Harbor	2–4′
Little Sand Bay	Wood, Harbor	3–4′
Manitou Fish Camp	Wood	6–7′
Michigan Lighthouse	Concrete w/Metal Pier	3–5′
Oak, West	Wood	4–5′
Otter, Southeast	Wood, U–Shaped	4–5′
Outer Lighthouse	Concrete	3–4′
Raspberry Lighthouse West	Concrete/Steel Bin	5–6′
Raspberry Lighthouse East	Concrete/Steel Bin	3–4′
Rocky, East	Wood	6–7′
Sand, East Bay	Concrete/Steel Bin	2–3′
South Twin, West	Concrete/Steel Bin	4–5′
Stockton, Presque Isle West	Concrete, Angled	6–7′
Stockton, Presque Isle East	Concrete, L–Shaped	4–7′
Stockton, Quarry Bay	Wood	5–6′

*Water depth ranges represent most usable sections of dock. Depths vary due to lake levels, shifting sediments, and storms. For current information see go.nps.gov/ApostleConditions. Note: Because of high water and winter damage, some docks may not be usable (e.g., Devils in 2021).

Distance in Miles Between Selected Points in the Apostle Islands

	Bayfield	Bass Dock	Bear N End	Bear Spit	Cat Spit	Devils Light	Devils Land	Gull Island	Ironwood spit	Longs Light	Manitou Island	Michigan Light	North Twin	Oak Island	Otter Dock	Outer Light	Outer Spit	Raspberry	Rocky Dock	Sand Light	East Sand Bay	South Twin	Stock Pl	Stock QB	York Spit	LSB Dock
Bayfield		4	16	14	18	22	20	20	16	6	12	16	22	10	14	28	24	14	18	20	20	18	16	14	16	18
Basswood	4		12	10	14	18	16	16	12	10	8	16	20	6	10	24	20	10	14	16	16	14	12	10	12	14
Bear North End	16	12		4	10	4	2	20	8	24	8	22	10	6	6	20	16	6	6	12	10	6	16	14	8	10
Bear Sandspit	14	10	4		10	4	4	20	8	20	4	18	10	6	4	16	14	4	6	10	8	6	14	12	6	8
Cat Sandspit	18	14	10	10		10	10	8	2	24	8	12	6	12	6	10	6	12	8	20	18	6	12	12	12	18
Devils Light	22	18	4	4	10		2	20	10	28	10	26	6	14	10	16	16	10	8	12	12	6	20	18	22	14
Devils South End	20	16	2	4	10	2		22	8	26	10	26	8	12	8	16	16	10	6	14	14	6	22	18	12	14
Gull Island	20	16	20	20	8	20	22		14	22	14	6	16	18	16	16	6	22	16	30	28	16	6	8	26	28
Ironwood Spit	16	12	8	8	2	10	8	14		22	4	14	8	10	4	14	8	10	4	18	16	4	12	10	12	16
Long Light	6	10	24	20	24	28	26	22	22		18	18	28	14	20	40	28	18	24	28	26	26	20	18	22	26
Manitou DK	12	8	8	4	8	10	10	14	4	18		12	10	8	2	18	12	6	6	16	14	6	8	6	10	14
Michigan Light	16	16	22	18	12	26	26	6	14	18	12		20	14	14	20	10	18	18	28	26	18	4	6	22	26
North Twin	22	20	10	10	6	6	8	16	8	28	10	20		16	10	10	10	14	6	24	22	6	20	18	6	22
Oak DK	10	6	6	6	12	14	12	18	10	14	8	14	16		8	24	18	4	12	10	10	10	12	10	6	10
Otter DK	14	10	6	4	6	10	8	16	4	20	2	14	10	8		16	12	6	4	16	14	4	10	8	10	14
Outer Light	28	24	20	16	10	16	16	16	14	40	18	20	10	24	16		10	22	14	26	28	12	18	20	26	28
Outer Spit	24	20	16	14	6	16	16	6	8	28	12	10	10	18	12	10		16	12	24	22	16	10	12	20	22
Raspberry DK	14	10	6	4	12	10	10	22	10	18	6	18	14	4	6	22	16		8	6	4	10	14	12	4	6
Rocky DK	18	14	6	6	6	8	6	16	4	24	6	18	6	12	4	14	12	8		16	14	2	14	12	12	14
Sand Light	20	16	12	10	20	12	14	30	18	28	16	28	24	10	16	26	24	6	16		2	16	22	20	4	6
Sand East Bay	20	16	10	8	18	12	14	28	16	26	14	26	22	10	14	28	22	4	14	2		18	20	18	4	4
South Twin DK	18	14	6	6	6	6	6	16	4	26	6	18	6	10	4	12	12	10	2	16	18		16	14	12	16
Stockton Pl	16	12	16	14	12	20	22	6	12	20	8	4	20	12	10	18	14	14	14	22	20	16		4	18	20
Stockton QB	14	10	14	12	12	18	18	8	10	18	6	6	18	10	8	20	12	12	12	20	18	14	4		14	16
York Sandspit	16	12	8	6	12	12	12	26	12	22	10	22	18	6	10	26	20	4	12	4	4	12	19	14		4
LSB	18	14	10	8	18	14	14	28	16	26	14	26	22	10	14	28	22	6	14	6	4	16	20	16	4	

Courtesy National Park Service

About the Author

Before my retirement from the practice of law in 2012, the natural beauty and solitude of the Apostle Islands National Lakeshore provided me with a series of wonderful escapes from the routines of work and everyday life. As I fell in love with the area in the early 1990s, I promised myself a kayak visit to each of the islands in the archipelago. Twenty years later that promise was fulfilled, and it seemed very natural to put some of the things I learned and experienced into a guidebook as a thank you gift to the National Lakeshore that I loved.

Some things have changed in the Apostle Islands National Lakeshore over the last thirty years, and they will continue to change in the future. While the Apostle Islands National Lakeshore will continue to be protected by governmental ownership, increasingly, in order to thrive, our public lands and parks will need greater support, both moral and financial, from the people who enjoy them.

The Apostle Islands National Lakeshore is lucky to have several nonprofit organizations dedicated to that support, and I invite those who use this book to consider helping them – particularly the Friends of the Apostle Islands – as a means of preserving these island gems in Lake Superior. The nonprofits may well be the key to maintaining the National Lakeshore as a welcome destination for escaping from everyday routines in generations to come.

If you enjoy the beauty, the solitude, and the basic lessons of the natural world, take a water trip and start your own love affair with the Apostle Island National Lakeshore.

Warning

In interviewing people for this book, one overriding theme was repeated again and again—safety, especially for kayakers. Lake Superior and the Apostle Islands are beautiful and wonderful, especially when explored in a kayak. But they are also dangerous and temperamental, and conditions can change and become life threatening quite quickly. Coast Guard personnel, local boat captains, kayakers, and outfitters are able to tell stories of people who required rescue after misjudging the weather, their equipment, or their own abilities. To avoid becoming the main character in one of their stories, use your head, plan carefully, and be careful and conservative in your paddling and boating. If you are on your first visit to the islands, take the ferry to Madeline or take a boat cruise to gain familiarity. If you are interested in kayaking, take a safety course suitable for paddling on the inland sea or engage an outfitter for your first trip. If you have not camped in a wilderness setting before, rely on the cruise boat or hire a water taxi to deliver you to a camping location for a couple of days to experience the absence of "civilization" before venturing out for a week to a remote island or islands.

Then enjoy.

Eagle Island (photo courtesy National Park Service).

Kayakers: Getting on the Water

Paddling in the Apostle Islands National Lakeshore can be one of the most satisfying semi-wilderness experiences in the midwestern United States. However, paddling on Lake Superior is unlike paddling most inland lakes. The big lake can replace a peaceful, calm sunset on one evening with a life threatening experience the next day. Safe paddling on Lake Superior requires the kayaker to learn new behaviors and to switch his/her mental state to conform to a new set of rules dictated by the whims of the lake. This section outlines some of the rules and the required behavioral adjustments.

If you have not kayaked on the big lake before, consider starting with a guided day trip or overnight camping trip using one of the outfitters in the area or consider a day kayak trip launching from a larger "mother ship"

A road less traveled (photo by Paul Matteoni).

(see the "Resources" section of this book). The outfitters have personnel experienced with Lake Superior rules and familiar with the islands. As a result, first-time paddlers will be more likely to have a safe and enjoyable trip.

Wind and Waves

Before leaving shore even for a day trip, check the weather report. A weather radio will provide the near shore weather report for waters within 5 nautical miles (about 5.75 statute miles) of the mainland as well as a Nearshore Marine Forecast for the Apostle Islands for the waters beyond 5 nautical miles. In the Apostle Islands area the forecast can be heard on channel WX7 (transmitting from Ashland). On the more distant islands the weather radio may also pick up transmissions from Duluth or Marquette, Michigan. The forecasts for the following two days are also posted by the National Park Service at its headquarters in Bayfield and at ranger stations throughout the National Lakeshore. The NPS posts current conditions online, including weather at go.nps.gov/ApostleConditions. The forecasts give wind direction, velocity, and anticipated wave height.

For the next twelve- to twenty-four-hour period the forecasts are generally very accurate, even providing some certainty for the timing of a change in the velocity and direction of the wind and the wave height. A careful analysis of the predicted weather changes allows the kayaker to produce a better daily float plan through the islands, taking advantage of a tailwind to provide easier paddling or seeking a protected shoreline during a windy period of the day. Delaying a crossing to avoid paddling into waves that have built up to 3 to 5 feet, or even 2 to 4 feet, is a wise choice, especially for solo paddlers or a less-experienced paddling group.

Weather changes can come very quickly on Lake Superior. The chapter on Rocky Island describes a rapid weather change that a friend and I experienced. As we were lying on top of our sleeping bags in our tents enjoying a calm, muggy 70-degree evening and dozing off to sleep, we were jarred awake by a sudden northeastern wind that built to at least 15 miles per hour and lowered the air temperature by about 20 degrees in about fifteen minutes. The previously calm water changed into a far less friendly 2- to 3-foot chop as the crews on the sailboats anchored just offshore scrambled to pull up their anchors and motor across the strait to find shelter on the southwestern side of South Twin Island. Within half an hour we were nestled deep within our sleeping bags and the cold wind and waves, followed by heavy rain, continued for the next eighteen hours, destroying our paddling plans for the next day.

Remembering that Lake Superior does not read the weather forecast and does not always abide by predictable laws, nonetheless there are a few general weather rules that can aid the kayaker's plans. First, weather generally moves from west to east. If you observe clouds building in the western sky, the clear sky will turn cloudy in the next twelve hours, and the clouds may be accompanied by rain and a change in wind direction. Second, a prolonged south or southwest wind may bring warm moist air with it, resulting in fog or possible thunderstorms. Third, a lasting wind from the north or northwest may mark the rapid approach of a cold front initially producing a thunderstorm followed by a clear, cooler period, perhaps with stronger steady winds. Fourth, if the prevailing wind direction changes by more than 90 degrees during the day, a weather change is likely in

Outfitter's kayaks lined up on Stockton Island Beach (photo courtesy National Park Service).

Not a good day for a rock shelf landing (photo by Mark Weller).

the next twenty-four hours. Fifth, generally in August and September, lighter morning winds will build to a higher level by noon to 2:00 p.m., diminishing again to a lower velocity about an hour before sunset until an hour or so after dark. Finally, as demonstrated by the Rocky Island account in the previous paragraph, a northeast wind, cooled by the long fetch across cold Lake Superior waters, will always bring a substantially cooler temperature to the Apostle Islands.

The waters of Lake Superior slow down the changes of the seasons in the islands, delaying spring and fall by as much as a month compared to the interior of the mainland. The surface water temperature remains in the forties in May and June, warming to the sixties by the end of August, and waves running surface water into some protected bays can bring the temperature to a very swimmable 70-degree Fahrenheit in late summer. The air temperature on the islands and the shoreline will reach a high in the sixties in May and June, the mid to upper seventies by July and August, and drop back into the sixties in September. A daytime high temperature above 90-degree Fahrenheit or below 55-degree Fahrenheit is not unusual in mid-summer.

Visitors at Sand Island rockshelf (photo by Robert E. Rolley).

Hypothermia

The danger of hypothermia to the Lake Superior kayaker cannot be over-emphasized. A capsized boat with a kayaker in the water is an emergency that must be remedied quickly. A kayaker's hand which initially can assist in the rescue will turn into five slow moving cucumbers attached to a cold watermelon in minutes. Numbed by the sudden immersion in cold water, the kayaker's mind may also seem to move at the pace of molasses. Lungs will rasp for more air as the immersed kayaker experiences breathing difficulty.

Dr. Gordon Giesbrecht, a Kinesiology and Recreational Management Professor at the University of Manitoba, has capsulized the physiological effects of hypothermia into a memorable 1-10-1 formula. During the first one (1) minute of immersion in cold water the victim will experience an increase in the breathing rate up to ten times the normal rate. Although the rasping will subside in about a minute, it is important to have the victim's head above water in this time period to avoid immediate drowning. In as little as ten (10) minutes, the victim will start to lose strength and flexibility of fingers and even arms and legs and the victim's mental function will slow, affecting the victim's ability to assist in the rescue. Finally, in as little as one (1) hour the victim may lose consciousness.[5] If a paddler's hands or other parts of the body have already been exposed to cold water before capsize, hypothermia may have already started and the one-hour time period until there is a loss of consciousness may be even shorter. If you or a co-paddler do capsize, the 1-10-1 effects on the body are important to remember.

The remedy for a capsized kayaker is a self-rescue or an assisted rescue. Getting the capsized kayaker back in the boat and out of the cold water quickly and efficiently is the object of the rescue. Ideally the rescue will result in the kayaker placed back in the seat of the kayak with paddle in hand and with a cockpit drained of water, ready to resume the trip which was interrupted by the capsize.

There are various kinds of rescue methods that can be studied in the many "how to" books available. Any kayaker paddling Lake Superior should practice self-rescue and assisted rescues to the point that almost no thought is required to proceed with the rescue process. Remember that the involuntary capsize is unlikely to occur in the warm water of a protected bay. Rather, it will come in open water at a time when the wind and waves make the rescue attempt more difficult. Dress for possible immersion by wearing a wetsuit or a drysuit (see "Equipment" below). *Never* go out on Lake Superior without wearing a personal floatation device (PFD).

Threading the needle (photo by Joy Chen).

Equipment

Certain equipment should be considered essential for even a day trip on Lake Superior. Additional equipment might be classified as important but perhaps not essential. Finally, there is some equipment that might be considered optional—items that will make any trip easier but what some kayakers will not consider worth their bulk or weight. At the end of this section, there is an equipment checklist for use by those who want to be thorough and who do not want to rely on a mere mental checklist. Each kayaker should consider making his or her own equipment checklist.

The first item on the essential checklist is, of course, a kayak. Depending upon the paddler's body weight and size the ideal individual sea kayak will be 15 to 18 feet long and 21 to 25 inches wide (its "beam").

While there are many competent paddlers who venture out on the lake in an open canoe, most of these paddlers have remained alive by picking their paddling weather carefully, covering the equipment and provisions in their canoe with waterproof tarps, or perhaps simply by luck. The closed hatches of a kayak provide an ideal all-weather small craft.

Similarly, kayakers who own only a recreational kayak (14 feet or less) or a whitewater kayak have ventured out on Lake Superior more as kayaking has increased in popularity. The use of these shorter kayaks can result in an enjoyable trip in relatively calm water, however, because of their shorter length, increased wave action on Lake Superior will obligate the paddler to spend too much time making directional corrections and too little time making forward progress on a longer paddle trip. The shorter recreational kayak also may carry a greater risk of capsize in heavy weather.

A kayak's ability to maintain direction in the wind and waves is called "tracking." The shape of a kayak's hull (bottom) determines to a large degree how well a kayak tracks. Most sea kayaks have rounded hull bottoms in the middle of the kayak to provide stability and hulls that are more pointed in the front (bow) and the rear (stern) of the kayak to assist in tracking. Many kayaks are also equipped with either a skeg (a retractable "fin" protruding into the water from the bottom of the hull) or alternatively a rudder mounted at the kayak's stern, which can be used to help the paddler maintain direction.

The hulls of most sea kayaks are also designed to "weathercock," that is, to point the bow of the kayak into the wind if the kayak is not being paddled. Weathercocking acts as a safety factor. If the unpaddled kayak automatically faces into the wind, it will allow the kayaker to see the approaching waves and avoid a capsize that would more likely come from riding the waves broadside to the wind.

The paddle is the second most important piece of equipment. The size of the paddle blade, its length, and the paddle's weight are all important variables to consider in choosing a paddle. Paddles come in one, two, three, and even four pieces and may have a straight shaft or a bent shaft. Paddle blades can be flat or cupped. While some kayakers may claim there is a "correct" or "perfect" paddle, generally the choice is personal to the comfort of the kayaker. The advice of an experienced paddler will be helpful, especially for the purchase of the first paddle.

The narrow blade of a "Greenland style" paddle will require less effort for each stroke, but will also require more strokes to cover a given distance. A broader blade will require fewer strokes to cover the same distance and, because its "bite" is bigger, it will provide quicker directional responsiveness for steering the kayak than the narrower blade provides. Physics tells us that generally it takes the same amount of work effort to move a particular kayak forward a given distance regardless of the amount of paddle blade exposure, so each kayaker should test various paddles to determine what blade size and shape works the best for the individual paddler and his/her kayak.

Loading up at Buffalo Bay Marina (photo by author).

Kayak launching beach at Little Sand Bay (photo courtesy National Park Service).

The length of a paddle also is subject to personal preference. The height and shape of the deck of the kayak in front of the paddler cockpit and on the sides of the cockpit can have a significant effect on the comfortable length of the paddle. As a paddler gains experience, his or her paddling style may change to a more vertical or more horizontal stroke, and the paddler may find that a longer or shorter paddle is preferable.

A kayaker may make about 20,000 strokes during an eight- to nine-hour paddling day, and even a small difference in paddle weight can make a significant difference in the amount of fatigue the paddler feels at the end of the day. Lighter generally is better, at least until the paddle feels like it will be blown out of your hands in a gust of wind or seems to flutter in your hands when you apply a strong power stroke through the water. A paddle made of lightweight materials like Kevlar and carbon fiber retains its strength and durability. Unfortunately, the cost of a paddle generally is inversely proportional to its weight, and the basic question may be how light of a paddle can you afford.

Most paddles also allow the kayaker to adjust the relative angle of one paddle blade to the other blade by up to 90 degrees. If the paddle blades are not in line with one another, the paddle is "feathered." The paddler in the picture entitled "A road less traveled" at the beginning of this chapter has his paddle feathered. Feathering a paddle allows the kayaker paddling into the wind to have the exposed paddle blade parallel to the wind while the other end of the paddle is being stroked broadside through the water, resulting in less wind resistance. Paddling with feathered blades requires the kayaker to flex either the right or left wrist with each stroke to place the paddle blade entering the water broadside to the paddler's stroke. The constant flexing easily becomes automatic, but it also may result in wrist fatigue or even injury after frequent paddle trips, a result that may outweigh the benefit of the reduction in wind resistance gained by feathering the paddle.

The third piece of essential equipment is a personal flotation device (PFD). Having a Coast Guard approved PFD on board is required by law. Not wearing the PFD while paddling is allowed in Wisconsin waters, but it is reserved only for paddlers who wish to act foolishly. The PFD should be adequate to float the user, it should allow the arm motion required for paddling without chaffing, and it probably should have some pockets for things like flares, a whistle, an emergency fire-making kit, and perhaps a marine radio.

The final piece of essential equipment is a wetsuit or a drysuit. Both body covers are worn for the purpose of providing warmth, particularly in the event of capsize while attempting and awaiting rescue. Either type of protection will lengthen the time before the capsized kayaker effectively loses the ability to assist in the rescue or succumbs to hypothermia.

The wetsuit is the cheaper alternative. When the paddler is immersed, cold water will leak in between the paddler's skin and the neoprene wetsuit. However, after the initial shock, the paddler's body will warm the water that has seeped inside the wetsuit, and the wetsuit will provide insulation against the cold lake water on the exterior of the suit. Under the wetsuit the paddler wears only a swimsuit and perhaps a T-shirt, with warmer clothing on the outside of the wetsuit if needed.

A drysuit has water-tight rubber gaskets around the neck and the ends of the sleeves and either gaskets or booties at the ankle. The drysuit is designed to keep the cold lake water out in the event of immersion so that insulating clothing can be worn inside the drysuit. Drysuits can be more comfortable for paddling, but if the air temperature changes during the paddle day, the drysuit, put on over clothing, makes the addition or removal of an insulating layer of clothing without stopping more difficult than it would be with a wetsuit. Also, on a hot day the inside of

Group paddle (photo by Don Hynek).

the drysuit will become more than clammy because of the paddler's sweating.

Spray skirts, keeping splashes of water from the paddle or wave action from filling the cockpit, and self-rescue equipment, such as a paddle float and cockpit pump, may also be considered essential equipment even though the equipment list shows them only as "important." Other items of important and optional equipment are listed with some comment on the equipment checklist.

Packing the Kayak

The equipment should be packed snugly into the kayak holds so that it does not shift and cause imbalance during the paddle trip. The equipment weight should also be distributed between front and rear holds so that the kayak rides flat in the water with neither the bow nor the stern riding lower than the other end. Heavier items should be on the bottom of the hold, thereby lowering the center of gravity and providing more stability. Minimize the amount of equipment riding on the top of the kayak since it will lower your stability, add to wind resistance, and perhaps become hazardous in landing. Finally, even in flat water, don't leave your hatches open.

Wreck of the H.D. *Coffinberry* on the north shore of Red Cliff (Schooner) Bay (photo by Don Hynek).

The (mostly) watertight hatch covers help maintain buoyancy, even if the kayak's hold is stuffed full of equipment.

Navigation

A map is an important aid to enjoying the Apostle Islands regardless of the amount of experience the paddler may have navigating in the National Lakeshore. The National Oceanic Service (NOS) chart #14973 covers the Apostle Islands. A smaller scale NOS chart (#14966), covering all of the Wisconsin coastline of Lake Superior from Duluth to Saxon Harbor, is less useful because it does not reveal as much shoreline detail of the islands. Other maps with additional information specific to the National Lakeshore include map A.I. Apostle Islands National Lakeshore published by McKenzie, and Trails Illustrated topo map for the Apostle Islands National Lakeshore. Although it is not recommended for navigation, many Bayfield stores sell a laminated map as a table placemat, which can be placed on the deck of a kayak to help navigate among the islands. No matter how well you seal the map in a plastic bag or a map holder, the map should be waterproofed with a latex preservative unless it is already printed on waterproof paper.

A compass is also important for navigation, especially on overcast days. A compass mounted on the deck of your kayak is ideal, but if such an investment is not in the budget, at least a hand-held compass should be part of the equipment checklist. A compass points to the magnetic north, which varies only a few degrees from true north in the Apostle Islands area. By knowing which direction is north the kayaker, of course, can also determine the other directions and compare visual observations of the landmasses to the map. For example, if a kayaker visually observes that the edges of two islands are aligned, the kayaker can draw an imaginary line on the map from the edge of the more distant island just past the point of the closer island and extend the line to find the kayak's approximate location on the map. The kayaker's location can be more definitely fixed by extending another line that crosses the first line using two other land mass points.

The magnet in a deck-mounted compass "floats" in liquid or on a pin and is marked in a manner to inform the kayaker the direction that the bow of the kayak is pointed. The compass is delineated clockwise from north in degrees, with 0 degrees (360 degrees) being straight north; 90 degrees straight east; 180 degrees south; and 270 degrees west. Thus, for example, a reading of 135 degrees on a deck-mounted compass tells the paddler that the kayak is headed in a southeastern direction.

In addition to the compass, a semi-waterproof wristwatch, sports watch, or other time-keeping device can assist the kayaker in "dead reckoning" navigation described in the next paragraph. Cell phones have become popular as a timepiece, but may not be useful for this purpose on a kayak trip when the paddler wants to check the time without a serious interruption in the paddling cadence.

Dead reckoning is really nothing more than the use of the principal that speed (i.e. miles per hour) multiplied by the time elapsed (i.e. expressed in hours or a fraction of an hour) will equal the distance traveled. To use dead reckoning the kayaker needs to know the average speed the kayak travels. The average speed may be tested by paddling at normal cruising speed between two points at a known distance apart. If the two points are a mile apart and the test trip takes fifteen minutes (1/4 hour) the average speed is 4 miles per hour. If the 1-mile test trip takes twenty minutes (1/3 hour), the kayaker knows that three such test distances may be covered in an hour's time and the cruising speed is effectively 3 miles per hour. In making use of the average cruising speed in dead reckoning, the kayaker needs to remember that the speed may be significantly reduced when paddling directly into a stiff breeze and similarly, that cruising speed may be

increased with a tailwind pushing the kayaker forward.

So if you maintain a constant heading using your compass and know how fast and how long you have paddled (and you know where you started from), you should be able to calculate roughly where you are on the map.

Dead reckoning can be used in trip planning as an ongoing monitor of the kayaker's current position and to estimate the time it will take for a segment of a trip or to complete the trip. Here is an example of the use of dead reckoning in a trip plan. Suppose that a kayaker is at the sandspit (a buildup of sand deposited by wave action generated by wind) on the southwest corner of Oak Island and is contemplating a trip to the previously reserved individual campsite on the northwestern shore of Manitou Island. There is little wind now and no change is predicted in the weather until late afternoon when thunderstorms may be approaching from the west. Checking the map the kayaker determines that the distance for the total trip will be about 6.5 miles. The kayaker estimates cruising speed conservatively to be about 3.5 miles per hour, and wants to take a short break from paddling before making the crossing from the east coast of Oak Island to the south end of Manitou Island. The kayaker decides to leave the Oak Island sandspit at 12:30 p.m. in order to be able to arrive at the Manitou Island campsite before 3:00 p.m. and set up tent and camp before the arrival of the predicted thunderstorms. Once the kayaker rounds the southeastern corner of Oak Island, the island will eclipse the kayaker's view of the western sky from whence the thunderstorm front will be approaching and the island will also disguise an increase in the westerly wind velocity, since the island will shelter the kayaker from the wind as he travels up the easterly shore of Oak. With this in mind, the wise kayaker plans to check weather conditions again during the break and before making the crossing to Manitou Island. As a contingency plan if the storm arrives earlier than predicted or the kayaker encounters other unexpected problems, the kayaker will remain at the Oak Island break area or stop at the dock on Manitou Island.

The ultimate aid to navigation and dead reckoning is a global positioning system (GPS) unit which can be used to determine the latitude and longitude of the current location, the current speed and "trip" speed, and the direct line distance (not necessarily the paddle distance) to another marked location. While paddling in a dense fog always exposes the kayaker to danger from other boat traffic, if it is necessary to travel in the fog, the GPS will help confirm the kayaker's dead reckoning calculations and possibly help the kayaker return to the original location if a crossing between two points fails for any reason.

Other Boaters

The inner islands—Sand, York, Raspberry, Oak, Basswood, and even Stockton—can seem almost crowded in July and August when sailboats and powerboats congregate for special events. Kayaks ride low in the water and may be hidden from the view of other boaters for about half the time in waves of 2 feet or more. In spite of the bright colors of most kayaks, personal flotation devices and paddles, a single kayak or even a group of kayaks are not always visible to the operators of the larger boats. In an encounter between a kayak and a larger boat, the kayak rarely comes away better off.

Some kayakers and some boaters can become arrogant about their "right" to use the waters on Lake Superior. Kayakers are smug about their use of the lake, moving along silently at a reasonable speed without the use of petroleum products and often practicing leave no trace camping. Some powerboaters view kayakers as a nuisance, acting as a largely invisible obstacle to the powerboats whose size, speed, and power make them safer to handle in the wind and waves that the lake has to offer. Sailboaters may have a special arrogance. They mostly use a renewable resource for silent propulsion, but still find kayakers troublesome as an obstacle to their freedom to tack back and forth at their leisure and discretion.

Resist such group arrogance. The lake is still big enough for every group's enjoyment. Boaters, keep a watch for kayaks ahead to avoid the damage and injury that can come from a collision or too close an encounter with your wake. Kayakers listen for powerboats and watch for sailboats. Anticipate their speed and direction and take steps to avoid the path of the larger boat. If a boat is approaching head-on, veer to your right to avoid the path of the boat and reveal the broadside of your kayak to the vision of the boater. If waves are more than 2 feet, wave the paddle back and forth in the air to increase your visibility. Kayakers, be especially careful if you cross a channel entrance to a harbor, since there is a greater likelihood of larger boat traffic and larger boat operators may be less attentive as they prepare their boats for docking or for advancing into the open water. Kayakers, use bright colored kayaks, paddles, PFD's, and clothing to draw attention to your presence while on the water.

Above all, render assistance to another boater in need regardless of the boat's size or pedigree. Boaters, don't let your arrogance lead you to think that kayakers can never render assistance to boaters.

Remember the story of the powerful lion that scoffed at the idea that a tiny mouse could ever offer him any assistance—that is, until the mouse freed the ensnared lion by chewing a hole in the net which held the lion. A true story—once a kayaker assisted in the rescue of the powerboat of an absentee owner that had come free of its mooring in a river harbor on Lake Superior and drifted into shallow rocky water. Another powerboat attempted an approach to the large unmanned boat stuck on the rocks, but it could not get close enough to attach a line to the foundering boat without the risk of scraping its own bottom in the shallow rocky water. After the failed rescue attempt by the large cabin cruiser, the kayaker approached the huddle of fishing boat captains stating that he had a kayak and a fifty-foot rope. One of the more arrogant captains derisively said, "So what are you going to do with that, pull that twenty-seven-foot boat off the rocks with your kayak? Ha-ha." "No," the kayaker replied in his best mouse-like manner, "but with my kayak I can go into the shallow water, attach my long rope, and bring the end of the rope out to deeper water so that one of the larger boats can pull the stranded boat off the rocks." With the help of a less arrogant boat captain and the park ranger, one end of the kayaker's rope was tied to the stranded boat, and the kayaker took the other end to the towing boat. With the help of a sturdy pole, the kayaker and the less arrogant boat skipper levered the stricken boat off the rocks and the park ranger, using his pontoon boat, was able to pull the boat loose and return it to its mooring. After the successful operation, the kayaker and all of the fishing boat captains shook hands and introduced themselves to one another. A short time later the kayaker

had trouble suppressing his own arrogance as he resumed his paddle trip.

Launch Sites

In order to get on the water and out to the islands, the kayaker will need to choose a launch site. The following launch sites with brief comments are arbitrarily listed in the order they would appear on a trip from south to north, then west around the top of the Bayfield Peninsula. Unless otherwise noted, there is a launch charge at the sites.

Sioux River—There is a boat ramp just off of Highway 13 about 7.5 miles south of Bayfield, and there is a short road to a nice beach on the lake that can be used free of charge for a softer, more relaxed launch. The launch site is useful primarily for access to Long Island.

Bayfield/Municipal Boat Ramp—Located at the end of Third Street in Bayfield, this launch site has a concrete ramp and features adequate day-use parking and a public restroom. Different launch fees apply for kayaks and larger boats.

Bayfield/Broad Street Beach—The improved portion of Broad Street stops at

Sailors delight (photo by Mark Weller).

Wilson Street, but the right of way extends to the water. While the beach is in use as a swimming beach in summer and launching a kayak is prohibited, it can be a convenient launch site in the offseason. There is only limited parking available with some street parking on Broad Street or Wilson Street. Currently there is no charge to use this off-season area.

Bayfield/Washington Avenue Beach— Next to the ferry landing, this beach can become too congested even for launching of a kayak during the summer months. Currently there is no charge for launching. Overnight parking is available off Washington Avenue up the hill from the beach.

Red Cliff/Buffalo Bay Marina—This site provides a shallow sand beach protected by a breakwater ideal for loading and launching a kayak. There is also a ramp for launching a powerboat. Registration and payment of launch fees and parking fees is currently done in the casino lobby.

Little Sand Bay—Launching at Little Sand Bay has become an experience in zoning. No kayak launching is allowed on the public beach. A larger boat (but no kayaks) may be launched for a fee at the Town of Russell boat ramp. The (free) kayak launch site is now located on a sandy beach west of the National Park Service dock. There is a new ranger station at Little Sand Bay with interesting exhibits and information.

Meyers Beach—Located about 4 miles northeast of Cornucopia off Highway 13 and at the end of Meyers Road, this sometimes-crowded launch site requires a National Lakeshore daily parking fee, but the fee structure may be changing in the future. The site has a beautiful sand beach for loading and launching kayaks, but currently equipment must be carried down (and more significantly back up) a wooden stairs between the parking area and the beach. Better accessibility is planned for the future. The site is primarily used for day trips to the mainland sea caves located about 1.5 miles northeast of the launch area.

Equipment Checklist

Essential Equipment
Kayak
Paddles
Personal Flotation Device (PFD)
Wetsuit with paddling jacket or drysuit

Important Equipment
Compass
Map
Spray skirt (to keep water and spray out of cockpit)
Paddle float (for self-rescue)
Cockpit pump (to bail out cockpit, especially after capsize and rescue)
Water bottle
Boots/footwear (probably neoprene for warmth)
Flares (for use to signal your location in an emergency)
Paddle gloves (for warmth and to prevent blisters)
Weather/marine radio
Sponge (to help remove water from cockpit and holds)
Watch or other timepiece
Sunscreen
Insect repellant
Sunglasses
Whistle (for signaling paddle partners or in rescue situations)
Head gear (for protection against the sun, perhaps covering head and neck)
Binoculars
Global Positioning Device (GPS)
Headlamp or other light
Duct tape (for repairing most anything)
Tow rope/rope/nylon cord, 50 feet (for rescue, towing, securing kayak, etc.)
Matches (waterproof) or lighter, fire-making aids
First aid kit: bandages, antibiotic cream, pain reliever, tweezers
Tools: locking pliers, screw drivers, knife for emergency repairs

Extras—optional equipment to make the trip safer or perhaps more enjoyable

Extra paddle (in case the main paddle breaks)

Deck bag

Extra batteries for radio, GPS, lighting, etc.

Water purification tablets

Head net for insects

Music playing device

Fishing equipment

Pen and notebook (for trip notes, deep thoughts, will draft)

Reading material (especially for wind bound times)

Kayaking to the Sand Island lighthouse (photo by Joy Chen).

Camping

Exploring all of the Apostle Islands would be difficult if the visitor to the National Lakeshore was limited only to day trips from the mainland. With the Outer Island lighthouse about 28 miles from Bayfield and the Little Sand Bay dock more than 26 miles from Michigan Island, the round trip distances from one end of the National Lakeshore to the other are simply beyond the daily paddling capabilities for most kayakers. Even for sailboaters and powerboaters the travel time from mainland ports to the more distant islands, done on a day trip basis without docking and anchorage, would rob them of valuable time otherwise available for the enjoyment of the islands. Overnight camping, dockage, and anchorage allows kayakers and other boaters more time for the leisurely enjoyment of both the inner and outer islands.

Camping in the National Lakeshore

Subject to temporary closures and site relocations, the National Park Service maintains over fifty-five individual and nine group designated campsites in the National Lakeshore (in 2021). The individual campsites are limited to seven or fewer campers and three tents. Eight to twenty-one campers are allowed in the group sites. Most islands have at least one designated individual campsite, but there are no designated sites on Raspberry, Bear, North Twin, or Hermit Islands. There are group campsites on Sand, Oak, Stockton, Rocky, and Basswood Islands. Only one individual campsite is located on the Mainland Unit, 6 miles in on a hike-in trail starting at Meyers Beach northeast of Cornucopia.

Accessible campsites with boardwalk transfers from dock to campsite are available on Sand and Stockton Islands.

Primitive or "wilderness" leave no trace camping for one-to-five people is also allowed outside the designated sites in camping "zones", however no camping is allowed outside of the designated campsites on Devils, Long and York Islands, and all camping is prohibited on Eagle and Gull Islands. No landing is even allowed at Eagle and Gull Islands between May 15 and September 1. Primitive camping zones and no-camping areas have been established to protect the enjoyment of campers in the designated campsites and hikers on designated trails, to protect bird nesting, threatened or endangered species and environmentally sensitive sites, and to protect the rights of remaining life lease holders.

All camping requires a permit. In 2021 the fees were $15 per individual campsite and

Oak Island campsite #4 (photo courtesy National Park Service).

primitive zone per night and $30 per night for group campsites. A $10 reservation fee is also charged for each trip. Each permit can cover up to fourteen consecutive nights. Permits for individual sites can be reserved up to thirty days prior to the first night of camping and a lottery for group campsites for the coming year is held each January. Permits may be obtained online at https://www.recreation.gov/camping/campgrounds/251865, or they may still be made over the telephone at (715) 779-3397 during normal business hours five days a week from October through Memorial Day and seven days per week from Memorial Day through September. Permits may also be obtained in person (or picked up after making a telephone reservation) at the National Lakeshore office at 415 Washington Avenue in Bayfield or at any ranger station.

All designated campsites have vault toilets (outhouses) or "stump toilets" (open air) except for the Trout Point campsite on Stockton Island. Most designated sites also have a picnic table at the site and raised tent pads which campers should use when available. Potable water may be available on Stockton and Sand Islands. Fires must remain in the fire rings provided at all the designated campsites, and campers should also use the bear boxes available at all of the designated sites.

Camping rules and fees change from year to year and it would be wise to check current camping permit rules and any temporary closures on the park service website (www.nps.gov/apis/) before seeking a camping reservation.

"Leave no trace" practices should be strictly followed for primitive zone camping and when using the many trails located on the islands and the mainland, and the camper should keep leave-no-trace principals in mind even in the designated campsites. Pack out all of your garbage; do not bury it, burn it, or throw it in the lake. Make your primitive camp only where there is little evidence of a prior leave-no-trace campsite. Where no vault toilet is available, dispose of human waste in a "cat hole" (imagine a cat using the

Stump toilet (photo by author).

Fire ring (photo by author).

Food locker bear box (photo by author).

litterbox), six to eight inches deep and located at least 200 feet from the nearest campsite, trail, or body of water, or use a portable toilet with a human waste bag to pack out. The National Park Service further requests that toilet paper used in conjunction with the cat hole be bagged and packed out of the park.

Fires in designated campsites should be limited to the fire rings. Backcountry zone campfires must be located at the water's edge on the beaches, and the size of *all* campfires should be limited to 3 feet in diameter and 3 feet in height. Better yet, use a camp stove for cooking and avoid *any* fire outside the fire rings at designated sites. In any case, no fires are allowed on the beaches on Raspberry Island, Julian Bay and Presque Isle Bay on Stockton Island, or on the northwest quarter of Outer Island. During times of extreme fire danger, the park service may actually prohibit the use of fire throughout the park. Gather dead and down wood only for your fire and don't transport any wood to the islands or even from island to island. Chainsaws are prohibited. No fires (including portable grills) are allowed on the park service docks or on the topside of boats tied to the docks. Leave no fire unattended, and extinguish the fire before leaving the area.

Wildlife and Other Hazards

A welcome guest staying at the house of a friend or relative is one who tries to abide by the house rules. Consider yourself a guest of the bear, deer, foxes, and even the annoying insects that call the Apostle Islands their home. Let their "house rules" influence your actions while camping in the National Lakeshore. If you follow their rules, you and those campers who come for a visit after you will continue to be welcome guests.

Bears

For human guests in the Apostle Islands, the black bear probably is the most feared wildlife host. A bear may weigh over twice as much as a human and may stand more than six feet tall when on its hind legs. A bear has a powerful swat and strong jaws, and in any human-bear fight, the safer bet is clearly on the bear. Luckily, most black bears in the Apostle Islands remain unaware of their

power and are fearful of humans. But sows (mama bears) can be aggressive in protecting their cubs, and bears that have learned to associate humans with food may lose their fear of humans.

There may be bears on any of the Apostle Islands as well as on the mainland sections of the national park National Lakeshore. However, the camper is more likely to encounter a bear on Oak, Sand, Stockton, Basswood, and Madeline Islands. Throughout the 1990s Stockton had the highest concentration of bears in Wisconsin and one of the highest concentrations in North America. By 2013, the highest concentration honor passed to Oak Island, followed by Sand and then Stockton.[6] In recent years, bear and human interactions have resulted in temporary closures of campsites, and even entire islands, to the public.

Bear sign on Basswood Island (photo by author).

So how do you avoid close encounters of the bear kind? Use the bear boxes at the designated campsites for your food, cooking utensils, and toiletries when you are not actively using the items. During any primitive camping, hang your scented items in a bag suspended 12 feet above the ground, either strung over a tree branch or preferably strung from a second taut rope tied between two trees as graphically demonstrated in the park service's camping brochure. Above all, don't feed the bears, intentionally or unintentionally. They won't know when to stop eating and will cause you and subsequent guests at the National Lakeshore a hardship that could have been avoided.

If a bear enters your campsite or picnic area, try to make noise (talk loudly, bang a cooking pot), look as big as possible, and try to scare the bear away while removing the delicious food-scented items to the bear box. By entering your campsite the bear is being as discourteous to you as it would be to have your human host enter the guest bedroom assigned to you without knocking. Trying to scare the bear away is appropriate and may keep the bear out of the campsite when it is occupied by future campers. But if a human host was to remain in your guest bedroom or the bear remains in your campsite after you loudly exclaim your displeasure, it probably is time to pack your bags and leave.

If you are hiking away from your campsite (outside the guest bedroom), you should make some noise so that any bear may hear you and avoid contact with you. If you encounter a bear away from a campsite, you are an intruder on his or her territory, and the loud get-out-of-here approach appropriate to the campsite invasion should not be used. Rather, use the "although I am a formidable animal, I realize I have invaded your space and will carefully back away now" approach. You still want to look big (but not threatening), and you want to avoid using a loud voice or challenging the bear with direct eye contact. Talk to the bear in a soothing tone and slowly back away from the bear, as long as you are not backing toward mama bear's cubs.

If a bear acts aggressively toward you at any location, leave the area immediately (but do not run) and report the incident to the park service as soon as possible.

Other Wildlife

White-tailed deer, red squirrels, beaver, fox, and possibly coyotes may also be encountered in the islands, however, they rarely will be interested in your presence and will flee if approached. See an exception to this rule in the Ironwood Island chapter of this book. There are no poisonous snakes in the National Lakeshore.

Mosquitoes, Flies, and Ticks

While much smaller than the mammals you will encounter in the Apostle Islands, the insects inhabiting the islands in summer can become a formidable detriment to the camping experience. Mosquitoes and ticks may be present on the islands from late May to mid-October, with the greatest numbers in late May and through most of June. Biting "beach" flies (stable flies), looking a bit like a common housefly, may go unnoticed during most of the season, except during occasional periods of hot humid weather. Larger "deer flies," more likely to be found away from the beach in wooded areas and clearings, enjoy a longer active season and will torment campers from sometime in June until September. The numbers of any variety of insect will vary from year to year depending upon the weather and the camper's location.

The amount of blood donated to the insects can be reduced by wearing long-sleeved shirts and long-legged pants. A mosquito net worn over the head may also provide welcome relief in times of particularly dense infestations. Insect repellants containing a high percentage of Deet also serve to ward off the mosquitoes, ticks, and deer flies, but there is a well-founded rumor of "beach flies" piled two deep from ankle to knee on a camper's pant legs, drunkenly laughing and still enjoying the orgy in spite of the Deet. Mosquitoes in the Apostles are usually most active in the evening, especially if it is humid and it seems likely to rain. Accordingly, one easy methodology to prevent blood loss is to get inside the mosquito netting of your tent even before the sun sets.

Fly hatch in late June (photo by author).

In the past couple of decades, campers have been made more aware of the infestation of smaller (more the size of a pinhead) deer ticks (*Ixodes scapularis*) and perhaps even lone star ticks (*Amblyomma americanum*). Ticks can be carriers of bacteria causing Lyme disease, babesiosis, anaplasmosis, and ehrlichiosis. Generally, to transmit the diseases, the tick needs to be attached to your body for twenty-four hours or more. It is wise to examine your entire body twice daily if you have spent any amount of time in wooded or grassy areas. If an inflamed red circle appears around a tick bite or you feel general malaise, fever, and body aches anywhere from twenty-four hours to two weeks after you suspect that you have been bitten by a tick, it is time see your doctor immediately. Any ticks should be removed as soon as possible in a manner that minimizes the possibility of the tick pushing its saliva back into the victim. The Center for Disease Control suggests using a tweezers, grabbing the tick as close to the victim's body as possible and removing it with a steady pull.

Poison Ivy

Poison Ivy may be found in areas that have been partially cleared by our human ancestors and particularly on Long Island. If you don't know how to recognize poisonous plants, remember the old saying, "Leaves of three, let them be."

Equipment, Clothing, and Supplies

The kind of equipment, clothing, and supplies needed for an overnight stay in the Apostle Islands National Lakeshore will vary with the method of water transportation used during your visit. If you are planning on staying in the cabin of a larger boat anchored in a protected bay or tied to one of the public docks in the lakeshore, you may have no need for a tent and sleeping bags and cooking equipment may be stored on the boat in spring and removed in fall, if at all. Even if a necessary food item has been forgotten on shore, the stores in Bayfield may be only a couple of hours away for the powerboat or sailboat. A forgotten item can become an annoyance, but not a trip ender.

On the other hand, if you are traveling to your camping location by kayak, water taxi, cruise boat, or on foot, forgetting an item of equipment or food can have a more significant effect on your trip. Inadequate equipment can become more than an annoyance and cause an early return to civilization.

For a camper hiking to a campsite or taking a water taxi or an island cruise boat, multiple small items may be packed into a backpack for transportation to the campsite. The kayak camper may not be able to combine multiple smaller items in a backpack because the backpack will not fit through the small hatch in the front or rear of the kayak. However, the kayaker may also use a duffel bag or backpack for transporting the smaller items between the kayak and the car or campsite.

The following discussion of equipment

items and food storage and preparation is more relevant to a camper traveling by kayak, water taxi, cruise boat, or on foot, but even campers who plan to spend the nights below deck on a larger boat might take note of the clothing discussion and develop a reduced or enlarged checklist of items to include for an overnight trip. Some of the items on the camping checklist will overlap with the checklist in the "Getting on the Water" section.

Tent

For overnight camping at one of the campsites in the Apostle Island National Lakeshore, the first piece of essential equipment is a tent. The tent should be a rugged, low-profile model with a watertight rain fly and mosquito netting. The low profile better enables the tent to resist high winds without becoming flattened or getting blown away. Keeping wind-driven rain and hungry insects away at night will give you the rest you need for the next day's activities.

While the size of the tent roll-up package is important for the kayak camper, the weight probably will not matter much unless you intend to be carrying the tent on your back for a long distance. Preferably you can slip the tent packed in its carrying bag through your kayak hatch so you don't have to stuff it in your hold unpacked or give your kayak the instability of a higher center of gravity by tying your tent to the top of your deck. Having to stuff un-bagged tents into your hold will more likely result in the tent becoming entangled with other equipment and possibly may also result in a torn tent.

While a single larger tent can accommodate more than two campers on a group outing, consider the level of love that may remain among the group members after spending most of twenty-four hours or more together in a tent waiting for the weather to clear. A number of tents with one or two campers per tent may be the better choice, keeping in mind that individual desig-

nated campsites are limited to a three tent maximum.

There are a number of covered hammocks on the market that may provide comfort and protection against the weather and insects. However, again consider the comfort level of spending a layover caused by bad weather in the more restricted position available in a hammock.

Avoid bright tent colors if you can. Other National Lakeshore visitors will appreciate not seeing your tent if it blends in well with the natural colors of the islands.

Sleeping Bag

Your sleeping bag should have a rating down to about 30-degrees Fahrenheit (lower if you will be camping early or late in the season) and should not be too bulky so that it cannot pass through your hatch opening packaged in the carrying bag. Since bad things sometimes happen, ideally your bag should retain its ability to keep you warm even if it becomes wet.

Sleeping Pad

Although perhaps not an essential piece of equipment, an air mattress or sleeping pad can increase your comfort and allow a better night's sleep to prepare for the next segment of your paddle trip. A closed foam pad avoids the loss of such comfort resulting from a leak in the pad or mattress, but it may also add to the bulk of the pad. If you use a mattress or an open foam pad, remember to add a simple repair kit to seal any punctures.

Clothing

In choosing clothing for a camping trip, think of warmth, including warmth when wet, and protection against rain, wind, and sun. This probably will mean using mostly synthetic fiber fleece, both light and heavy, and some type of a waterproof, light windbreaker for both the upper and lower body. A heavier fleece that can keep you fairly comfortable down to about 40 degrees is a good idea even for a summer trip. The heavy fleece coupled with a waterproof nylon jacket and pants will make rain and wind-bound days more tolerable.

For normal summertime camping, a lighter polypropylene shirt with long sleeves (for minimum warmth and sun protection) worn over a short-sleeve shirt of the same material is most useful. The light synthetic fabric is easily rinsed in the lake at the end of the day; it dries quickly overnight and unless it is raining, will be available to wear again the next morning. For the kayaker the lower half of the body, protected from both the sun and cold by a wetsuit, drysuit, and a spray skirt, may not need more than a swimming suit or shorts during the daytime paddle, but a pair of light trousers (again, quick drying is useful) or jeans will provide comfort and some protection from insects for evening wear around camp.

A good pair of hiking boots may be worth the packing space, if any significant hiking is planned for your trip. If no hiking is planned, footwear may be limited to paddling boots and a pair of sneakers. Sandals may feel luxurious for walking along the beach while the sun is out, but the exposed feet may become an appetizer for hungry insects in the evening.

A broad-brimmed hat will serve to minimize exposure to the sun during daytime paddling, and will also serve as a reservoir for insect repellant around camp.

Food and Cooking Utensils

Food taken on camping trips should fit personal preferences. Food preparation can be made simple or complex. Although attention to healthy nutrition is important, most of us could easily survive on less nutritious items for the period we are camping, since presumably we will soon be returning to a better balanced diet after we return home. But good food can enhance the camping experience and elevate the sense of well-being. The sug-

gestions in this section are quite general and mostly reflect the preferences of the author.

First, it may be helpful to subdivide the camp food into five different categories of "foods"—breakfast, lunch, dinner, beverages, and snacks. For convenience, that may mean packing five different smaller containers within a larger food drybag. The smaller containers may be color-coded to identify the type of food they hold or may be made of clear plastic so that it is easy to see what is in them. Keeping five different categories of containers in a larger drybag simply enables the camper to more easily find the desired food item without having to unpack the entire food bag.

Next, count the days you will be camping to come up with the number of "meals" you will need. Add meals for one more day (or two for a longer trip) because you may become wind bound at some point of the trip and need extra food.

For breakfast consider oatmeal (or another hot cereal), granola or commercial breakfast cereal repacked from the box, or perhaps a bagel with peanut butter (or humus, etc.). Package the oatmeal or dry cereal in separate individual bags the size of a single daily ration. Try adding a small amount of powdered milk to the dry oatmeal to make it creamier, and consider adding dried apricots (usually rich in vitamin A), other dried fruit, or even sugar and cinnamon to the mixture for enhanced nutrition and flavor. Also consider dried egg mix or pancake mix for a more leisurely, substantial breakfast of scrambled eggs or pancakes on the mornings when paddling is delayed by weather. For a morning beverage consider coffee or tea if caffeine is part of your morning routine, and perhaps some kind of a powdered fruit drink fortified with vitamin C.

Lunch is likely to be eaten before the next camp is set up and may be prepared while eating breakfast. Consider a sandwich type of meal that can be accessed easily from a deck bag or other handy location. Bagels, because they seem to resist spoilage better than bread, offer a good basic sandwich material, but don't rule out crackers, pita, or regular bread. Sausage, cheese, humus, and peanut butter all make good choices for the middle third of the sandwich providing some protein for energy later in the day. Carrots cleaned the day before the trip and refrigerated in a plastic jar with water for twenty-four hours prior to leaving on the trip can enhance lunch and add vitamin A to your diet. If drained before you leave on the trip, carrots can remain good for three or four days without refrigeration. Apples and oranges also are a juicy treat to enhance your lunch. For a cooler weather lunch variation, consider taking along a small vacuum bottle that can be filled with leftover hot water from breakfast and made into a warm instant soup for lunch.

There are several manufacturers of freeze-dried meals that come in a "just add boiling water" pouch for an easy evening meal. The pouch meals are light and compact, and some are even nutritious and tasty. Pouch meals are a bit pricey but can become an easily prepared evening meal in the event of a late arrival at the campsite or if the evening meal becomes rushed because of a threatening thunderstorm or a cloud of insects.

Unless hiking (and carrying your food) for some distance is part of the trip plan, a wider variety of heavier, but still compact evening meals can be made to fit your food preferences. Start with a boxed rice or noodle based starch for carbohydrates, usually cooked in boiling water and simmered for five to fifteen minutes. Add some canned meat (chicken, turkey, corned beef, ham, or a vegetarian protein) and perhaps dried or canned vegetables (beans, peas, corn, sun dried tomatoes, broccoli, you name it). Fresh vegetables such as onion, peppers, or carrots can also be added to the boiling water when the rice or pasta is added to enhance the nutrition and flavor of the concoction. Basic seasonings can also be used to enhance the flavor, including salt, pepper, garlic powder, chili powder, etc. Experiment with recipes you like at home,

realizing that the same food that tastes bland when cooked over your home stove may seem more savory when prepared and eaten on a camping trip.

Snacks may be packed in an accessible location on the kayak to provide extra energy for morning and afternoon paddle breaks. These are indulgences to meet your tastes. Chocolate, nuts, dried fruit, jerky, spicy sausage sticks, perhaps "energy" drinks and concentrates; oh, and lots more chocolate— all fit the requirements. The sweeter items can also serve as an evening dessert.

Beverages go in a separate container because the same beverage may become a part of several different meals. Depending upon your preferences, consider coffee or tea for breakfast and (perhaps decaffeinated) for evenings. Powdered drinks, including powdered milk made in camp the evening before and stored overnight for use with breakfast cereal, can also enhance lunch and snacks and help rehydrate the body in the evening. Colder, wetter weather makes warm cocoa a special treat. Although heavy and bulky, a can of beer or soda or a box of wine, cooled in the lake, can enhance the evening meal or increase the beauty of the sunset.

Utensils

Each person on the trip should have a plate or bowl, a drinking cup that can handle a hot or cold beverage, and a knife, fork, and spoon. For cooking, take a kettle of the size that is appropriate for preparing food for the number in the camping group and a large spoon for stirring and serving. The kettle or a separate coffeepot will be useful to boil water in the morning for coffee or tea and for hot cereal, using the leftover to supplement the day's water supply or put in a vacuum jar for soup at lunch.

Water

While it sometimes may be safe to drink water directly from the lake if it is collected away from shore and from below the surface, don't risk it. Boiling or filtering all of your water, using water purification tablets, or treating the lake water with an ultraviolet purifier will avoid possible intestinal problems and an early and unpleasant end to your trip. Good trip planning means having a primary as well as a back-up system for purifying water. Of course, if the cooking process involves boiling water, the cooking water need not first be purified.

Hiking

Hiking the trails in the Apostle Islands National Lakeshore can be the principal reason for planning a visit to the islands. The hiking option also provides the kayak camper with a source of exercise and means to satisfy the exploratory itch on a foggy or windy day when paddling is not possible.

There are over 50 miles of hiking trails on the islands and the mainland section of the National Lakeshore. Over 33 trail miles can be logged on three of the larger islands, including Stockton (14.50), Oak (11.85), and Basswood (7.20). Basswood, Oak, and Stockton Islands offer looped trails so you do not have to retrace your steps. Four islands have no marked trails (Cat, Ironwood, North Twin, and York), but even Cat and York have

long stretches of beach to satisfy the desire to explore on foot.

Most of the trails in the National Lakeshore are well marked and easy to follow, and unless there has been a significant amount of recent rain, most trails can be hiked without getting wet feet. Some trails on Stockton and Oak traverse sandy eco-sensitive areas, and in such sensitive areas it is extremely important for hikers to remain on the boardwalks forming the trails. Because the forest is reclaiming some of the trails (e.g. Outer Island), the hiker should inquire about the current state of repair of any trail to be used.

Even without a kayak or other boat, a wilderness backpacking and camping trip is

Tree huggers in old growth forest on Sand Island (photo by author).

Oak Island Trail (photo courtesy National Park Service).

possible by taking a cruise boat to Stockton Island and backpacking the 6.3 miles to the remote Trout Point campsite, or by taking a cruise boat or water taxi to the Oak Island dock and walking 2.8 miles up to campsite #4 or 3.9 miles to the North Bay campsite (#6). Landlubbers may drive to the Meyer's Beach parking area and hike up the Lakeshore Trail, camping along the way at the remote mainland campsite.

Usage of the island trails will reward the hiker with interesting sights including lighthouses (Devils, Outer, Michigan, Raspberry, and Sand); historical sites (Basswood, Sand, Manitou, and Oak); ecologically unusual areas (Oak and Stockton), and always a great wilderness adventure.

Fishing

Successful sport fishing has become a technological endeavor usually done on a powerboat with a large engine and perhaps a trolling motor and armed with depth finders, sonar, and GPS units. During the summer months, sport fishermen usually do daytime trolling with multiple lines, planers to keep the lines spread apart in back of the boat, and downriggers to take artificial lures down to fishing depths of 60 to 90 feet. Fishing at shallower depths, even from shore, can be successful early or late in the season and very early or late in the day, even in summer. If you do not own a fishing-equipped powerboat or are inexperienced in fishing the waters around the islands but want to experience a successful fishing trip, hire a charter boat and guide for a rather pricey full or half-day fishing trip. Although none of the charter captains will guarantee results, their knowledge of island waters will increase the chance of catching a trout or salmon.

The nets of commercial fishermen are marked by floats and appear from time to time at various locations throughout the islands. Most of the commercial fishing is now done by setting a linear gill net almost a quarter mile in length. Commercial fishermen are now using trap nets which lie entirely under the surface of the water instead of the Pound or Pond Netting (with part of the net remaining above the waterline) used in the past. While a kayak rudder or skeg typically will not become fouled in crossing a set net (except possibly at the very ends) avoiding the nets is the better option. For sport fishermen dragging trolling lines, anticipating the net locations and avoiding them is essential.

While it may sound attractive to drag a fishing line on a kayak trip among the islands in order to collect a trout or two for dinner, the reality is that the likelihood of success may not warrant the rigging required to troll at the proper depth and to make the changes

Successful afternoon on a charter fishing boat (photo by author).

Sandspit sunset (photo by Don Hynek).

A merganser mother's watchful eye (photo by
Don Hynek).

necessary to accommodate the changes in
depth. Further, retrieving a fouled line could
require backtracking several times along
the route. Still a few early morning or late
evening casts of a spoon or other lure from a
rocky sandstone shore may provide satisfaction for the fishing urge and prove successful
to the kayaker or backpack camper.

A Wisconsin fishing license and a Great
Lakes fishing trout/salmon stamp are required for fishing in the National Lakeshore.

Campgrounds Outside
the National Lakeshore

Although there is a wide variety of indoor
overnight accommodations available in
Washburn, Bayfield, Red Cliff, and
Cornucopia, camping outside the bound-
aries of the National Lakeshore may be

appropriate for a late arrival on the evening
before the start of a National Lakeshore trip
or for the night before returning home. The
following is a list of campgrounds (from
south to north traveling along the coast of
Chequamegon Bay and around the Bayfield Peninsula) that can be used for such a
purpose. Although camping fees are subject
to change, the fees mentioned below are for
the 2021 season. Recheck the fee schedule,
campground rules, and amenities available
in a campground before leaving home, since
there may be seasonal changes and restric-
tions due to disease control measures.

Birch Grove Campgrounds—A National
Forest campground located on the isthmus
between two small lakes. Start 1 mile south
of Washburn on Highway 13; go west on
Wannebo Road for 8 miles, then turn right
(north) on Forest Road 252 and go 2 miles
and right again (back to the east) on Forest Road 435 for 1 mile. Sixteen drive-in
campsites for tent or RV; well water; vault
toilet; fire rings; picnic tables; no electricity; fee required ($15.00); no reservations.
https://www.fs.usda.gov/recarea/cnnf/
recarea/?recid=27831

Thompson's West End Park—A municipal park located at the end of South
8th Avenue in Washburn (go south from
Highway 13 at the intersection with County
Road C). An open park with little screening
between the 50 sites for tents or RVs; water;
flush toilets; pay showers; fire rings or raised
fire box grills; picnic tables; electricity; Wi-Fi;
Cable TV; fee required ($27.00-$35.00); no
reservations. http://www.cityofwashburn.org/
parks--campgrounds.html#prwestend

Memorial Park—A municipal park
located next to Lake Superior off Highway 13
at the north end of Washburn. An open park
with tall pine trees but little screening between
50 campsites for tents or RVs; water; flush toilets; pay showers; fire rings or raised fire box
grills; picnic tables; electricity at many campsites; Wi-Fi; fee required ($27.00-$35.00); no

reservations. http://www.cityofwashburn.org/parks--campgrounds.html#prwestend

Big Rock Campground—A county park on the Sioux River northwest of Washburn offering more primitive tent camping. From Washburn, take County Highway C about 3 miles northwest, then north on Big Rock Road 1.5 miles. Thirteen tent campsites; hand water pump; pit toilet; fire rings; picnic tables; no shower; no electricity; fee required ($15.00); no reservations. https://www.bayfieldcounty.org/240/Big-Rock-Campground

Apostle Islands Area Campground & RV Park—A family-owned campground on the hillside just south of Bayfield at 85150 Trailer Court Road, Bayfield, Wisconsin. Sixty-three total RV and tent sites; water; dump station; firewood; pay shower; electricity available; Wi-Fi fire rings and picnic tables; tent sites around $30 per night (check website for rates) for two adults and up to six children, extra $5 for each additional adult; no one-night reservations in July or August. Phone: (715) 779-5524. http://www.aiacamping.com.

Dalrymple Park Campground—A municipal park with good campsite separation. Located on the Lake Superior shoreline about a mile north of Bayfield on Highway 13. Twenty-eight tent or RV campsites; water; vault toilet; fire rings; picnic tables; no shower (pay shower available at recreation center in Bayfield); electricity available; fee required ($30.00); no reservations. http://www.cityof-bayfield.com/dalrymple-campground.html

Buffalo Bay Campground—A tribal campground on the Lake Superior shoreline with open campsites. Located just north of the casino grounds in Red Cliff, about 3 miles north of Bayfield on Highway 13. Forty-three total campsites; 6 tents only sites, 4 tent or RV sites, and 33 RV sites; flush toilets in casino; fire rings; picnic tables; shower in casino; electricity available; fee required ($30.00 tent; $45.00 RV); reservations, (800) 226-8478. https://legendarywaters.com/campground-marina/

Point Detour Campground—A rustic tribal campground on a bluff above Lake Superior along the rocky mainland shoreline just across the channel from York Island with some brush screening between campsites. Take Highway 13 north out of Bayfield about 5 miles to Old County Highway K, then right (north) on Old K for close to 3 miles, then right (north) again 1.5 miles on Raspberry Road which turns into Ridge Road as it turns west. After 0.5 mile on Ridge Road turn right (north) on Blueberry Road, and finally after a mile on Blueberry Road, turn left (west) on the winding Point Detour Road almost 2 miles to the campground. Twenty-four primitive campsites, pit toilet; fire rings; picnic tables; no shower; no electricity; fee required ($25.00); no reservations. https://legendary-waters.com/campground-marina/

Town of Russell Little Sand Bay Recreational Area—A municipal park and campground on Little Sand Bay next to the National Lakeshore branch office and kayak and boat launch sites. Take Highway 13 north out of Bayfield about 5 miles to Old County Highway K, then turn right (north initially, then west) on Old K and follow it 4.5 miles to Little Sand Bay Road, turn right on Little Sand Bay Road (a windy road for the last mile) north and west for 1.5 miles to the campground, picnic area, and boat launching area. Forty-eight RV sites and 6 tent-only sites; flush toilets; pay showers; fire rings or raised fire box grills; picnic tables; electricity available; fee required ($22.00 tent, $25.00 RV); reservations: (715) 779-5233; sandbaycampground@centurytel.com.

Camping Checklist

Tent (including poles and stakes, rain fly)
Sleeping bag
Air mattress or sleeping pad
Matches and/or lighter
Materials for starting a fire in damp weather
Camp convenience kit with:
      Hand compass
      Headlamp/flashlight
      Light nylon cord (for clothesline or other uses)
      Trowel (for digging "cat holes")
      Toilet paper
      Repair kit for tent, air mattress
      Biodegradable soap (*not* to be used for bathing in the lake)
      Toothbrush and paste
First aid kit:
      Bandages
      Antibiotic cream
      Pain reliever
      Tweezers
Rope (for hanging food and scented items for sites without food lockers)
Water filter and/or water purification tablets
Map
Insect repellent
Sunscreen
Book (for reading on bad weather days)
Optional Items:
      Camera
      Binoculars
      Locking pliers
      Regular and Phillips head screwdrivers
      Nylon or plastic tarp (for cooking shelter during rain)

Clothing Checklist

2 Synthetic fiber T-shirts
2 Synthetic fiber long-sleeved shirts
Underwear
Warm and light socks
Heavy fleece top
Heavy fleece trousers
Waterproof jacket
Waterproof "storm" pants
Tennis shoes (possibly also hiking boots)
Towel
Insect head net

Cooking Equipment Checklist

Camp stove
Fuel for stove
Cooking pot(s) of appropriate size for group
Pot cover
Large spoon for stirring and serving
Large knife
Coffee pot (for heating water in the morning)
Water bottles or storage "bag"
Cutting board (for slicing and dicing fresh ingredients)
Biodegradable dish soap
Dishcloth or scratch pad
Plastic garbage bag
For each camper:
      Plate
      Cup (perhaps with built-in French press coffeemaker)
      Knife
      Fork
      Spoon
Optional additions:
      Frying pan
      Spatula
      Additional pot or saucepan
      Dishtowel
      Strainer to separate food particles from dishwater

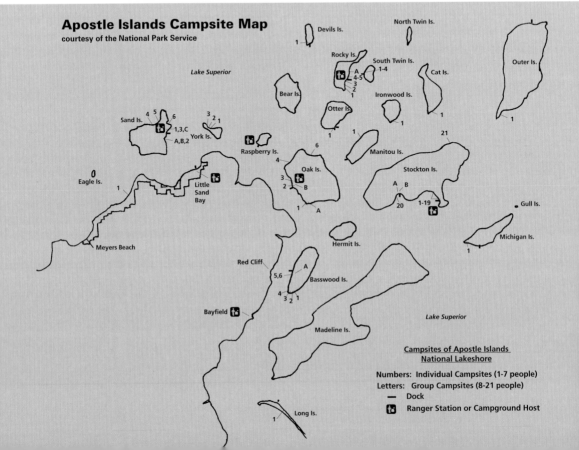

Apostle Islands Campsite Map
courtesy of the National Park Service

Campsites of Apostle Islands National Lakeshore

Numbers: Individual Campsites (1-7 people)
Letters: Group Campsites (8-21 people)
— Dock
🛉 Ranger Station or Campground Host

Island Size & Trail Length	Well Water	Toilet (Stump or Vault)	Accessible Site?	Picnic Table
Basswood – 1,917 acres, 7.2 miles of trails				
Sites 1-4: South end of island	No	Shared V		Yes
Sites 5 & 6: 200 yards south of dock	No	Shared V		Yes
Group Site A: 200 yards south of dock	No	Shared V		Yes
Cat – 1,348 acres, no trails				
Site 1: at sand spit south end of island	No	S (mouldering privy)		No
Devils - 318 acres, 1+ mile				
Site 1: at dock, south end	No	V		Yes
Ironwood - 659 acres, no trails				
Site 1: sand spit south end of island	No	S		Yes
Mainland Unit - 2,568 acres, 6.2 miles				
Site 1: 6 miles NE of LakeshoreTrailhead	No	V		Yes
Manitou - 1,363 acres, 2.75 miles				
Site 1: Beach 2 miles N of Fish Camp Dock	No	S		Yes
Michigan - 1,578 acres, 1.5 miles				
Site 1: Beach Area .9 miles W of Lighthouse	No	S		Yes
Oak - 5,078 acres, 11.85 miles				
Site 1: Sandspit 1.5 miles SE of Dock	No	Shared V		Yes
Site 2: .1 mile NW of Dock	No	Shared V		Yes
Site 3: .25 miles NW of Dock	No	Shared V		Yes
Site 4: NW beach 2.8 miles from Dock	No	V		Yes
Site 6: North Bay 3.9 miles from Dock	No	V		Yes
Group Site A: Clearing near Sandspit	No	Shared V		Yes
Group Site B: North of Dock	No	Shared V		Yes
Otter - 1,333 acres, 1.9 miles				
Site 1: Sandspit near Dock	No	Shared V		Yes
Outer - 8000 acres, 8.7 miles				
Site 1 : S end of island E side of Sandspit	No	S		No
Rocky - 1,100 acres 1.9 miles				
Site 1: Sandspit .5 mile S of Dock	No	S		Yes
Sites 2,3: w/in .25 mile S of Dock	No	S		Yes
Sites 4,5: w/in .25 mile N of Dock	No	Shared V		Yes
Group Site A: .25 mile N of Dock	No	Shared V		Yes
Sand - 2,949 acres, 3 miles				
Site 1: 200 yds N of E Bay Ranger cabin	Yes	Shared V		Yes
Site 2: 100 yds S of E Bay Ranger cabin	Yes	Shared V		Yes
Site 3: East Bay Dock	Yes	Shared V	Yes - from Dock	Yes
Site 4: W end of Lighthouse Bay	No	S		Yes
Site 5: Lighthouse Bay E of Site 4	No	S		Yes
Site 6: Justice Bay 1 mile N of E Bay Dock	No	S		Yes
Group Site A: 200 yds S East Bay Dock	Yes	Shared V		Yes
Group Site B: 300 yds S East Bay Dock	Yes	Shared V		Yes
Group Site C: 100 yds N East Bay Dock	Yes	Shared V	Yes - from Dock	Yes
South Twin - 362 acres, .35 mile				
Sites 1-4: .25 mles from dock	No	Shared V		Yes
Stockton - 10,154 acres, 14.5 miles				
Site 1: Near Presque Isle Dock	Yes	Shared V	Yes - from Dock	Yes
Sites 2-19 along Presque Isle Bay	Yes	Shared V		Yes
Site 20 - Quarry Bay .25 mile W of Dock	No	Shared V		Yes
Site 21 - Trout Point, N side of Island	No	none		No
Group Site A: Quarry Bay 500 ft S of Dock	No	Shared V	Yes - from Dock	Yes
Group Site B: Quarry Bay 600 ft S of Dock	No	Shared V	Yes - from Dock	Yes
York – 321 acres, no trails				
Sites 1-3: Beach on N side of Island	No	Shared V		No

BASSWOOD ISLAND

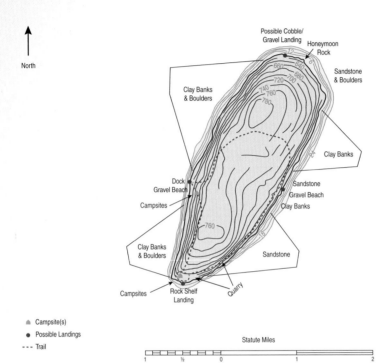

North

Possible Cobble/
Gravel Landing

Honeymoon
Rock

Sandstone
& Boulders

Clay Banks
& Boulders

Clay Banks

Dock
Gravel Beach

Campsites

Sandstone
Gravel Beach
Clay Banks

Clay Banks
& Boulders

Sandstone

Campsites   Rock Shelf
Landing   Quarry

🏕 Campsite(s)

● Possible Landings

- - - Trail

Statute Miles

Location

Basswood Island is located about 1.5 miles east of the mainland and is easily accessible from a launch at the Buffalo Bay Marina. Because of its location and accessibility, Basswood Island may be the first of the Apostle Islands visited by most novice paddlers. The island also serves as a steppingstone to Hermit Island lying about 1.5 miles northeast of the northern tip of Basswood Island and to Stockton Island and beyond.

Geography and History

Basswood Island is about 3.5 miles long, north to south, and 1.5 miles wide. Its southerly tip is less than 0.5 mile wide. Basswood Island is the fifth largest island within the National Lakeshore with an area of 1,917 acres. Its highest point about a quarter of the way from north to south down the island rises 188 feet above the surface of the lake.

The southerly half of the island was used in the past for several farms and the clearings for the farm buildings still exist, although the forest is slowly reclaiming the open areas. The clearing for the group campsite near the dock is one of the former farm sites. The agriculture on the island included a dairy farm and an orchard where a few remnant apple trees remain. Milk from the dairy farm was transported by boat across the channel to customers on the mainland.

The island has two stone quarries along the southeastern shoreline. Red sandstone from the quarries was cut into blocks, hoisted out of the quarries, loaded by overhead cranes onto barges and shipped to Minneapolis-St. Paul, Milwaukee, Detroit, and Chicago.

Basswood campsite at rockshelf landing (photo by author).

Shoreline and Landings

The National Park Service dock is located on the westerly shore of Basswood Island a bit south of the midpoint between the north and south ends of the island. The dock, about 70 feet long with a water depth of up to 4 feet provides access for powerboats and sailboats, and a kayak can be landed on the shoreline at a small gravel beach adjacent to the dock. The shoreline from the dock to the southwesterly tip of the island consists of clay banks with medium and large boulders in the water making it difficult for a kayak landing.

There is a rock shelf just east of the southerly tip of the island that can be used for a kayak landing or for mooring a larger boat on a temporary basis in calm water conditions. The notations scratched into the sandstone at the rock shelf serve as a reminder that others have used the landing before. Another possible rock shelf landing area lies about 0.25 mile to the northeast next to the abandoned shoreline quarry.

Along the southeasterly portion of the island to about the midpoint of the island's easterly shore there are sandstone shelves high enough above the water level to prohibit any landing. Paddling about midway up the easterly shore, a few clay banks mark the approach of a small cobble beach where a seasonal stream drains into the lake from the middle of the island. The remainder of the eastern shoreline north of the cobble beach is a mixture of clay banks with boulders and sandstone ledges, giving way to sandstone cliffs, shelves, and boulders on the northeast shoreline of the island.

The picture-perfect, vertical "Honeymoon" Rock dots the northerly shore.

Along the northwest shore of the island are low clay banks with some boulders and cobblestones. The northwest corner is the location of a former fish camp, and a careful landing could be made in shallow water if there is little wind or the wind is from southwest to east. From the northwest corner southerly back to the dock area the shoreline

Basswood rockshelf etching (photo by author).

Bayfield viewed from Basswood Island campsite (photo by author).

Basswood's Honeymoon Rock (photo by Robert E. Rolley

has high clay banks with boulders, generally making landing difficult except for a few small, flat, sand and pebble beaches that may disappear below shoreline vegetation if the lake level is high. In calm weather a landing could be made on the small beaches, keeping a watch for obstructing boulders just below the surface and at the waterline.

Camping

A group campsite lies in a clearing on a hill above the National Park Service dock, and two individual campsites are located below the group site on the hillside above the dock. A second set of four individual campsites is located along the southerly tip of the island, and the southerly campsites are accessible for kayak landing at the rock shelf at the southeasterly corner of the island depending upon wind and wave action. Each campsite has a fire ring, food locker, and a picnic table. Each set of campsites (at the dock and at the southern end of the island) share a vault toilet. No well water is available at the dock or any of the camping areas.

There are bears on Basswood Island. It is important to use the food lockers located at each campsite to store your food and toiletries.

A single primitive camping zone more than 0.25 mile away from the designated campsites, the dock, and the quarries is allowed on Basswood Island.

Hiking

A hiking trail leads from the campsites near the dock southerly about 1.5 miles along the westerly shore of the island. The trail then hooks to the east for 0.5 mile across the south end of the island and provides land access from the dock to the individual campsites along the south shore. The trail then heads north past the two stone quarries. The first stone quarry is worthy of careful exploration—although the quarry closed in 1893, a couple of large, cut blocks of stone still await shipment. After the second quarry, the trail continues north to the small seasonal stream

Basswood Island Trail (photo courtesy National Park Service).

midway up the east shoreline, then switches back to the west for about 1.8 miles across the center of the island and through the former orchard back to the camping area above the dock.

Kayak Trip Suggestions

Basswood Island represents a good destination for the novice paddler's first trip to the Apostle Islands National Lakeshore. By kayak, the crossing from Buffalo Bay Marina at Red Cliff or from Roy's Point should take only thirty to forty minutes, resulting in a minimal time for the exposed crossing. In examining the water before making the trip to Basswood, remember that a westerly wind will produce only a ripple on the protected lee side of the mainland highland, but could be producing 3-foot waves by the time the paddler approaches the Basswood dock. Check the direction and velocity of the wind and obtain the wave forecast before leaving the mainland.

Basswood could be a day trip, leaving from Bayfield or Buffalo Bay in the morning, having lunch in the dock area with a short hike on one of the trails, and returning to the launch point in the afternoon. From Buffalo Bay the round trip would be only 3 to 4 miles and from Bayfield the trip along the eastern shore of the mainland to Roy's Point, the crossing to Basswood Island, and the last mile or so up the western coastline of the island would result in a round trip distance of about 10 miles.

Another two- or three-day weekend trip would start with a crossing to Basswood, setting up camp in the dock area, and taking a hike on the trails during the first day. The second day would include a circumnavigation of the island with a watchful eye for the change in wind and waves that may occur as the direction of exposure changes during the paddle around the island. The second day may be a long day for the novice since the trip around the island could be 10 to 11 miles. After the circumnavigation, the wait-

ing campsite in the dock area will appear to be an invitation to a good camp meal and a good night's rest. The second night camping on Basswood Island will give way to a morning paddle for the return trip to Buffalo Bay or Bayfield to complete the novice's weekend trip.

The campsites on Basswood Island can also serve as a steppingstone for a trip to the islands more distant from the mainland. If the paddler arrives at the National Lakeshore later in the day or needs a shakedown first day cruise to make sure that there is no missing equipment, Basswood is a good choice for the first night out on a longer trip.

The Crossing

"Crossing." The word that kayakers use to describe the traverse across water between two land masses. The word implies more than the mere passage from point A to point B. A crossing also implies increased exposure to danger.

The kayaker's crossing may be from mainland to mainland across a bay, across a channel from mainland to an island, or any other combination. The crossing exposes the kayaker to the elements of wind, waves, currents, possible equipment failure, and to other human beings in boats more massive than a kayak. The danger is real.

Unlike the many warning signs we have on our highways, there are few signs warning of the dangers of a crossing posted along the shorelines of Lake Superior. Consider a highway sign that warns of a deer crossing ahead. The purpose of the sign is to warn the car driver to slow down and watch for deer. The deer don't read the signs and sometimes seem oblivious of the approaching automobile. It's up to the car driver to watch for deer. Like the oblivious deer, the lake won't read the warning signs either. The lake cares not at all about the welfare of the kayaker. It is up to the kayaker to heed the warnings provided only in the wind and waves and the report of present and future weather conditions.

The flat water conditions observed by the kayaker next to the starting land mass may quickly change during a crossing. Conditions on Lake Superior can change in minutes. Wind conditions that cause only a ripple in the lee of the starting land mass can become a constant blow of 15 miles per hour at the destination, kicking up 3-foot waves and making a landing difficult and risky.

An equipment failure, such as a broken paddle or rudder failure, in calm seas 50 yards offshore may be an annoyance, but the same failure on a crossing could become a much more serious event in bad weather.

Powerboats traveling at ten times the speed of a kayak may not be a threat to the kayaker cruising along the shoreline. But will that powerboat operator, perhaps intent on his or her own destination, identify the kayaker's bright colors and the flash of the paddles and be able to avoid the kayak in the open water on a crossing?

Perhaps one of the most significant hazards the kayaker faces in making a crossing is internal—simple fear. Even if the surf is pounding as the kayaker cruises along near a rocky shoreline, there is comfort knowing that land, although in reality inaccessible because of the rocky surf, lies only a short distance away. Until kayakers are able to extract oxygen from water like fish, the proximity of even an inaccessible shoreline preserves the myth that the kayaker will continue to be able to breathe oxygen directly from the air.

The fear of the crossing may be diminished by making the crossing with others. Unless the wind and waves are too loud, a good conversation can ward off the kayaker's fear.

For the experienced kayaker, the crossing may span the entire width of one of the Great Lakes or 14 miles from the mainland across open water to one of the major islands of Lake Superior. The longer the crossing, the more exciting it may seem. A kayaker's confidence level increases with time and experience. Once-frightening crossings become easier as time passes and the fear subsides.

Perhaps the most exciting crossing is the first crossing. For the inexperienced kayaker in the Apostle Islands, the first crossing may be only 1.5 miles from Red Cliff's Buffalo Bay to Basswood Island.

This is a story of the first crossing of two inexperienced kayakers.

In June of 1992, my wife, Signe, and I made our first crossing from Red Cliff to Basswood Island. It was somewhere around 11:00 a.m. on the last day of the Inland Sea Symposium. Sea kayaking was just starting to become popular, and the Apostle Islands National Lakeshore was mostly just another place to visit on a Lake Superior Circle Tour. We were inexperienced and under-equipped.

We carried our equipment to the sand beach behind the breakwater for the marina at Buffalo Bay, going over the mental checklist of our equipment. Kayaks, of course. Paddles. PFD's, although then we referred to them as "life preservers." Wetsuits. Neoprene booties. Spray skirts. Paddle float and hand pump to pump out the water in the cockpit in the event we capsized. Long-sleeve shirt or jacket and hat. Sunglasses. Suntan lotion. Water and perhaps a snack.

Even without camping equipment and food, we put on our paddling clothing and assembled the equipment slowly. The anxiety of making the crossing to Basswood weighed heavily upon us. It was as if by packing slowly, someone or something might intervene to provide us with a reasonable excuse for not making the crossing at all.

No intervention. Signe fastened her spray skirt and became free floating as I gave the stern of her kayak a push off the sand. Now I would have to follow.

We paddled to the edge of the breakwater. Intervention was still possible; the wind and the waves might somehow be higher than we anticipated beyond the breakwater and be more than we could handle. I thought that it was important not to show the fear that I felt for both of us since Signe was probably as frightened as I was.

Aware that some of the uneasiness was simply unreasonable fear of a lengthy exposure to danger, I checked my watch. The previous day we had paddled a shoreline trip from Bayfield to Roy's Point and back. We had paddled about 3 miles per hour on that shakedown trip along the shoreline. I calculated that it would take us at most forty minutes to make the crossing to Basswood Island at that speed. My unreasonable fear would be diminished by measuring the progress we were making in the crossing in terms of minutes paddled and minutes remaining.

"So where are we headed?" Signe asked, as we passed the breakwater and headed east toward Basswood Island.

"I think just to the right of that pine tree," I responded, nodding toward Basswood Island.

"Well, that doesn't help me very much. From here I can't tell what's a pine tree and what's not a pine tree. Which pine tree?"

"See that kind of V-notch in the middle of the island skyline? I think we head just to the right of that. The tallest tree in the crest of the skyline notch is the pine I was talking about." I sounded confident even if I wasn't.

"But how would I know?" I thought. I've never been to Basswood Island. All I have is a little map under the bungee cords on my kayak deck that was laminated to form a table placemat purchased yesterday in Bayfield. Prominently displayed on the placemat are the words, "Not for Navigation."

About half way across (I could tell from my watch), the waves became more prominent, and we both experienced the power of Lake Superior. Signe's boat had no rudder or skeg, so I purposefully kept my rudder up to try to be sure I was feeling the same effects of the wind and waves that she was feeling. It was easy for both of us to be careened 45 degrees off course by a quartering wave hitting our kayaks.

The crossing seemed to last forever. Perhaps we would be so tired when we reached Basswood Island that we wouldn't be able to paddle back to the mainland. Friends and relatives would eventually call the Coast Guard or the National Park Service and after a diligent search, perhaps they would find us on Basswood Island in tattered wetsuits eating berries. After several days in our smelly wetsuits, the tracking dogs would find us easily. After the rescue, the local paper would report that the kayakers stated, "We should have never attempted the crossing. We are basically coastline and inland kayakers. In the future we will stick to the coastlines of small inland lakes that have a continuous sandy beach."

About two-thirds of the way across (my watch was still working) we heard a powerboat traveling north to south in back of us along the mainland shore. It was probably close to 2 miles away when we first heard it. Our first unreasonable fear, of course, was that the powerboat would run over the top of both of our kayaks. If it didn't hit us directly, its wake would cause enough of a wave to upset both of our kayaks. Our self-rescue techniques were far from perfect.

"Those …," Signe muttered inaudibly, referring disapprovingly to the powerboat and claiming the entire channel for our sole use.

I was much more reasonable. I thought that the powerboat intentionally had remained out of sight until we were well into our crossing and most vulnerable. Then it closed in for the attack.

The powerboat passed along the mainland shoreline about a mile away from us. We didn't even notice its wake.

Soon we could identify the dock on Basswood Island, and we modified our course slightly to reach the dock. The last quarter mile should have taken five minutes. It felt like five hours to reach the safety of land. We were already tired from what at that time seemed like a long paddle.

At last we were at the Basswood dock, a pebble beach and the safety of hard ground. We shared a new bond. We had been exposed to the danger of a crossing and we had survived. It seemed at the time that we had survived a substantial challenge to our courage and perhaps even to our marriage. To enjoy the fruits of our victory over danger we walked uphill to the campground, ate a snack, and drank water.

The elation over conquering fear and the accompanying chitchat soon dissolved into the anxiety of the return crossing. But hey, we survived once, we could survive again. We went back to the boats after a respectful rest. Now how can we delay leaving the shoreline of Basswood Island? We paddled along the shore to the south a short distance, exploring.

The inevitable came—the trip back to Buffalo Bay. If the wind and waves jostled us, I do not remember. Probably there was another motorboat threatening us, perhaps even from a closer distance, but it made no lasting impression on us. Waves which turned our bow 45 degrees off course on the way back were only an annoyance, they did not appear to be life threatening. By the time we got back to the breakwater at the Buffalo Bay Marina, we were exhilarated by the triumph of having met the challenge of our first crossing.

On the way home, armed with new confidence, we talked about the camping equipment and food we would need for a longer trip lasting several days and including multiple crossings.

BEAR ISLAND

North

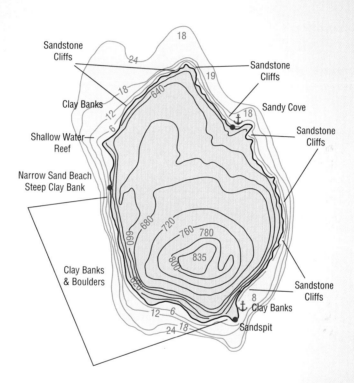

Sandstone
Cliffs

18

24

19

Sandstone
Cliffs

18

Sandy Cove

18

640

Clay Banks

18

12

6

Sandstone
Cliffs

Shallow Water
Reef

Narrow Sand Beach
Steep Clay Bank

680

720

760 780

660

835

800

Clay Banks
& Boulders

Sandstone
Cliffs

8

Clay Banks

12   6

Sandspit

24   18

● Possible Landings

⚓ Anchorages

Statute Miles

1   ½   0   1   2

Location

The south end of Bear Island is about 2 miles northeast of Raspberry Island and 2 miles northwest of Otter Island. The boathouse on the south end of Devils Island, easily visible from the northeastern shore of Bear Island in the afternoon sunshine, lies about 2.5 miles north-northeast of Bear Island. Rocky Island is 2 .5 miles just north of east from Bear Island, and the north shore of Oak Island is about 2.5 miles south of the Bear Island sandspit.

Geography and History

At about 233 feet above the surface of Lake Superior, Bear Island is second only to Oak Island in elevation. The island's highest elevation is about three-quarters of the way down the island, north to south, and centered on the island's east to west axis. Bear Island contains approximately 1,824 acres, and is about 2.5 miles wide and 4 miles long (north to south).

Bear Island is shaped like a raindrop with an indented bottom and three dimple-like points breaking the semi-smooth outline. Traveling around the island clockwise from the southern indentation (bay), the first dimple is a high clay bank protruding from the western shoreline. After crossing the rocky northern tip of the raindrop, the second dim-

ple is a sandstone rock shelf extending from the northeastern shoreline. The third dimple protrudes from the southeastern "corner" of the island in the form of a sandspit.

Although it was logged as late as the mid-twentieth century, the second and third growth has returned most of the island to a fairly wild state. Some artifacts from logging operations remain in the woods up the drainage area from the seasonal creek entering the lake on the north end of the cove nestled just above the northeastern dimple of the raindrop. A silent, deteriorating log cabin remains at the top of the northern rocky embankment above the creek. The life lease for the land area around the sandspit and dock terminated in late 2013, and the Park Service continues to evaluate what use will be made of the area.

Shoreline and Landings

Perhaps the best place to land on the island would be the sandspit, but landing there may be restricted, and visitors should treat the remaining structures with respect. From the sandspit along the southern and western shore there are eroding clay banks with boulders fallen into the water. Just below the western dimple there is a narrow sand beach backed by a steep clay bank. Because of the high clay bank, this sandy area perhaps better serves as a site for a break from paddling rather than a possible primitive camping area. It also is exposed to a westerly wind so that launching from the narrow beach in more than a light breeze could be problematic.

A few hundred yards north of the narrow beach, shallow water extends out from the western dimple well into the lake. Even a shallow draft vessel like a kayak may scrape a rudder or a skeg, and the area should be avoided or crossed with caution, especially in wavy conditions. Northeast of the dimple the clay banks turn into sandstone shelves that continue up to the northern tip of the island and then southeast to the rocky dimple on the northeastern shoreline. A beautiful quarter

East shore of Bear Island (photo by author).

mile of sand beach has evolved in the cove north of the rocky dimple, and the beach provides easy access for an unmarked wilderness camping site and for the exploration of the rock shelves on the dimple itself. Sandstone cliffs cover the eastern shore from the dimple south almost to the southeast corner of the island, where there are again clay banks until the land flattens at the sandspit. Off the sandspit to the south and east the water remains shallow well out into the lake.

Camping

There currently are no designated campsites on Bear Island, but one leave-no-trace, primitive camping permit is available for the entire island, except camping at the sandspit is still prohibited. Primitive camping is probably best at the sandy cove north of the northeastern dimple. In the busiest part of the season the prime location probably will have to be shared with a sailboat or powerboat anchored in the small bay. Sunbathing on the beach or on the rocks on the dimple can be very relaxing either as a stop-over on a trip ending at another island or as an overnight wilderness camping experience.

Camping on the narrow beach just south of the western dimple also is a possibility if the weather is calm and a late arrival and early launch is contemplated. If the wind and waves are calm, a landing and camp on the northern rock shelves may also be possible.

Hiking

Currently there are no hiking trails on Bear Island. The trails used by loggers more than half a century ago have been grown over.

Kayak Trip Suggestions

Bear Island is centrally located among the islands and can be used as a relaxing overnight stopping point, or a place to rest and relax in the middle of a longer paddle, before proceeding to the next camping location. It may also serve as a good stopping point for the first or last night of camping on a multi-day trip since the northeastern dimple is about a one-day, 12-mile paddle from Little Sand Bay and a 14-mile paddle from the Buffalo Bay Marina.

Bear Island's northeast Cove Beach (photo by author).

CROWDED^

Perhaps the grammarians who make rules for the English language should declare a new rule for adjectives to warn the reader when the context of the adjective should be carefully considered to establish its intended meaning. The adjective warning could be identified by marking it with a caret (^). Why use a caret? Well, asterisks are already taken for use in footnotes and sadly, carets are largely unused in the English language, although readily available there on the upper case "6."

The use of a caret for the proposed new "consider this adjective in context" rule can be demonstrated using the adjective, "crowded" in the following sentence: "John closed the tavern door and made his way across the crowded^ barroom to an open spot at the bar." The purpose of the caret would be to invite the reader to stop and read the adjective in the context of the sentence, visualizing the adjective's meaning. "Crowded" in the context of the barroom sentence would nudge the reader into imagining John changing directions several times as he crossed the barroom trying to avoid other human beings, mouthing a few "excuse me's" along his way to the bar.

Similarly, but at the other end of the continuum for the meaning of the adjective "crowded^" consider: "John paddled around the last rocky point on Bear Island and entered the crowded^ cove, viewing with increasing concern a powerboat anchored a hundred yards off shore and two catamarans with two sailors sunning themselves on the sandy shore." In the context of a remote bay on an island of mostly wilderness in the Apostle Islands National Lakeshore, two people from a powerboat and two sailors with two catamarans can make the cove seem crowded^.

Becoming Crowded^ at Bear Island. White spot is Devils Island boathouse (photo by author).

The loading/unloading area, the kayak launching beach, and park service dock at Little Sand Bay seemed crowded^ in the morning when I wanted to unload my car and launch for my kayak trip to Bear Island. One of the powerboat owners using the transient dock had left her car in the two-car parking space above the path that served both the dock and the kayak landing beach. I waited. One of the local outfitters was using the second parking space. While the outfitter group had lots of equipment and a number of single and double kayaks to unload from the van and trailer, the group leaders were very efficient in unloading the equipment and soliciting members of the group to help move the equipment to the beach. I took over the second parking spot opening when the outfitter group finished unloading. Righteously vowing that no one would have to wait an unduly long time for the parking spot I was now using, I unloaded my kayak and equipment and left it on the grass, moved my car to the parking lot, and returned to my kayak and equip-ment to carry it down to the beach.

The paddle across Little Sand Bay and out to the Raspberry Lighthouse did not feel crowded in any sense of the adjective. The wind was light and the morning was sunny and bright. The crowded^ launch area at Little Sand Bay was soon forgotten.

After inspecting the shoreline improvements in the dock area and taking a tour of the refurbished keeper's quarters at the Raspberry Lighthouse, I paddled around the south-western tip of Raspberry Island heading northeast toward the backside of Bear Island. As I angled away from Raspberry, I felt like distant eyes were watching me. I scanned the sandy shoreline where the northern shore of Raspberry takes a turn from the northeast to the north. There, on the sandy beach about a mile away from me there were, count them … seven, eight, nine kayaks. The large^ group of paddlers were taking a lunch break. It was the middle of the week in mid-July. Although there were no other boats in sight, the feeling of being crowded^ returned.

An encounter with a kayak group the size of the one on lunch break on Raspberry Island would be unlikely where I was headed. I planned to make a crossing from Rasp-berry to the southwest side of Bear Island and proceed up the west shore of the island heading east across the northern rocky tip and then head back southeast to the sandy cove tucked into the shoreline just north of the northeastern dimple. It is a wilderness campsite, and no large groups would be allowed to set up camp on Bear Island.

Before starting the crossing I evaluated the weather. The westerly wind had increased since I launched, but it was early afternoon—usually the windiest time of the day—and the weather forecast had predicted waves of two feet or less. I would be exposed for an hour or possibly two if I chose to continue paddling all the way to the northeastern cove without a stop. The conditions were manageable and stable enough to make the solo crossing.

As usual when crossing a bay or when crossing from one island to another, if I plan to continue along the destination coastline, half way across the crossing I start altering my heading to points farther away along the coast toward my ultimate destination. Chang-ing the heading lengthens the paddling time for the crossing but ultimately shortens the total time to the destination. On this crossing my heading gradually eased to the north along the west shore of Bear. Ultimately the change in my heading stopped at the is-land's dimple on the northwest shoreline. I moved closer to shore to inspect the possible landing site just south of the dimple.

There was a somewhat short and narrow sand beach below the dimple. Backed against a steep and high clay bank the landing would best serve to provide a paddle break, but not an overnight campsite. To carry a tent, sleeping bag, and other equipment up the embankment to the tree line would be strenuous^. To merely set up an exposed camp on the narrow beach would potentially serve to mar the wilderness enjoyment of anyone else passing by in the water.

The general feeling of well-being and contentment that comes with a longer paddle trip made me eschew a stop at the dimple. I continued north close to the shore, but no-ticed that my rudder slid across a rock or two as I crossed a shallow section. I veered to port to gain more depth beneath my kayak.

The sound of the waves, intensified by the shallow water, created the feeling that the velocity of the wind had increased. But looking out to the deeper water to my west I observed that the wave height in open water was the same as it had been.

A constant vibrating, humming sound underlay the sound of the wind and waves. It had too deep a resonance to be an airplane. I scanned the lake and located a large com-mercial vessel on the horizon to the north. It looked like a floating matchstick, featureless except for small peaks on either end. I imagined someone standing on the laker's deck, examining the north shore of Bear Island from perhaps 5 miles away. If a ship 700 or 800 feet long looked like a matchstick to me, would the imagined deckhand, even with binoculars, observe me as a tiny pin? Or would my kayak, resting so low in the water, be invisible below the horizon? Perhaps my bright yellow drysuit would appear to be a tiny fishing bobber drifting along the island's shoreline.

The thoughts of my reverie moved on to a time and distance consideration. The wake generated by such a large vessel probably would be noticeable as a break in the more regular wave action on Bear Island even 5 miles away. How long would it take for the wake to reach me? The ship would already be out of sight when the wake reached me, well on its way to the Duluth-Superior harbor. If the peaks of the wake-generated waves coincided with the peaks of the normal wave action, the result could be a series of several "rogue" waves, observed on Bear Island long after the ship itself had passed and was forgotten. There must be mathematical formulas for the speed of wakes and the diminution of wake-generated wave intensity, but the formulas were not intuitively apparent to me as my heading veered more southeast, then south, following the shoreline to my remote protected cove.

It was hot. I was hot. I had paddled about 11 miles, 7 miles since the last stop. I had not done any conditioning to prepare for this paddle trip. I was not as young as I used to be. I was feeling fatigued. I was looking forward to a cool refreshing dip in the lake to wash off the sweat and cool my sunburned face. All of the above. As I rounded each rocky outcropping, I anticipated the solitude of the remote beach that I remembered from years before.

Then I rounded the last set of rocks and saw a powerboat with a tall^ cabin located close to the bow. A park service boat? Was there a crew working on the old log cabin site at the north end of the cove? Was a crew creating a new designated campsite? As I passed more of the rocks along the shore, two sailboats came into view. They materialized into catamarans nudged up on shore at the north end of the cove. As I approached the cove, the powerboat lost its park service appearance and became a private boat; its two occupants were sitting in lawn chairs at the south end of the cove. Their dog was tethered on a leash near them.

My paddling cadence slowed as I crept into the crowded^ cove, trying to decide where on the sand beach I should land. The landing choice was obvious—between the catamarans on the north end of the beach and the couple sitting in the chairs at the south end. My approach had slowed because I was only semiconsciously allowing time for me and the rest of the crowd to adjust our collective mindsets to the addition of yet another party on the beach.

The catamarans were preparing to leave even as I landed and transferred the weight of my body to wobbly legs. Socialization with the couple at the south end of the beach would have to wait until I relieved myself beyond the beach tree line into the woods.

By the time I returned to my kayak on the beach the catamarans had launched, but were having difficulty finding enough wind on the lee side of the island to push them north along the shore. I needed to know something about the couple in the chairs, and they probably needed to know my intentions. As I approached them, their dog growled and took up a defensive posture to protect the couple from the intruder. I reminded myself that in spite of having my body still encased in a drysuit, to the dog I probably smelled like the worst kind of Bigfoot. I had taken off my cap and my matted, uncombed grey hair probably reinforced the dog's perception that I was a wild, threatening being. After reassurance for the owners and a rough hand-combing of my hair, the dog decided I was merely interesting, not threatening—a smelly human, to be sure, but not a Sasquatch—and he laid down again next to his master and mistress.

"Wonderful beach, beautiful afternoon." I opened the conversation with an obvious neutral comment. I could have said, "I am pretty harmless to you and your dog, I carry no weapon, and I probably can get along with most anyone for at least a short time." But in the midwestern United States you rely on the location and the weather to convey the "I come in peace" message, especially if both are positive.

"It couldn't be better," the man agreed. ("We are also peaceful and accept your presence.") "Where did you paddle from today?"

"I launched from Little Sand Bay this morning. I stopped at Raspberry Island to take the lighthouse tour this morning. How about you? Did you come out just today or have you been on the lake for a while?"

"We've been out since Sunday," he replied.

We continued through mutual questions and answers for: "Where are you from?" "What do you do for a living?" "Do you have family?" They were on a week's vacation. They had returned to Wisconsin with a boat purchased while they had been living in California (hence the unusual profile of their powerboat). They had been coming to the Apostle Islands for seventeen years, and we were mutually acquainted with at least one local boater. Their boat was equipped for fishing, but they had not spent much time fishing and had not caught much when they did try. They were familiar with all of the islands and had more current knowledge of the National Lakeshore administration than I did. They cringed when I mentioned that I was about a year into retirement from the practice of law ("Are you sure that you are peaceful and carry no weapons?"), but accepted the fact that I nonetheless did have some redeeming qualities.

Although they and I both were seeking the solitude of a wilderness experience, our conversation allowed us to reach the level of mutual tolerance of the other party's presence so that we could share the crowded^ public beach and bay each of us previously had psychologically viewed as our "own." With the catamarans now long gone, I moved my kayak to the opposite end of the beach from the couple in chairs, set up my tent, shed my drysuit and enjoyed a delicious cleansing swim in the clear, tolerably cold^ lake.

The couple and I each prepared an evening meal, and they packed their chairs and equipment into a very small rubber dinghy and returned to their California boat anchored in the bay.

About an hour before sunset a sailboat entered the cove under motor power, anchored and prepared to spend the night. With the addition of the anchored sailboat, the cove again had become crowded^. I noticed that the activity of the couple in the California boat increased. Eventually they weighed anchor, started their engine, and slowly left the cove, cranking their engine higher as they left the shallow cove and hit open water. I watched their boat become a speck as the engine noise became faint, and the local mosquitoes discovered my presence in the waning twilight. I lost sight of them as they were passing the north coast of Rocky Island. On their way to South Twin, perhaps? Or Cat, an island that was part of the fond memories they had shared in our conversation? Or perhaps even Outer? As I crawled into my tent to avoid the mosquitoes, I wished them well, understanding why they had left the cove and hoping they would find a new anchorage in a less crowded^ bay or cove.

Aurora (photo by Mark Weller)

CAT ISLAND

North

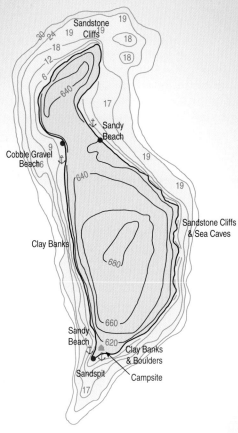

Sandstone Cliffs

30 24 19 19 19

18

12

6

640

17

Sandy Beach

9

Cobble Gravel Beach 6

640

19

19

Clay Banks

Sandstone Cliffs & Sea Caves

680

660

Sandy Beach

620

Clay Banks & Boulders

Sandspit

Campsite

17

 Campsite(s)

● Possible Landings

⚓ Anchorages

Statute Miles

1   ½   0   1   2

Location

Cat is one of the outer islands of the archipelago, 16 miles on a straight northeastern line from the mainland's Buffalo Bay out past the southeastern tip of Oak Island. To the east, Cat's only neighbor is Outer Island, its sandspit and lagoon lying almost 4 miles distant. Slightly west of north, North Twin Island is about 2 miles from the top of Cat Island and Ironwood Island is 2 miles southwest of Cat.

Geography and History

They say that Cat Island derives its name from its shape. If that is the case, the cat lending its name to the island was a flat headed, thin-necked Manx with a stubby tail portrayed by the island's thin sandspit point at its extreme southerly end. The cat is sitting and facing the northeast with its neck initially heading northwest from its body and its head and nose facing northeast. Most of the cat's body must be submerged, since the island lies relatively low in the water, its highest point only about 80 feet above the waterline. With its long neck the cat may be larger than it looks, however, having a surface area of 1,342 acres.

One of the island's former names was Hemlock Island. It doesn't look much like a hemlock tree either, although that name probably derived from the nature of the island's early vegetation.

At some point in Cat Island's history there was a fish camp on the east side of the island along a thin sandy beach where the cat's chin meets its neck. There was a trail across the thin neck of the cat to a gravelly beach on the west side of the island probably to allow the fishermen easier access to the lake if there was an easterly wind.[7]

There used to be a shack at the south end of the island, now removed, which locally had been referred to as the "Cat House." The Cat House also has been the source of stories mostly limited only by the imagination.

The island was last logged in the 1950s, and the trails left by the loggers are grown over and no longer recognizable.

Shoreline and Landings

The sandspit at the southern tip of Cat Island juts out into the lake far enough to allow a landing even in windy conditions on either the east or the west side. Going counterclockwise around the island, after the sandspit, there are eroding clay banks with boulders at the waterline. By the cat's front paws there are sea caves and sandstone cliffs northeast to the flatter area at the start of the cat's neck. In calm seas, there are a few spots to land on small sand beaches nestled between the large sandstone boulders around the cat's paws. Going up the cat's neck there is a sandy beach at the site of the old fish camp. The shoreline goes back to sandstone rocks and overhangs across the top of the cat's head. The back of the cat's neck is a cobblestone and gravel beach, and along the cat's back the shoreline again features high clay banks as the island's elevation rises higher above the waterline. As the western shoreline again slopes down to reach the start of the sandspit, the clay banks disappear.

The sandspit offers protection for anchorage from northeast to southeast winds on its west side, and protection from southwest to north winds on the east side. The bay on the underside of the cat's chin could also be used for anchorage when protection from a westerly to northerly wind is needed.

Cat Island sandspit (photo courtesy National Park Service).

Camping

There is one campsite on Cat Island accessible by landing on the west side of the sandspit. Its amenities include a food locker, fire ring, and a "moldering privy," an experimental less-energy and less labor-intensive approach to campsite disposal of human waste (as described in the park service camping brochure for Cat Island). The sandspit is a good place to swim in the afternoon sun, and the campsite usually comes with a beautiful sunset.

There is one primitive camping zone for Cat Island outside the designated site at the sandspit.

Hiking

The trails that served the last loggers sixty years ago have disappeared, but the long beach on the sandspit provides an opportunity for almost a mile (round trip) of leisurely hiking and pebble hunting.

An octopus pine (photo by Don Hynek).

Cat Island path from campsite to beach (photo courtesy National Park Service).

Kayak Trip Suggestions

The Cat Island campsite can be a destination site if one is looking for a secluded beautiful beach for absorbing the sun, beachcombing, and book reading. While you may share the beach with mariners from a boat anchored on either side of the sandspit, the sandspit is large enough and the island remote enough that crowding should not be a problem.

The Cat Island campsite also can be a weigh station for a crossing of the northern tier of islands from east to west or vice versa. When paddling between Devils, Rocky, or South Twin Islands and Stockton, Outer, or Michigan Islands, Cat's campsite can become a welcome overnight stop.

WHERE'S THE CAT HOUSE?

The four of us had already completed our paddling for the day and were looking forward to spending the last night of our four-day trip in Cat Island's only campsite at the sandspit.

We had paddled from Stockton that day with a stop at the Outer Island sandspit for some lunch before being driven off Outer Island by an enthusiastic hatch of beach flies. While the flies attacked our legs and ankles, they could not bite through our wetsuits. Even so, the flies were bothersome enough to give us the incentive to move on to our reserved campsite on Cat. We finished chewing lunch while starting the crossing to Cat. Oddly, there were very few flies at the Cat Island sandspit. A 4-mile flight apparently was too long for them and none of them had the patience to ride for an hour or so on our kayak decks.

We were self-absorbed in the teasing banter that had permeated the last three days of our long July weekend and were reaching the end of the "For Men Only—In Bad Taste" trip that started with a thunderstorm on Michigan Island on our first night out.

We all had jobs and ideally we wanted to paddle back to Red Cliff in the morning and drive home by late the next evening. Other than the obligation we felt to return to work, our only worry in the world was the memory of the Michigan Island storm and the high winds that followed the next day, marooning us for an unplanned wilderness camping night on Stockton Island. But our weather radios promised a clear to partly cloudy day with light and variable winds until mid-day, so we planned to rise early and paddle long before there was any significant breeze.

We had already set up our tents, had a refreshing swim, or at least a dip in the cold water, and were ready to prepare the evening meal. In a more civilized setting it might have been happy hour.

We barely noticed a sailboat approaching the sandspit from the west, using its small, quiet outboard to edge in toward the beach. Our group's conversation lapsed as we watched the sailboat approach and start to put down both bow and stern anchors. Our wariness of the sailboat was probably close to primal in its nature. The approaching boat is different from our boats. We were not acquainted with the several sailors on the boat. Would they be friendly? Did they carry weapons? Why were they coming so close into "our space"? None of us asked these questions or even consciously thought of them. We just became less talkative as we watched two sailors scramble into their dinghy to come ashore. Our silent watchfulness must have arisen from some basic ancestral instinct for self-preservation.

But these are more modern times and this was the Apostle Islands National Lakeshore, not a primitive encounter with a raiding group from another tribe.

"Ahoy there, permission to come ashore," called one of the dinghy occupants respectfully, as he observed the four of us all staring out at the sailboat. It was a call without real meaning, but served to tell us that the invaders carried no weapons and were respectful of the fact that we were the first occupants.

"Hey to you, too," Don replied. "Come ashore. But dinner is not prepared yet." It was as nonsensical a reply as was their call to shore. But Don's words also carried the message that we also were a peace loving, no-weapon group with only a temporary claim to the sandspit and perhaps not enough food planned to accommodate the several people on the sailboat as guests for dinner. Neither group would be attacking the other that night.

After we exchanged information about where we had been and what the rest of our trip would be, the sailors got to the point.

"Have you been to the Cat House?" the dinghy rower asked.

"No," one of us kayakers responded. "What's the Cat House?"

"Well, we were told that there is a place near the Cat Island sandspit where you can get a beer. At the tavern in Bayfield last night we were told that the Cat House was a 'must stop' while we were sailing around the islands."

"Well, we haven't really gone into the woods to explore, but we have looked around enough to have seen a building back there, if there was one," I said.

"Maybe there used to be something," offered Don. "Remember when we paddled down the eastern shore of the island, there was a shed that looked like it was ready to fall into the lake."

"Oh yeah, it looked like it might be an old outhouse," Jim recalled.

"Definitely no beer though," I said. "Believe me, after three days of paddling, I would have been aware of the presence of a cold beer anywhere within about half a mile. I think someone was messing with you at the tavern last night."

"Yeah, probably so."

After we exchanged a few more pleasantries and other stories, the sailors hopped aboard the dinghy again and slowly made their way back to the sailboat.

"Have a safe paddle back in tomorrow," the dinghy passenger kindly wished us.

"You have a safe trip, too," Don called back. "We're leaving early, but we will rap on your hull when we leave to give you a wake-up call." Then, in a lower voice to the other three kayakers, "It sounds like someone in the tavern last night gave them a good story."

In the morning, there was not even enough breeze to raise a ripple and the lake was a mirror. As we were leaving, the early morning silence made the "shave and a hair-cut, two bits" rap on the sailboat hull sound even louder than intended. We felt like we were hydroplaning by the time we paddled past Stockton Island, and reached Red Cliff by 11:00 a.m.

A comment from Bob Mackreth on The Retread Ranger blog from "Among the Islands" at http://www.bobmackreth.com/blog describing the rescue of a Madeline Island resident named Carl Olson in a small rowboat between Madeline and Michigan Island based on an article in *Bayfield County Press*, December 29, 1938, fills in the story of the Cat House:

Most likely Olson sought refuge not in the lighthouse [on Michigan Island], *but in one of the fishing cabins near the island's southern tip. It was a local tradition that island cabins were left unlocked during the winter, with a supply of provisions sufficient to sustain anyone seeking emergency shelter.*

The National Park Service honored this tradition until recently, maintaining a small emergency cabin on far-out Cat Island. Affectionately known as the Cat House, the cabin was built by the NPS in 1988 to replace an earlier shelter that had stood there as long as anyone could remember. Current management tore it down a few years ago; having cabins on the islands no longer fit with the new vision of the archipelago as unexplored wilderness.

DEVILS ISLAND

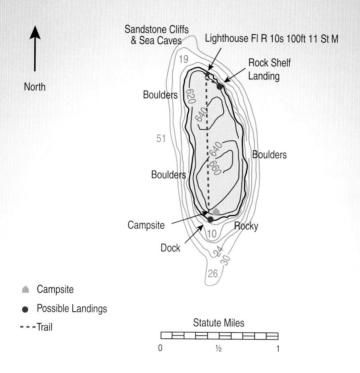

Sandstone Cliffs
& Sea Caves

Lighthouse Fl R 10s 100ft 11 St M

North

19

Rock Shelf
Landing

Boulders

620

640

51

640

Boulders

660

Boulders

Campsite

Rocky

Dock

10

24

30

26

▲ Campsite

● Possible Landings

- - - Trail

Statute Miles

0   ½   1

lights of Devils Island (photo by Mark Weller and John Rummel—prints available www.friendsoftheapostleislands.org).

Location

The north tip of Devils Island is the northern most point in Wisconsin and the temperature and wind conditions at the lighthouse site reflect conditions on the open lake more than the conditions on the Bayfield Peninsula almost 9 miles to the southwest. It is a lonely island with Bear Island about 2.5 miles to the southwest and the unprotected side of Rocky 2 miles to the southeast.

Geography and History

The lighthouse grounds located on the rocks above the sea caves at the north end of the island seem to rise high above the surf, belying the fact that the island's highest elevation is less than 60 feet above the lake surface. Devils Island is shaped like an uncut cigar, lit on its north tip by the lighthouse. It is about 1.25 miles long, north to south, and only about 0.5 mile east to west at its widest point. The lake has taken its toll on Devils Island, leaving its area at only 318 acres, one of the smallest islands (not counting Eagle and Gull Islands) in the National Lakeshore.

Devils Island's name probably originates from the ungodly compression noises produced when the rollers off the lake trap air in the cavities in the sea caves. At water level the groaning noises can easily strike fear in the hearts of unsuspecting kayakers and boaters even on a calm day.

The history of Devils Island centers around its light station, the last light station built on the islands. (The Ashland breakwater light, recently added to the National Lakeshore, was built in 1915, and the second tower at the Michigan light station was erected in 1929.) A 60-foot tall temporary wooden light tower was first lit in 1891. The original steel tower now seen on the island was completed in the fall of 1898. The exterior steel braces were added to the 80-foot cylinder in 1914 to stabilize it and alleviate the vibration that the tower was experiencing in heavy winds.

On September 20, 1901, a third order Fresnel (pronounced without the "s") lens

Fresnel lens atop Devils light (photo by Mark Weller)

View from Devils Island light (photo by Don Hynek).

manufactured in France was placed into service at Devil's Lighthouse. The Fresnel lens is an eight-sided, egg-shaped set of prisms that intensifies a small light from a kerosene lamp into a beam that can be seen for miles. The Fresnel lens was replaced in 1989 when the Coast Guard installed a modern beacon mounted on the tower railing outside the enclosed lantern room and removed the Fresnel lens from the lighthouse. The Fresnel lens was returned to the top of the tower in 1992. Unfortunately, an October storm in 2019 caused a portion of the lens to fall from its mounting and shatter. The balance of the lens has been stabilized by the Park Service, and repairs to the lens should be completed in 2021.

Nine head lighthouse keepers served between 1891 until 1951, when the Coast Guard took over control. The lighthouse was fully automated in 1978 and was left without staffing. The National Park Service has usually stationed a volunteer at the lighthouse in current times.

Hans F. Christianson was the head keeper in September 1928 when a vacationing President Calvin Coolidge visited Devils Island, and signed the keeper's log after having lunch on the flat sandstone rock shelf just southeast of the light station.

No evidence of the President's visit was etched in the stone, but at least one probably bored teenage daughter of head keeper James W. Bard did carve her name in the sandstone shelf sometime before she left the island in an emergency Coast Guard evacuation.

Marjorie, the teenager, suffered a fractured hip in a fall at the light station in late September, 1939. Her father, fearing the worst since he had already lost another daughter when her pneumonia had gone untreated while he served as a lighthouse keeper at Whitefish Point in Michigan, used his primitive radio to call for help. Although a stiff northwesterly wind prevented him from launching his small cabin cruiser to take Marjorie to a mainland hospital, the Coast Guard cutter, *Diligence,* responded. Guardsmen carried Marjorie strapped to a box spring from the lighthouse over a mile down the trail to the dock at the south end of the island, and the *Diligence* delivered her to Bayfield and eventually an ambulance took her to Ashland for treatment.[8] Before she could return to Devils Island, her father was assigned to a new lighthouse post. Indeed, Marjorie Bard Coons never did return to the island until July 27, 1997, a year before she died.[9]

The light now flashes red every ten seconds and, at 100 feet above the lake surface, is visible for 11 statute miles.

Devils Island sea arch (photo by Mark Weller).

A calm day for exploring caves (photo by Don Hynek).

Emerging view of Devils Island sea caves (photo by Don Hynek).

Devils Island sea arch (photo courtesy National Park Service).

Shoreline and Landings

There are only two good landing areas on Devils Island – the dock area at the south end of the island and the rock shelves just southeast of the light house site. The dock area can provide a safe landing for larger boats even in somewhat rough conditions, and the sandy shore inside the protected small harbor makes for an easy kayak landing. Unfortunately, the dock area has suffered severe winter damage, and the dock area will remain closed until a replacement dock can be constructed.

At the northeast corner of the island, the height of the rock shelves is varied enough to allow temporary "docking" for power-boats and sailboats at the higher shelves, and also to allow the safe entry and exit and temporary storage for a kayak hauled up out of the water on the shelves more even with the surface level of the lake. The landings on the rock shelves will not be possible in the event of a strong wind from the northeast, southeast, or east.

The sea caves and cliffs around the northern end of the island below the lighthouse perhaps are one of the most spectacular experiences in the islands, but the sea caves require a smaller boat or a kayak and calm seas or a light southerly breeze to enter.

The easterly and westerly shorelines of Devils Island are mostly inaccessible, with both shorelines marked by rocks along the waterline. The rocks increase in size and height above the water toward the north end of the island.

Camping

The one individual campsite just above the dock area at the south end of the island may be closed because of repairs to the dock. The campsite has a vault toilet, fire ring, picnic table and food locker.

Hiking

A trail just over a mile long runs from the dock area north to the lighthouse site. An unofficial crossing trail leads generally southeast along the top of the cliffs and through the lighthouse site at the north end of the island down the bank east of the lighthouse to the rock shelves.

Devils east rock shelf landing (photo by author).

Devils Island Trail (photo courtesy National Park Service).

Kayak Trip Suggestions

Devils Island could be a destination site in a three-day window of good weather, perhaps paddling all the way out to the Devils campsite from Little Sand Bay on the first day (14 miles), exploring the lighthouse and caves by paddling up to the shelves at the north end of the island on day two, and taking the long paddle back to the mainland or to another island campsite on day three.

Devils Island is also within easy reach from the campsites on Rocky and South Twin for a single day trip excursion as part of a longer trip.

Inside Devils Island sea cave (photo by Don Hynek).

ETCHED IN STONE

The trip from the Rocky Island sandspit campsite to the dock at the south end of Devils Island was an easy paddle into a quartering westerly wind. Still, Bob and I both were a bit light on paddling experience and like little boys wishing we were there already, our anticipation of the trip's end made the 2-plus mile crossing seem longer. Bear Island was visible ahead to our left, but to the north on our right, no landfall broke the distant conjunction of sky and water. Devils Island seemed to remain distant and small even as the western shore of Rocky receded from our view. There were no other boats in sight during our early morning crossing.

Our plan was to paddle to the dock on Devils and walk the trail up through the center of the island to explore the lighthouse grounds. We landed in the sand in the "harbor" protected by the dock on the west and a breakwater on the southeast. After investigating the dock area and the single unoccupied campsite on Devils, we followed the trail north up the hill. Our plan could have been improved by the inclusion of better footwear and shore clothing (rather than hot wetsuits) for the hike.

We were the first visitors of the holiday weekend to arrive at the lighthouse, and the volunteer keepers, a husband and wife team, showed us through their temporary quarters as well as the lighthouse tower. The couple, backed by excerpts from the keeper's log, dazzled us with stories from the past. The stories, expanded by our imaginations, changed us into the lighthouse keepers ourselves, facing the power of a gale force wind out of the north, managing the tedium of the day-to-day maintenance of the light and lighthouse facilities, trying to keep our sanity during lengthy periods of isolation from the rest of the world, and protecting our family from danger.

"Now in 1928, they had a special visitor named Calvin Coolidge," the keeper intoned. "They served him lunch at a table right southeast of here on the flat rock shelf. Do you know who Calvin Coolidge was?"

While neither Bob nor I were old enough to personally remember 1928, we hadn't slept through all of our history classes in high school.

"He was the President of the United States." Bob answered.

"That's right," continued the volunteer as he filled in the details of the luncheon. The volunteer's description was so vivid that Bob and I felt ourselves craning our necks to try to see Coolidge's table on the flat rock shelf. Trees and time made the confirming view of the presidential table setting on the rock shelf impossible to see from the entryway of the keeper's quarters.

The isolation must have been especially acute for the children of the keepers and assistant keepers. Generally home-schooled and required to participate in household chores and gardening to raise some of the family's food, the isolated life of the pre-teen at the lighthouse probably got boring very quickly. There is no reason to believe that at that time a few generations ago, parents were not already suffering from deteriorating wisdom in the eyes of their teenage children. So the children, including Marjorie, the teenage daughter of one lighthouse keeper in the late 1930s, invented things to do. Like lowering their brave little brother down from the edge of the rocky cliff in a bucket tied to a rope. Like laboriously carving her name on the sandstone rock shelf near Coolidge's lunch spot.

After ascending the lighthouse tower and viewing the Fresnel lens and the vastness of the lake north of the island, we thanked the keepers for the great stories and detailed tour of the grounds and lighthouse and headed back down the trail to the south end of the island. The walk back to our kayaks seemed much shorter as we processed the stories that the volunteer keepers had told to us and added our own silly comments and embellishments. The lure of an escape from our current jobs to an entirely different life played on our imaginations. We concluded that while we would enjoy a job as a light-house keeper, our spouses would soon assist our quest for isolation and the simple life by divorcing us and returning to the mainland.

We had only viewed the sea caves from above while we were on the lighthouse grounds, so when we reached the dock again we reentered our kayaks and paddled up the east shore of the island around the rock shelf to the sea caves. Although the wind remained light, the rollers coming off the lake made deep gasping noises as they com-pressed air into the rocky caves below the lighthouse. The claps and deep groans were unnerving—like the evil commentary made by the devil himself. Intellectually, we knew that the wave action was light and that it would not be difficult to control the kayak even in some of the narrower cave openings. Emotionally, however, we fought the irrational fear of the ungodly noises that seemed to be warning us to leave the caves immediately. By now it was mid-day, and there were a few powerboats and even a sailboat or two to share the absorption of the noise of the sea cave booms.

There are sea caves throughout the islands and on the mainland northeast of Mey-ers Beach. The Devils Island caves are probably the most impressive and intimidatingly beautiful.

Before we made the crossing back to our campsite at the Rocky Island sandspit we decided to stop for a rest and a snack, pulling our kayaks out of the water on the rock shelves southeast of the lighthouse. The light and teasing banter Bob and I had engaged in since morning slowed to a stop as we munched and drank in the afternoon sun on the rock shelf. Our minds rolled backward through the memories of the day. We remem-bered the groans and sights of the caves, the stories of the life of the lighthouse keepers and their families, and the boredom of their teenage daughters.

"Do you suppose there really was a teenager named Marjorie," Bob wondered out loud. "Let's see, she would have to be in her mid-seventies now. I wonder if she is still alive."

"Hmm," was all I could reply.

How much of the volunteer keepers' tales were true and how much were simply good stories enhanced by our imagination? Then our silent reverie was jerked away.

"Look. Look," was all I could muster.

Our eyes focused on a name scratched in the sandstone around sixty years ago. It read, "Marjorie," and suddenly in our imaginations the very vibrant teenage daughter of the lighthouse keeper was there sitting on the sandstone shelf, looking up at us from her name carved on the rock shelf, smiling, and enjoying the afternoon sunshine with us. Marjorie's story was real.

HERMIT ISLAND

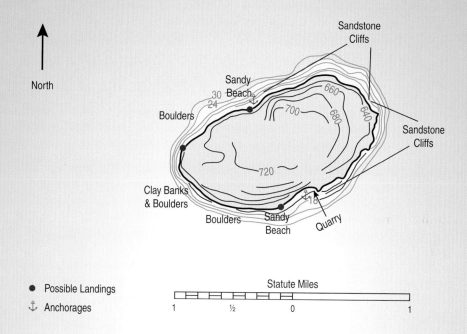

North

Sandstone Cliffs

Sandy Beach

Boulders

30
24

700

660

680

640

Sandstone Cliffs

720

Clay Banks & Boulders

Boulders

Sandy Beach

Quarry

18

● Possible Landings

⚓ Anchorages

Statute Miles

1   ½   0   1

Hermit Island quarry viewed from the water (photo courtesy National Park Service).

Location

Hermit Island is located about 1.5 miles northeast of Basswood Island, about 1.5 miles southeast of Oak Island, and about 1.5 miles southwest of Stockton Island. The northwest shore of Madeline Island lies about 2.5 miles southeast of Hermit Island. While Hermit Island is somewhat protected by neighboring islands, its neighbors can also serve to funnel and intensify winds from the north, east, northwest, and southwest.

Geography and History

Hermit Island is oblong in shape with its long axis running about 1.75 miles from southwest to northeast. On its short axis, running northwest to southeast, it is a bit under a mile wide. Hermit Island covers about 800 acres.

Most of Hermit Island slopes fairly steeply from its shorelines up to about 175 feet above the lake at the center of the island. From a distance it looks like an egg floating lowly in the water, pointy end to the southwest. As with most of the Apostle Islands, the northerly and northeasterly shoreline of the island is generally inaccessible from the water. Centuries of waves driven by winds from the north have eroded the soil, leaving only sandstone shelves and cliffs facing the prevailing wind and waves.

The island's name derives from a man named William Wilson who lived alone on the island after he was either shamed or forced into exile from the Madeline Island community of La Pointe in the mid-1800s.[10] After his expulsion the island was known for a time as Wilson Island, but later became the more generic "Hermit Island." For years people believed that Wilson had left treasure buried on the island.

An abandoned quarry lies about midway along the southeasterly shoreline of Hermit Island. Large blocks of sandstone still await shipment at the quarry site. Frederick Prentice, the former owner of the quarry, built a substantial three-story lodge near the quarry in the 1890s, but after his death, the building, intended as a residence, remained underused until it was razed in the 1930s. Other building sites are located about 3/8 of a mile southwest of the quarry, just north of the most westerly point of the island, and about half way up the northwestern shore.

In 1910, the Lake Superior Land & Development Company platted lots on Hermit Island and tried to market the lots as an ideal place to grow fruit and spend the summer months, but the plan mostly did not come to fruition.

Shoreline and Landings

Just north of the southwesterly tip of the island there is a sandy beach that offers a soft place to land and if the shoreline brush can be penetrated, it could also serve as a possible backcountry zone campsite. From the southwestern tip of the island, paddling southeast, east, and finally northeast, high clay banks with boulders give way to larger boulders along the shoreline.

A second small sandy beach about a third of the way around the southeasterly shoreline ("Second Beach") offers a landing site in calm weather, although the shoreline explorer needs to remain alert for boulders that lie close to the surface in approaching the beach. Proceeding counterclockwise around the island from the second beach to the northeast along the southeasterly shore, the explorer will again find clay banks rising 10 feet or more above the surface of the lake. The clay banks become sandstone shelves and cliffs around the northeasterly tip of the island and along the northerly shore. The shelves and cliffs, some 20 feet or more above the water level, make landing impossible. As the counterclockwise explorer heads north along the easterly shoreline, "Lookout Point," a collapsed sea arch, comes into view.

A bit more than midway along the northwesterly shore of the island, a third small sandy beach ("Third Beach") provides a landing area that is well protected from southerly, southeasterly, or southwesterly winds and waves. Between the Third Beach midway down the northwesterly shoreline and the first sandy beach at the westerly tip of the island, there are boulders in the water with narrow intermittent gravel beaches that could serve as a landing area, unless the winds are from the northwest.

Depending upon wind direction, larger boats may anchor near just north of the southwestern tip of the island and off either the Second Beach or the Third Beach described above.

Camping

There are no designated campsites on Hermit Island; however, each of the three small sandy beach areas described above offers a possibility for a primitive zone campsite, although it may be difficult to find a flat area for pitching a tent. Only one primitive zone permit is allowed for all of Hermit Island. No camping is allowed near the quarry site.

Hiking

There are no hiking trails on Hermit Island. The old trails in the building areas have been reclaimed by woodland vegetation and a trained eye is necessary to even locate the former paths.

Kayak Trip Suggestions

Hermit Island serves as a good steppingstone for a lunch stop or for spending the first night after launching from either Buffalo Bay Marina in Red Cliff or from Bayfield. The southwestern tip of Hermit Island is located about 5 miles from Red Cliff and about 8 miles from Bayfield. If the kayaker seeks a secluded camping experience in an undesignated campsite on the first night of a longer trip to the outer islands, particularly in July and August when the designated campsites may be already reserved by others, Hermit Island will usually be available.

The "Third Beach" on Hermit Island (photo by author)

GOING ALONE

For some paddlers the ultimate kayak camping experience is a trip without any companions. A successful solo trip both requires and builds self-confidence. For kayakers who tolerate or even welcome solitude, a solo trip serves to calm and rejuvenate their spirit and allows them to return to their more hectic everyday lives with a renewed tolerance for other human beings.

There are several advantages to paddling with a group of kayakers. Conversations with other paddlers can make long crossings seem shorter, and sharing an evening campfire can create strong bonds among people who share a common interest in kayak camping.

There is also safety in numbers. In the event of an equipment failure, even a single companion can help with the repair. Once on a coastline trip in Isle Royale, my companion's rudder seemed to be stuck in a slightly askew position on a long bay crossing. The foot pedals just did not seem to be working, condemning him to a wide circle, unless he constantly overcompensated with a broad sweep stroke. I pulled alongside my friend's kayak to help diagnose the problem and try to help him free the rudder, something that would be more difficult if he was paddling alone. When we determined the problem to be attributable to a stuck foot peddle, I "rafted up" our kayaks by leaning across the foredeck of his kayak and grasping tightly to the bungee cords of his deck. Lashed together by my arms, the two kayaks became a pontoon boat providing the stability he needed to break the seal of his spray skirt and rearrange the equipment stored at his feet in the cockpit, which was causing the restriction on the use of the foot pedals.

Group paddling also has its downside. Ideally, the decision-making in a group paddle trip can lead to wiser paddling decisions. However, in reality the decision-making is frequently relegated to the group leader, leaving disgruntled members of the group who would prefer a different result. Group decisions tend to be heavily influenced by the ability of the paddler with the lowest skill levels, and they should be. The nature of the membership of the group also tends to influence its willingness to take risks. On a day of marginal paddling safety because of the weather, imagine the difference in the group's discussion of the question, "Do we paddle today?" in a group consisting of younger, experienced male paddlers compared with an inexperienced group of mixed abilities. The young male paddlers, loaded with testosterone, are more likely to venture out on the water.

Paddling alone also has its advantages and disadvantages. With careful planning the single paddler runs less risk of something going wrong. While there is safety in paddling with companions, as the size of the group increases, there simply is a greater likelihood of a misadventure, such as illness, equipment failure, or failure to meet group expectations. Although it is less likely that something untoward will happen to a single paddler, a bad decision or problem with weather or equipment can immediately become more serious than it would be if paddling with companions. On the Isle Royale costal trip it would have been impossible for my companion to free his rudder if he had been paddling alone.

With only one voice to offer an opinion, decision-making should be easier on a solo trip. But the lone kayaker may find that uncertainty seems to increase without the ability to discuss matters with companions. On a longer trip before leaving shore in the morning, I find myself listening to the mechanical voice of the marine weather forecast over and over, trying to decide how the wind and waves will affect the planned trip for the day. Should I be paddling at all? Will I be able to arrive at a certain protected location before the wind changes? Will an alternative camping site be available if a weather change occurs earlier than anticipated?

The solo kayaker should tolerate a lower level of risk than would be tolerable when paddling in a group. There is no one to provide assistance in the event of equipment failure or other difficulties. However, for some paddlers conquering the risk and uncertainty of an extended trip alone provides them with greater satisfaction than they would receive from a comparable trip as part of a group.

While a checklist of equipment is always useful, it becomes essential for the solo trip. If the camp stove is forgotten at home or in the car, there will be no companion on the solo trip to suggest the sharing of his or her stove. The solo paddler's checklist should include back-up items and systems. If the water filter does not work, will the resources be available for boiling water or for using purification tablets? If a paddle breaks, was a back-up paddle included on the checklist? Is there an extra meal or two packed in the event that weather delays the completion of your trip?

For some kayakers, the ultimate reward beyond the anticipated solitude is the satisfaction of becoming totally self-reliant for a period of days relying only on what you brought with you in a kayak. The sweetest moment of the solo trip may be the arrival at the final destination, realizing that you again tested the big waters of Lake Superior, and the waters did not injure or kill you.

My first solo trip in the Apostle Islands was a springtime overnight trip appropriately spent on Hermit Island. Kayak camping was relatively new to me.

For years I practiced law and dealt with people every day. The busiest time of the year started in early February and continued through the middle of May. As the hours of daylight increased in the spring months, midwesterners would seem to awaken from winter hibernation and realize that there would be another summer for recreation, another season to plant and harvest crops, and longer days and better weather ahead for another business venture.

This awakening of human spirit in late winter and early spring always seemed to increase exponentially the amount of contact I had with other human beings, and by mid-April, I would long for a kayak camping trip to separate myself from people and their problems. My own psyche also awakens during the early spring, and I yearn for the seasonal rejuvenation that occurs in the forests of northern Wisconsin. Like a germinating seed, my spirit seems to reawaken in the soft, damp duff on the forest floor, tapping into the earth's nutrients and absorbing new energy from the sun.

It was mid-May and I had been planning this trip since mid-April, preparing a checklist and daydreaming about various paddling scenarios and camping routines, anticipating and relishing the seclusion provided by the big lake and the forests of the Apostle Islands. I took three days off from work. It was before the days of cell phones. There would be relief from any significant human contact for three whole days.

My plan was simple. I would launch from the Buffalo Bay Marina at Red Cliff, paddle to Basswood Island, and set up a "base camp." The second day I would paddle to Hermit Island, explore Hermit and return to my campsite on Basswood for a second night. The third morning I would return to Red Cliff to complete the trip.

After spending the night in a campground in Washburn, I stopped at the National Lakeshore office in Bayfield to get a camping permit. In the mid-1990s there was no need to reserve a campsite early, especially for a camping trip in the middle of May. At the Buffalo Bay Marina and campground, I had to seek out the caretaker in order to pay the launch and parking fee. There were a few hardy campers in the campground next to the marina, but mostly they were hidden in camper trailers, and many of the trailers seemed to be temporarily abandoned, patiently waiting for the summer season.

It took almost an hour to remove the kayak from the car top, carry the equipment from the car to the beach, load and pack the kayak, and put on my wetsuit. With canoe camping you pack the knapsacks at home, and you can be on the water in ten minutes. Put the canoe in the water, grab the paddles, load the fully packed knapsacks in the canoe and you are off. Kayak camping is different. Each item of equipment is carried to the water and packed into the kayak. Sure, some of the smaller items can be carried together in a duffel bag, but each item goes into the kayak individually, passing through a hatch hole that seems barely large enough for your arm.

There is a benefit to the length of time it takes to pack the kayak for a camping trip on Lake Superior. It gives the kayaker an opportunity to adjust the mind to the new set of "lake rules" that become effective upon launching a kayak on the big lake.

Our daily lives are filled with "everyday rules." When the car's gas gauge reads close to empty, you stop to buy gas. You get up at a certain time in the morning in order to make it to work on time. When a client calls, you try to return the call before you go home in the evening. After a while we become so accustomed to our everyday rules that we may not even continue to recognize them as rules at all.

The everyday rules from our daily lives have little application to kayaking on Lake Superior. Here the rules change and the only important rules are the "lake rules." Get the weather, wind, and wave report before leaving shore. Double-check the equipment list. Try to think of all of the "What if's" that may occur on your planned trip. Above all, if you paddle alone, don't take chances. No one will save you. You need to rely only on yourself.

Before I got into the kayak and pushed off from shore at Buffalo Bay, I stood on the beach absorbing the sounds, sights, and smells of spring, apprehensively concentrating on the impending change in rules. Migrating warblers chanted their songs. Poplar trees displayed the yellow-green of emerging catkins. The smell of damp earth and leaves, not unlike the smell of late fall, mixed with the slightly fishy smell of the lake recently freed of its ice cover.

The weather forecast called for partly cloudy to cloudy sky, only a 20 percent chance of rain that day and no significant wind and waves for the next two days.

I launched and paddled beyond the breakwater into the open lake. There was only a ripple created by a northerly wind, and the surface of the water sparkled. As I headed for the Basswood Island dock, the morning sun filtered through a thin layer of distant cotton clouds, and I soon overcame the ubiquitous fear of crossing open water alone. About two-thirds of the way across the channel, it occurred to me that I could be flexible enough in my planned schedule to take advantage of the current paddling conditions and paddle directly northeast past the tip of Basswood Island and on to Hermit Island. I could return to Basswood later in the afternoon after exploring Hermit. There would be sufficient time to set up camp on Basswood before sunset. My confidence level was high, buoyed by the feeling that I had finally escaped the everyday set of rules applicable to the workplace. Why not go for it? I changed direction slightly to aim the kayak toward the northwest corner of Basswood and beyond to Hermit Island.

As I went beyond the northwest corner of Basswood Island, I met a commercial fishing boat returning to Bayfield with the morning catch. A trail of seagulls followed the boat in the water and the air. The catch must have produced at least a few fish; their entrails attracted the gulls. As I passed the fisherman, clad in a heavy, yellow rubber apron, he leaned out of the boat's side door and waved. I let go of my paddle and waived back. I took the wave to be a salute to me paddling alone this early in the season. Or perhaps the wave was intended to say, "Goodbye, solo paddler. I hope you fulfill your apparent death wish." The everyday work rules for the fisherman resembled my lake rules more than my regular everyday rules. A part of me was filled with envy for the fisherman.

As I paddled toward Hermit Island, I remembered the stories of buried treasure on the island. One story has a stolen French military payroll buried on the island in the 1700s. Another story involves a man named Wilson who was banished from the Madeline Island community of La Pointe in the mid-1800s to live out the rest of his days alone (and bury his treasure) on Hermit Island.

If I were to bury treasure on the island, would I not bury it in the clay near the shoreline? The clay does not yield well to a shovel, but it would be easier to dig a hole in the clay rather than soil laced with hard rock. And if the treasure was buried in a clay bank near the edge of the lake, would not the most likely person to spot the exposed treasure trove be a solo kayaker examining the clay banks while paddling along the shoreline in early spring just after the winter thaw and the spring erosion left the ancient treasure chest newly exposed to view? What would I do with the treasure? Would I secretly hoard it for my personal use or notify the National Lakeshore authorities? I knew my conscience and the law would require the latter.

Soon I reached the southwest end of Hermit Island, congratulating myself on my flexibility of making changes in my plans. I paddled along the southeasterly shore, keeping an eye out for the newly exposed treasure. I passed the small beach, noting it for a landing on my way back, and stopped briefly at the quarry site to wonder at the difficulties of loading such large blocks of stone on barges back in the 1890s. The water depth dropped off quickly near the quarry, and with the water clarity so high in the early spring, it was hard to distinguish between water that was ankle deep or waist deep. I continued to the northeastern end of the island and contemplated paddling all the way around the island. But I sensed that something had changed, reducing my confidence level for paddling alone; perhaps it was a slight change in the weather. I turned around and paddled back to the small sand beach.

Sitting on a rock eating my lunch, I realized that there probably was no other human being within 3 miles of me at this time of the year. I fell into a near stupor as I contemplated the change to lake rules, the unfound Hermit Island treasure, and the trip back to Basswood Island. My stupor was interrupted by the realization that the thin layer of clouds had become thicker and the sun had disappeared. Although it was not raining on Hermit Island, a light rain or mist now completely obscured the mainland, and the outline of Basswood Island, less than 2 miles away, remained barely visible.

Lake rules dictated another change in plans. While the mist probably would clear before sunset and the wind was still light, I considered simply staying on Hermit Island for the night instead of returning to Basswood. I did not want to risk a solo crossing back to Basswood Island relying on my compass alone, especially in uncertain weather.

I explored the slope above the beach for a flat area to pitch a tent. The woods consisted mostly of poplar growth with a few maples and an occasional oak. The slope was mostly barren of underbrush and any flat spot for pitching my tent. A couple of hundred yards up the slope I found a spot flat enough for the tent and returned to the beach to collect the things I would need for the night. Basswood Island had now also disappeared in the mist, reinforcing my decision to stay.

After a day of paddling, I always have enjoyed a quick dip in the clear waters of Lake Superior to wash off the sweat and rinse the wetsuit. The key word is quick since the lake is usually too cold for any extended swimming. In mid-May the water temperature was only about 40 degrees, and I found that my feet began to hurt when I was in water barely up to my knees. I dipped the top of my head into the shallow water to wash my hair. In less than a second I had the splitting headache that one gets from eating too much ice cream too quickly. I put on warm clothes for the evening and resumed the stupor.

As I lit the camp stove to prepare an evening meal, the sun came from behind the clouds and warmed my body and spirit. With several hours of daylight left I could still paddle back to Basswood Island for the night, but that would mean putting the cold wetsuit back on and packing the tent and other equipment back into the kayak.

After eating, I packed my food and other things that might prove interesting to a bear's nose in a drybag and chose a sturdy oak branch high above the ground and away from my tent to hang the attractive package. First, I tied a rock to the end of my rope and then threw the rock over the branch, ultimately hoisting the drybag tied to the other end of the rope and filled with bear goodies so that it was suspended more than 10 feet off the ground and more than 5 feet below the branch. While there probably were no bears on Hermit Island, if one had awakened from hibernation early on neighboring Stockton Island or Basswood Island, it could have walked across the ice to Hermit Island less than two months ago.

I was asleep in my tent before it was completely dark.

In the grey light of the morning an inhuman sound woke me with a start. Either the ghost of the person who hid the treasure on the island had returned to defend it or a child was calling out in anguish. I waited for a repetition of the screech. It came again, but this time sounding more like the call of a pileated woodpecker, not a common sound to be heard even when living under lake rules. A peak outside the tent door confirmed the woodpecker theory.

I worked diligently to pack up the tent and the sleeping bag and pad. I lowered the un-molested food pack to the ground. Breakfast and coffee tasted great in the cool morning air. The sun came up and I looked forward to the exercise of paddling back to Basswood Island and perhaps skipping the second night of camping and paddling all the way back to Red Cliff. Even with my diligent attention to packing, I was not ready to push off until an hour and a half after waking.

The paddle back to Basswood and ultimately to Buffalo Bay Marina was over water that only rippled and glistened in the sun. On the trip back to the marina, I thought again about the treasure of Hermit Island. Indeed, I *had* found treasure on Hermit Island. But it was not measured in gold or silver. Rather it was measured by the seasonal restoration of my spirit and marked by a change in the rules of life.

Stranded on the rocks (photo by author)

IRONWOOD ISLAND

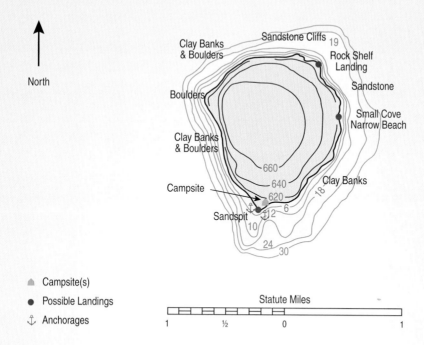

North

Clay Banks & Boulders

Sandstone Cliffs 19

Rock Shelf Landing

Sandstone

Boulders

Small Cove
Narrow Beach

Clay Banks & Boulders

660
640
620
6
12
18

Campsite

Clay Banks

Sandspit

10
24
30

Campsite(s)

Possible Landings

Anchorages

Statute Miles

1   ½   0   1

Ironwood Island path to campsite (photo courtesy National Park Service).

Location

Ironwood Island is centrally located among the islands in the Apostle Islands National Lakeshore, lying 1 mile northeast of Manitou Island and equally distanced 1.75 miles east of Otter Island, southeast of South Twin Island, and west of Cat Island. The northern coast of Stockton Island is about 3 miles south of Ironwood just past the northeastern tip of Manitou.

Geography and History

Ironwood is nearly round in shape and about 1 mile in diameter, measuring about 659 acres in area. The circular shape is marred by two protrusions into the water—the one on the northwest is an extension of boulders; the other on the southerly or southwestern "corner" of the island is a sandspit. The island is relatively flat, rising only about 78 feet above the elevation of the lake.

About 10 feet above the sandspit is a flat area that probably served as the base for the logging activity on the island. Now the island has a mixture of hardwoods and conifers, but it may have derived its name from the hard ironwood trees constituting part of the original forest.

Shoreline and Landings

If you imagine the round island to be a clock face, except for the sandspit located at about 6:30, there are high clay banks from about 4:00 o'clock to about 9:00 o'clock. From 9:00 o'clock to 12:00, north of the protruding boulders, the steep clay banks change to sandstone and at about 11:00 o'clock ultimately become sandstone cliffs. From noon to 4:00 there are sandstone shelves with ledges 5 to 25 feet above the water, making a landing impossible with two possible exceptions. The first exception is a rock shelf located at about 1:00, although it may be easier to use the shelf as a landing for a boat larger than a kayak even in calm seas. At about 3:00 o'clock there is a small cove with a sandy landing.

Larger boats can find partially protected anchorage on either side of the sandspit, depending upon wind direction. Keep in mind that the shallow water south of the sandspit extends several hundred yards into the lake and it will be important to make a wide loop if it becomes necessary to cross over to the other side of the sandspit.

The best landing and perhaps the only all-weather landing is at the sandspit. The flat area that was formerly used for the logging operations is adjacent to the sandspit and the island's only campsite is now located on the east side of the sandspit.

Camping

There is one designated campsite on Ironwood Island with a tent pad, fire ring, food locker, and stump privy. The camping area is about 10 to 12 feet above the water and offers a nice view across the water to Stockton Island to the south and Manitou Island to the southwest. Ironwood has one primitive camping zone outside the area of the designated campsite.

Hiking

There are no hiking trails on Ironwood Island. The old logging trails from the clearing at the sandspit have been reclaimed by woodland vegetation.

Kayak Trip Suggestions

The campsite on Ironwood Island could serve well as a secluded, contemplative destination site. The site offers about a 150-degree view of the lake and the nearby islands. The sandspit provides a great beach for a cooling dip in the afternoon, and an easy soft spot for a landing or a launch. Perhaps because of its seclusion, the campsite may have more than its share of hungry mosquitoes waiting to take advantage of exposed human skin.

Because of its central location among the islands, it can also become a welcome overnight way station for a continuing trip in any direction.

SABRINA, THE RABID DOE

Somehow I ended up getting a late start on my solo trip over the long Fourth of July weekend. Although I arose early on the first day of the trip, there were some morning obligations involving physical labor that left me sweaty and even a bit tired. When I arrived at the Buffalo Bay Marina just after noon, the note on the caretaker's door said, "At lunch. Back at 1:00." I drove my car down to the marina beach anyway and prepared to launch, thinking that it would take me most of the hour to pack the kayak for the three-day trip.

By the time I finished packing the kayak, there were only about ten minutes to wait for the harbormaster's return, and there was ample entertainment since Red Cliff was hosting its annual Fourth of July pow-wow with drums, singing, dancing, and traditional holiday dress. At the time, the festivities were held in an open area now occupied and replaced by a new hotel and casino. I couldn't blame the caretaker for being a few minutes late.

After paying the launch and parking fees, parking my car, and wiggling into my wetsuit, it was close to 1:30 before I got into my kayak and pushed off from shore into the calm, protected marina harbor. I had determined that the paddle trip to Ironwood Island with stops on Hermit Island and possibly Stockton would take me close to four hours. There was no more time to waste. While the weather forecast was good, the wind was not a problem, and it would be daylight till well past 8:00 o'clock, I remembered the ranger at the Park Service Headquarters in Bayfield suggesting that it would be wise to occupy even a reserved campsite by 5:00 p.m. on a holiday weekend. The fatigue from the morning's physical labor along with the beat of the pow-wow drums faded away behind me as my kayak glided northeast, aimed toward the western shore of Hermit Island. The sun reflected bright diamonds on the lake surface, rippled by only a slight southerly breeze.

This was a trip of greater significance than some because at the time, there were only two islands in the park that I had not previously visited—Ironwood and North Twin. I planned to camp two nights on Ironwood before returning to Red Cliff. On the intervening day I would paddle to North Twin, circumnavigate the island, and return to my campsite on Ironwood by way of the west side of South Twin Island. For almost fifteen years I had promised myself a visit by kayak to each of the accessible islands in the National Lakeshore. This trip would complete that quest.

My paddle cadence was strong and steady at about forty strokes per minute, and I was approaching the western shore of Hermit Island in an hour. A quick break on Hermit Island would relieve my bladder and give me renewed vigor for the next leg in the trip.

As I approached Hermit Island's sand and cobble beach, I saw a few lily pads in the water near shore. I remember seeing lilies in swampy lagoon areas around the islands, but I did not remember any such plants in the cold, open water of the big lake. Getting through the brush to the woods was no easy task, since the brush line, hanging oppressively over the cobble beach, seemed to want to push me back into the lake. Once I climbed the steep bank beyond the tree line, the mosquitoes and flies provided the brush with reinforcements to resist my intrusion. Soon I was back in my kayak resuming the paddling cadence, not because I still felt the need not to waste time—that civilized compulsion had drifted away behind me with the sound of the pow-wow drums—rather, now I was fleeing from the victorious insect defenders of Hermit Island.

I continued northeast from Hermit Island about 3 miles to the western tip of Stockton Island and then continued about a mile along the shoreline, noting for future reference a couple of small sandy landing areas formed by the deltas of seasonal creeks that emptied into Lake Superior. I stopped again for an exploratory break from paddling on a sandy beach along the northwest shoreline of Stockton Island where my topographical map seemed to promise a flatter and more level shoreline. I found a soft, sandy landing and the flat sandy shore dotted with alders and other smaller brush that might serve as a wilderness campsite for a future paddle trip. Indeed, there were numerous flat sandy areas that would work well for pitching a tent. Unfortunately there also was a lot of bear scat, and the nearest large trees to hang bear attracters beyond the bear's reach for the night were a good distance away.

Back on the water for the final 3.5 miles, I played mind games with myself, trying to keep my paddling cadence up to the level it was when I started the trip by reminding myself of the admonition of the park ranger about arriving at the campsite before 5:00 p.m. The admonition really was only a mind game that dulled the real craving for the total relaxation that comes with a rehydrating cool drink, an even cooler dip in the lake while rinsing out the hot wetsuit, and the leisurely preparation of the evening meal. I reached the campsite at about 5:15.

Usually I carry my equipment from the landing area to the campsite and set up the tent and sleeping arrangements even before I take off my wetsuit. Setting up camp first allows my body to cool off and reduces the shock of a cold swim in the lake. Setting up camp first also shortens the time it takes to actually get into the welcome sleeping bag when I can no longer keep my eyes open after dinner, and it provides immediate shelter if the weather becomes stormy during the evening. While no inclement weather threatened that evening, with the morning's physical activity and nearly four hours of paddling, I knew sleep would creep silently into my camp and drag me into the tent and sleeping bag, perhaps even before the sun had a reasonable time to set.

Although it was one of the warmest evenings of the summer, the cold waters of Lake Superior left me refreshed but shivering after only a few minutes of immersion. I felt cool and relaxed as I pulled on my evening "camp clothes" and hopped along the sandspit trying to put on my tennis shoes without getting them wet and full of sand. I carried my rinsed wetsuit, towel, and the last remnants of what I needed for the evening meal from the beach up the sand hill to the campsite on the flat area above the sandspit.

As I lit the camp stove and started to boil some water for some rice or pasta-based meal at the campsite picnic table, a feeling that I was not alone slowly crawled up the hairs on the back of my neck. A brown mass with three dark spots in the corner of my field of vision materialized into a yearling doe with her coal black eyes and nose forming the three dark spots. She stared at me intently not 20 yards away just at the edge of the tree line surrounding the open campsite. For perhaps a minute we studied each other. I wanted to reach for my camera, but feared that our visual reverie would be easily interrupted by my movement.

Sabrina, the rabid doe of Ironwood Island (photo by author).

Finally I got up from my seat at the picnic table and took a couple of steps to reach my camera. The doe—I named her Sabrina—continued her eerie stare while I took her picture several times. The boiling water summoned me back to the task of preparing dinner. While my movements during cooking were relatively slow and not threatening,

Sabrina generally showed no fear of my normal camp activity and continued to watch me closely, taking only a few steps in and out of the trees now and then. Sabrina was not displaying the usual whitetail fear of humans.

Why was Sabrina so casual? Had no one told her that humans were predators? Was she suffering in a rabid mental haze, waiting for me to put down my guard so she could charge and pass on the disease to me? I had never heard of a rabid deer. It was spooky. I felt the need to make sure that I would not feel a sudden cold nose nuzzling the back of my neck while I ate my dinner. I looked at Sabrina, took a step toward her and gave her a half yell, "Hey!" Sabrina bounded to the tree line, reacting to my aggressive actions. I was almost relieved that she had acted in a manner I considered more normal for a whitetail deer. I didn't expect to see Sabrina again.

After finishing dinner and cleaning up the dishes, I knew I would not be able to stay awake long sitting on the picnic table watching the sunset. A few mosquito bites would be all the excuse I would need to crawl into the insect-free tent and the inviting sleeping bag. To avoid falling asleep by 8:30, I decided to take a short walk on the sandspit. The walk would allow me to escape the mosquitoes for a few minutes and to relieve myself before I succumbed to the relaxed sleep that would come so easily after the day's exercise and a stomach so recently filled with a wonderful amount of carbohydrates.

As I walked along the sandpit, I heard Sabrina's hoofs in the sand behind me. I even thought that I could hear her breathe. I stopped. She stopped. I walked. She walked. I even did a short sprint for about 20 yards. Sabrina followed closely, at a distance of only about 10 yards, stopping short when I stopped my sprint and planted my feet in the sand. My ideas about Sabrina's rabidity returned. Or perhaps she was a deer infused with the spirit of something other than the spirit derived from her whitetail ancestry. Sabrina now was planted squarely between me and the return to my camp, giving me the same eye contact we had while I was cooking at the picnic table.

"What's up with you?" I asked Sabrina out loud, hoping that she would not answer me in any understandable fashion. The sound of my own voice seemed to break the spell that Sabrina had cast over me.

I urinated and continued to search my mind for an explanation for Sabina's unusual behavior.

I walked in a direction perpendicular to my former path to the packed sand at the waterline. If Sabrina was attempting to block my return to camp, maybe I could circle around her along the beach.

Sabrina followed my former path to the place I had urinated and stopped, choosing not to follow me on my detour to the waterline. Her nose was at the ground and her tongue seemed to be licking the sand. I realized instantly that Sabrina was not rabid. She was not infused with a strange spirit. Island bound in a pure freshwater sea, she was after the salts I had left on the ground. She apparently had learned that humans visiting the campsite left the tent area to relieve themselves, and she learned to follow them and watch for the deposit of the salts she craved.

The revelation immediately restored Sabrina and me to our proper positions in the food chain. I was reminded of several spring trips to Oak Island when members of the paddle group startled deer on their trips to the forest to relieve themselves in the middle of the night. In the morning we observed hoof prints and pawing marks in the soil in the spots the humans had visited the previous night. As gross as the delivery system seemed to be, we concluded that after a long winter, the Oak Island deer craved the salt.

I slept well that night, unconcerned about a rabid or enchanted Sabrina. When I left the campsite early in the morning two days later, I left a small amount of table salt on a flat rock near the fire pit. I didn't know if Sabrina's senses would lead her to the small saltlick, or if she would rely on her memory waiting to welcome the next human camper who would provide her with a salt fix. But if she found the salt gift I had left, I hoped she would consider it a token payment for the companionship, mystery, and entertainment she had provided me on Ironwood Island.

LONG ISLAND

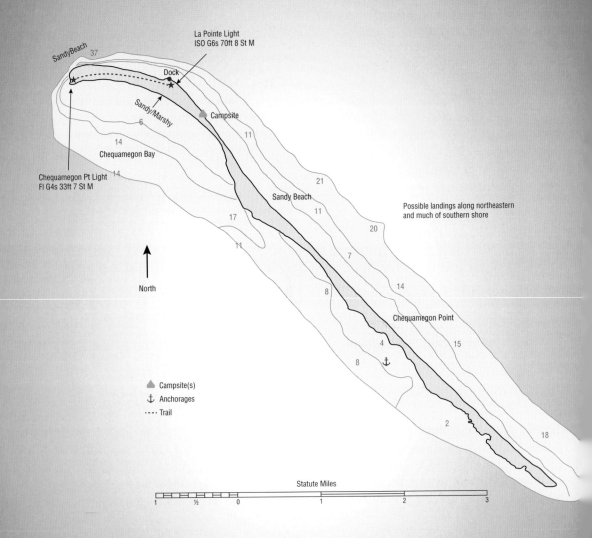

SandyBeach

37

La Pointe Light
ISO G6s 70ft 8 St M

Dock

Sandy/Marshy

Campsite

6

11

14

Chequamegon Bay

14

Chequamegon Pt Light
Fl G4s 33ft 7 St M

21

Sandy Beach

11

Possible landings along northeastern
and much of southern shore

17

20

11

7

North

8

14

Chequamegon Point

4

15

8

△ Campsite(s)

⚓ Anchorages

----- Trail

2

18

Statute Miles

| 1 | ½ | 0 | 1 | 2 | 3 |

Location

The northerly beach of Long Island lies about 6 miles south-southeast of Bayfield and about 3.5 miles east of the mouth of the Sioux River and the beach along Highway 13 between Washburn and Bayfield. Grant's Point on the southwestern tip of Madeline Island is about 1.5 miles north of Long Island.

Geography and History

Long Island looks like a broken hockey stick with the tip of its handle pointing to the southeast and its flattened and broken blade at its northwest end oriented in a more easterly-westerly direction. While "island" remains part of its name, sometime in the late fall of 1976, sand deposited by the waves and wind of a geographically changing Lake Superior joined the handle of the hockey stick to Chequamegon Point, part of the Bad River Reservation. The portion constituting Long "Island" contains about 300 acres, depending upon sand deposits and lake levels, and it is about 3.5 miles long but only about a quarter-mile wide at the blade of the hockey stick. Long Island is made entirely of sand and rises only about 15 feet above the level of Lake Superior.

While the exact date is uncertain, according to Ojibwe oral traditions, sometime in the early 1800s, a Dakota Sioux war party was trapped and destroyed on Long Island by a group of Ojibwe after the Sioux had attacked and killed two Ojibwe teenage duck hunters who had crossed over to Long Island from Madeline. According to the account, only two of about 150 Dakotas escaped from Long Island by swimming across Chequamegon Bay.[11]

Long Island was added to the National Lakeshore in 1986, some sixteen years after the National Lakeshore was created.

Two automatic lighthouses now operate on Long Island—Chequamegon Point Lighthouse located at the western tip of Long Island and La Pointe Lighthouse located on the north shore of the island about a mile east of the Chequamegon Point Lighthouse.

Chequamegon Point light (photo by author).

La Pointe light station (photo by author).

The Chequamegon Point Lighthouse, 33 feet above lake level, flashes green at four-second intervals, and is visible for 7 statute miles. The La Pointe Lighthouse is visible for 8 miles, it is 70 feet above the surface of the lake, and also flashes green six seconds on and six seconds off. Both lights are visible from Bayfield.

The original La Pointe light was built in 1858 as a tower on top of a one and a half story wood frame dwelling, but in 1897 the original La Pointe light was removed from the building and the building was later abandoned and is now in ruins. It was replaced with a 67-foot cast iron tower and other buildings located about 2/3 of a mile east of the original light-house site.[12] The Chequamegon Point light, a pyramidal skeletal tower of iron and steel, was also added in 1897. In 1987, the original Chequamegon Point light was dragged by a Coast Guard helicopter back away from the eroding shoreline and the newer cylinder topped by the current light was added.

A small triplex house next to the current La Pointe Lighthouse that served as the keepers' quarters has not been occupied by park service volunteers during the summer months. The La Pointe Lighthouse also has about a 60-foot dock that is mostly unusable because of shallow water around the dock. When the lake level is high, the end of the dock becomes separated from the shoreline. Boats drawing less than 3 feet of water may be able to use the end of the dock, but a sand beach landing may be easier.

Just east of the current location of the Chequamegon Point light there was a family fish camp run by the LeBel family from about 1869 to the 1940s. In recent years a lagoon still remained on the protected south shore of the island that the fishermen may have used for live storage of their catch.[13]

A variety of oaks and pines have found root at the crest of the island away from the waves, and beach grass and beach peas stabilize the lakeside shoreline. On the more protected Chequamegon Bay side of the island, alders grow almost to the waterline and are backed by swampy areas. Bushes and vines grow among the underbrush throughout the island. Some of the bushes yield blueberries. Some of the vines have the telltale "leaves of three" of poison ivy, warning you to "let them be."

Shoreline and Landings

Although the location of Long Island is not particularly remote, it remains relatively pristine. While its long sandy north shoreline may beckon larger boats, it is surrounded by shallow water, making landing a larger boat difficult. The long fetch of a north or northeast wind can create a wide surf zone on the northerly shore of the island, but the water remains shallow well out into the lake and a kayaker can safely land almost anywhere on the sandy shore of the island in normal conditions. At the La Pointe dock it will be easier for the kayaker to land on the sand beach adjacent to the dock rather than attempt to land on the dock itself.

Traveling southeasterly up the handle of the inverted hockey stick on the Chequamegon Bay side of Long Island, the shoreline becomes marshy. Protected landings for a break from winds may be possible on the south side of the hockey blade, but the insect residents of the marsh, also protected from the wind, may consider the intrusion to be an invitation to lunch.

Camping

There is one designated campsite on Long Island, located 0.5 mile southeast of the La Pointe light. The individual campsite has a stump toilet, fire ring, food locker, and a picnic table. No primitive camping is allowed outside the designated campsite area.

Hiking

The old concrete path between the two lighthouse sites has become mostly buried under the sand, but a mile-long wooden boardwalk makes for an easy hike between the two lights. Almost endless hiking, exploring, and beach combing is available along the beach. In May and June, hikers should avoid fenced areas along the shore that protect nesting sites of piping plovers, an endangered shorebird.

Kayak Trip Suggestions

Long Island could be combined with a trip to or from the south shore of Madeline Island, but because it stands alone, in the absence of a reservation for the designated campsite, it is likely to be a destination island for a day trip from the Sioux River beach, Bayfield, or Grant's Point at the southwestern tip of Madeline Island. When crossing from Grant's Point to Long Island, be aware that the shallow water between the southwest tip of Madeline Island and the red navigation buoy can produce some unexpected wave action and currents.

If a visit to Long Island is to be integrated into a multi-day trip, the kayaker will need to be prepared for paddling a longer distance. Madeline Island's Big Bay campground is about 10 miles from Long Island, and the south end of Basswood Island is about 8 miles north of Long Island. The paddle trip between Long Island and Basswood Island could be divided into two legs with a stop for refreshments at one of the restaurants within walking distance of Joni's Beach at La Pointe on Madeline Island.

WHERE DID I COME FROM?

By sometime in the mid-1990s after several kayak camping trips to the Apostle Islands, I had resolved to visit each of the islands by kayak. My wife, Signe, and I were staying in Bayfield for several days on a mini-vacation. While I had brought along my kayak for some possible day trip paddling, we were not planning any overnight camping.

Signe wanted to take a shopping trip to Ashland to pick up some things not available in Bayfield or Washburn. I thought the shopping trip offered me a perfect opportunity for adding Long Island to the list of the islands I had visited. I could make a day trip to visit Long Island while my wife continued down Highway 13 to Ashland to do the shopping. She would drop me off at the Sioux River beach on the way down to Ashland and pick me up two or three hours later after her shopping was done. I would have time for a nice day trip, paddling the 3.5 miles from the Sioux River beach to Long Island and returning to the beach for the pick-up.

The "road" from Highway 13 to the beach can be tricky. It cuts across an alder swamp, and the surface can range from slippery when it is wet to low-traction loose sand when it is dry. It is the kind of road that can quickly ensnare two-wheel-drive vehicles. If the drive wheels start spinning in the sand, the vehicle quickly may be buried to the axle, requiring a tow truck or several strong humans to be able to return to Highway 13. I stopped the car 75 yards short of the beach before the start of the loose dry sand.

"So, let's see," I said somewhat absentmindedly as I removed my kayak from the top of our car. "It's 1:30. It will take me about an hour to paddle to Long Island, perhaps a bit longer to return because of the westerly wind. Paddle time plus about half an hour to explore would put us at about 4:00 to 4:30. Will that be enough time for your shopping?"

"That sounds like good timing," Signe answered.

"Okay, I will meet you back here at 4:00 or 4:30 at the latest. Have a good time shopping."

"And you have a safe and enjoyable trip," she responded. She turned the car around in a wider opening in the alders and headed back to Highway 13.

I wiggled into my wetsuit and carried the kayak, my paddle plus a back-up paddle, paddle float, cockpit pump, and other equipment to the beach. As always, it took longer than I would have anticipated to stow the limited day trip equipment and rig the kayak. My timing for the trip and pick-up did not include the fifteen to twenty minutes of rigging time. While stowing and rigging, I realized that the map that I usually carry on a trip to the Apostles had been left in the car. No matter, this was a short trip, the sky was clear, and the destination was visible from the starting point.

Finally I slipped into the cockpit and pushed off the sand beach. The low outline of the trees and beach of Long Island were visible on the easterly horizon. I aimed the kayak toward the Chequamegon Point Lighthouse at the tip of Long Island.

I was still somewhat of a kayaking novice, and I still lacked the confidence in making a crossing alone that I felt later in my paddling career. On a solo trip like this it made me nervous to look back toward the perceived safety of the receding shoreline where I had launched. Backed by a relatively light westerly wind, I paddled aggressively toward the Chequamegon Point Lighthouse, a pinpoint on the dark outline of Long Island across Chequamegon Bay. I have often thought that the faster you paddle, the less time you are exposed to the dangers of a crossing. I measured my progress by occasionally checking my watch to determine what portion of the estimated crossing time had elapsed and what time remained.

As I approached the tip of the island, the details of the lighthouses, both current and older, and what I took to be a foghorn emerged from their general outlines. I scanned the beach to see if there were better places to land and chose the north side of a shallow sandspit extending from the tip of the island. Now that it had a few miles of fetch behind me, the westerly wind was stronger at the shoreline of the island than it was when I launched from the mainland, but it was not enough to cause concern in the shallow water extending out at least 100 yards from the shore.

I pulled my lightly loaded kayak up the beach to keep it well above the reach of any wave action to ensure that it would be waiting for me when I chose to return to the Sioux River beach.

Both lights at Chequamegon Point seemed to be in need of some maintenance. As I viewed the older nonfunctioning light as well as the newer cylinder light, I realized that repairs and painting probably could be made almost on a constant basis. All the buildings on the island are buffeted by wind, ice and snow in winter and sandblasted by the island's own sand in the squalls of summer. While it may never be that hot on the tip of Long Island with a cooling breeze from almost any direction, the unrelenting summer sun could dry and blister even the best paint.

At the time I thought that the cylindrical light also included a foghorn. I imagined it ready to blast a groan across the channel at any time. As I contemplated the horn, I wondered what it would be like to experience a foghorn's sound at the close range. It would be literally deafening, as in capable of creating deafness in the hearer's ears. It was easy to imagine the sand under my feet vibrating with the deep resonating sound of the fog horn. I looked to the sky and across the channel. It was still clear; no chance of fog.

I returned to my kayak and thought about extending the trip along the northern coast of Long Island for about a mile to explore the La Pointe Lighthouse and keepers' quarters. No, the pick-up time is too close. Exploring the La Pointe Lighthouse would wait until the next trip to Long Island.

I retrieved my snack and water from my kayak and sat down on the beach looking west toward the mainland. That is when I realized that the thin white line of the mainland's sand beach 3.5 miles across the bay seemed to extend for well over a mile. Since I had not looked back when I left the mainland shore, I had no clue about what part of the long sandy shoreline I should be aiming for to return to my Sioux River launch site. Without the forgotten map, I could not determine the appropriate compass bearing for the return trip. For such a short trip I had not packed binoculars. I tried to remember elevations along the Sioux River "valley"—map details that I did not recall ever studying. No help. These were the days before either my wife or I had a cell phone.

There seemed to be two choices. I could paddle with a heading somewhere in the middle of the long sand beach, hoping to identify details of the Sioux River beach area before the end of my return trip and make directional corrections as I approached the shore, or I could paddle to one of the ends of the beach and then follow the shoreline until I recognized the Sioux River pick-up point. With the first choice there would be a risk that I would not recognize any details of the Sioux River beach area as I approached the shore and would decide to cruise parallel to the shoreline paddling in the wrong direction, only to lose faith in my choice and reverse my direction. With the second choice I might have to paddle a longer distance, but there would be greater certainty of actually locating the Sioux River pick-up point, and I would not use up more time wandering up and down the shoreline repeatedly losing faith in my chosen direction.

Choosing the second option, I packed the snack and water back into the kayak, launched and paddled hard in the direction of the northerly edge of the long sandy coastline.

Because I was paddling into a light wind heading back to the west, I was traveling slower on the return crossing. Even if I was lucky and did not have to paddle far to reach the pick-up area, I might be ten to fifteen minutes late for the pick-up. Without luck I would be even later. I started to think about a number of questions: "What would Signe do if I was more than half an hour late and she did not see me completing the crossing or cruising the shoreline looking for her? Initially would she be angry at my tardiness? Would she later conclude that I had encountered problems on my trip and return to Bayfield to alert the Coast Guard while I continued to cruise the near shore of the mainland looking for her? How long would she wait before abandoning the pick-up and taking the Coast Guard option? How much worse would this whole experience be if she got stuck in the sand while trying to turn back up the road?" Each unanswered question produced a new vigor in my paddling cadence.

As I approached the northerly end of the sandy mainland shore I saw a road and some cabins, but I still did not recognize my location relative to the Sioux River. I beached the kayak and walked up the road to Highway 13. I was at Bayview Park Road north of the mouth of the Sioux River.

I went back to my kayak and hastily and awkwardly launched again for the half mile or so paddle south to the Sioux River. By now I was more than half an hour late, still in time for my wife's ire but probably before she would head for Bayfield and the Coast Guard.

When I reached the beach for the anticipated pick-up, I left my kayak abandoned at the beach and hurried across the sand path between the beach and area where cars could be parked. Neither Signe nor our car was anywhere on the road between Highway 13 and the beach. In my mind's eye she was already headed to Bayfield to report the loss of a husband.

I returned to the beach to remove the equipment from the kayak and carry it to a point on the path that should be safe for the car. While I was carrying the last load from the beach to the path, Signe turned onto the path from the highway in our car.

I felt my own anger building. I had worried about her anger if I was late, and now she shows up almost an hour after the scheduled time. My anger dissipated quickly like air rushing out of a balloon. She apologized for being late.

"I'm sorry that I'm late, but it just took more time than I thought it would, and I didn't want to have to return to Ashland to complete the shopping."

"Well, I was late myself," I responded, "and I thought that you would be angry with me for being late for a while, but ultimately you would head to Bayfield to report your missing husband to the Coast Guard. I was late enough that I figured you already had been here for the pick-up and had left for Bayfield. The sand beach here on the mainland is about a mile long and looking west from Long Island, I couldn't tell where I had come from."

"Oh no, John," she said, "I wouldn't report to the authorities for some time. At this point I'm confident that you can take care of yourself on your paddling trips."

While I did not yet share her confidence in my paddling abilities at the time, the dinner conversation at Maggie's Restaurant that evening was great, as the topic of my uncertainty as to where on the long mainland beach I had launched from broadened to a more philosophical inquiry. Indeed, where had any of us come from?

In the time since the Long Island trip, it has become a symbolic focal point for a review of the more general questions of where did we come from as the human race, where are we now, and where are we headed for the future. While the question, "Where did I come from?" could easily have been answered on the Long Island trip by reference to the map left in the car or by simply turning around several times on the initial crossing to Long Island to fix a landmark on the Sioux River beach for the return trip, the broader question of where did we come from as human beings or as the planet Earth remains more elusive.

Indeed the analysis of where we came from, where we are now, and where we are headed seems to be based on the assumption that time itself is linear. It seems inherent in our very nature that we perceive time as if we are passengers in a moving vehicle always experiencing "current time" while constantly traveling along a timeline leaving the past behind us as we move into the future. While viewing time as linear is a convenient way to analyze our own existence, is not the broader picture of time one in which the existence of all points on the timeline—past, present, and future—are ever present as all of our perceived "nows" roll from the past into the future.

Individually we possess a memory of past events that frequently proves to be substantially inaccurate because of the way our mind tries to reconcile our experiences and changes them ever so slightly to make them consistent with other experiences. The history of our ethnic groups, our species, and our planet, preserved in our writing and the physical evidence of the earth's past history, similarly becomes less clear as the usage of words changes and our own current thought processes interpret the writings and archeological evidence.

While our memory of the past becomes more uncertain as the distance between the past and the "current" increases, most of us treat our perception of the future to be nonexistent. Perhaps the future has always existed, and will continue to exist even before our travel along the timeline reaches it. Perhaps our perception of the passage of time is nothing more than the manifestation of our unwillingness (but not inability) to recognize the current actuality of the "future" events.

For example, surely our ultimate physical death exists as a fact immediately upon our birth. Yet we spend most of our lives blissfully ignoring the already existing fact of our ultimate demise. Perhaps we have taught ourselves, individually and as a species by natural selection, to ignore all already existing, but perceived as future, events. Our treatment of future events as unknowable may serve as good medicine for our mental health and preserve us in a hostile environment. Certainly acknowledging the current existence of all "future" events tends to negate the existence of our free will to change and shape the events we have not yet experienced on our trip down the timeline. The negation of our free will is not a currently popular philosophical point of view.

For some of us the time we spend kayaking in the Apostle Islands allows us to rise above that vehicle steadily hauling us along linear time and attempt, at least, to examine more broadly where we came from, where we are now, and where we are going.

Long Island Boardwalk (photo by author).

MADELINE ISLAND

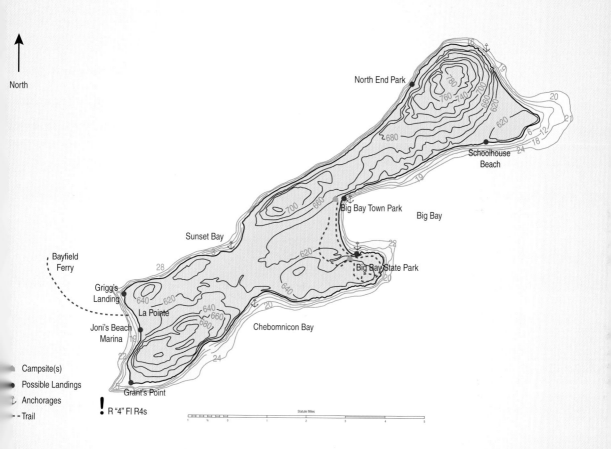

North

North End Park

Schoolhouse Beach

Big Bay Town Park

Big Bay

Big Bay State Park

Sunset Bay

Bayfield Ferry

Grigg's Landing

La Pointe

Joni's Beach Marina

Chebomnicon Bay

Grant's Point

▲ Campsite(s)
● Possible Landings
⚓ Anchorages
- - Trail

❗ R "4" Fl R4s

Statute Miles

Location

Because of its size, the location of Madeline Island needs to be described by stating the distance between specific parts of Madeline Island and other islands or points of interest. The La Pointe community on the southwestern end of the island is a bit over 2 miles southeast of the city of Bayfield. Grants Point at the southwestern tip of Madeline Island is about 1.5 miles north of the La Pointe Lighthouse on Long Island. The mid-northwestern shore of Madeline is 1.5 miles southeast of Basswood Island. The more northern reaches of Madeline's northwestern coast are about 2.25 miles southeast of Hermit Island and about 2.25 miles south of Stockton's southern shore. Michigan Island's sandspit is 3 miles east-northeast of Amnicon Point at Madeline's most eastern extension.

Geography and History

Madeline Island was not included in the federal government's acquisition of land for the Apostle Islands National Lakeshore. By the time Congress authorized the land acquisition in the 1970s, a significant superstructure of improvements and roads as well as residential and commercial development had made the island a politically and economically unattractive addition to the National Lakeshore. Although Madeline is not part of the National Lakeshore, it is included in this book because it provides many summer visitors with a less rustic alternative to the near wilderness camping experience in the Apostle Islands National Lakeshore.

Perhaps the shape of Madeline Island can be compared to a long-necked goose taking flight from the water in a northeastern direction. While the goose's neck and head are roughly in the correct proportions, its lower body and wing are disproportionately undersized.

Madeline covers a large area, about 15,360 acres or 24 square miles. Its northern shore (the back of the goose's neck and around the crown of its head) rises sharply up from the lake, reaching 70 to 170 feet above the water within a quarter to a half-mile from the shore. The rapid increase in elevation along much of the north coast is broken by mostly seasonal streams that have eroded paths through the bluffs. From the goose's lower back, all around its tail, and back up past its wing to the top of its bill, most of the island's shoreline rises more gradually, although there also are some sandstone cliffs overlooking the water along the southeastern shore.

Although Madeline Island and the rest of the Apostle Islands probably were occupied at least seasonally perhaps as early as five thousand years ago, William Warren, who collected oral Ojibwe history in the mid-1800s, calculated that the Ojibwe people arrived at Madeline Island in the late fifteenth century. The Ojibwe raised corn and pumpkins on the island, gathered wild rice, and hunted moose, bear, elk, deer, and perhaps even bison (buffalo) on the mainland (living at that time in the pine barrens of what is now northwestern Wisconsin).[14] The oral traditions of the Ojibwe people record a migration from the salty sea in the east (probably the St. Lawrence River) across the Great Lakes, ultimately to the shores of Lake Superior. The Ojibwe may have mostly abandoned their village at La Pointe in the early 1600s before the start of the extensive fur trade.[15]

Etienne Brule may have been the first European to visit the west end of Lake Superior around 1620. Fur trade and the desire to spread Christianity brought French explorers and missionaries to the area in the mid and late 1600s, after the brothers-in-law, Pierre Esprit Radisson and Medard Chouart, Sieur des Groseiliers, returned to Quebec laden with furs in 1660. La Pointe again became a thriving trading village, with a garrison of French soldiers stationed there until 1759.[16]

French influence at La Pointe declined in the late eighteenth century, replaced by the British and ultimately the Americans. As the fur trade economy declined and the fishing and lumber industries became more important, the economic "capital" of the area switched from La Pointe to mainland towns that were accessible by rail.

The island's current name derives from a delightful story. Michel Cadotte, who ran a trading post in the early nineteenth century for the British Northwest Company, married Equasayway, the daughter of Chief White Crane, and changed her name to Madeline. The chief was so pleased with the marriage that he changed the name of the island to "Madeline."[17] The name of La Pointe, previously used to describe the whole island, remained as the name for the village.

In current times, the rich history of the island may be revisited at the Madeline Island Historical Museum in La Pointe and at the cemetery across from the Madeline Island Marina. The cemetery is the final resting place for both Ojibwe and European settlers (including Michael Cadotte, who died in 1837).

Shoreline and Landings

Much of Madeline's shoreline is privately owned and for the kayaker is inaccessible except for emergency landings or unless the landowner has given permission to land or launch. The shoreline itself varies from two areas of sandstone cliffs—one stretching around the goose's forehead and the other around the goose's wing south of Big Bay—to long sand beaches (Big Bay, Chebomnicon Bay, known locally as Russell Bay, and most of the southwestern part of the island from Grant's Point north to Grigg's Landing). In between there are ledges, cobble beaches, and rocky shorelines.

There are three boat launch sites near the Village of La Pointe along the southwestern shore. Joni's Beach Memorial Park is located about half a mile south of the ferry landing on Main Street. To reach the second public access, Grigg's Landing, from the ferry dock, go left (north) a block at the first intersection, then east a block and turn left on Whitefish

Street traveling first north, then northeast for about 0.5 mile. The third public access near Grant's Point is at the end of Old Fort Road across the South Channel from Long Island about 1.25 miles south of the ferry landing (south on Main Street, then turn right and continue south on Old Fort Road).

Madeline Island seasonal transportation parked near Grigg's Landing (photo by Don Hynek).

North End Park provides carry-in access on Madeline's north shore, albeit impractical because of its length (600 yards) and the steepness of the last 250 yards down to the water. North End Park is located on North Shore Road about 2.5 miles northeast of the intersection of North Shore and Benjamin Boulevard, about 10 miles northeast of La Pointe on the back of the goose's head. Schoolhouse Beach provides public access to the lake on the southeastern shore about 10 miles east of La Pointe where the goose's bill meets its neck at the end of County Road H and the beginning of Schoolhouse Road. Carry-in access is available at Big Bay Town Park at the north end of Big Bay. The carry-in to the beach from the parking area at the Big Bay Town Park includes a stairway and is several hundred yards to the water, depending on how full the parking area is. Big Bay State Park also can provide a carry-in access

Rock shelf at Big Bay State Park on Madeline (photo by Robert E. Rolley).

on a more gradual sloping pathway, but it is also several hundred yards to the water.

For larger boats, the primary access is at the Madeline Island Yacht Club about a mile south of the ferry landing, but Grigg's Landing also has a concrete ramp suitable for launching from a boat trailer.

Camping

Madeline Island has two major campgrounds—Big Bay State Park at the south end of the Big Bay sand beach and lagoon and Big Bay Town Park at the north end. Both campgrounds are heavily used in July and August, but both offer some opportunity for reserving campsites. Both campgrounds also offer a

Group camp at Big Bay State Park on Madeline (photo by Robert E. Rolley).

variety of sites, including walk-ins, sites with or without electric service, tent-only sites, and RV sites. Both also have standard campground amenities including fire rings, picnic tables, potable water, pit and flush toilets, and showers.

Camping fees at Big Bay Town Park in 2021 are $40 per day for sites with electricity and $33 without. Big Bay State Park has fees of $20 to $37 depending upon the residency of the guest, the day of the week, and the availability of electricity. The campground also requires the purchase of a state park use sticker. All fees, of course are subject to change.

Email contact for the Town Park is bbtp@townoflapointewi.gov and the phone number is (715) 747-3031. For State Park reservations, visit https://wisconsin.goingtocamp.com/ and for more information about Big Bay State Park camping, see https://dnr.wisconsin.gov/topic/parks/bigbay.

Hiking

Even during the high season of July and August walking the long Big Bay sand beach usually will not feel crowded. In addition to the beach, Big Bay State Park offers over 6 miles of nature trails for hiking. Madeline Island Wilderness Preserve also maintains almost two miles of trails just northeast of LaPointe. For more civilized hiking try walking around the village of La Pointe, visiting the museum, the cemetery, and the shops, pausing for lunch or a cold beverage at one of the restaurants.

Hiking does not need to be the only exercise on Madeline Island. Bicycle rentals are available in La Pointe, and canoe and small boat rentals are also available at Big Bay Town Park, but the open canoes should be used only for exploring the lagoon at Big Bay, not the open water of Lake Superior.

Kayak Trip Suggestions

Integrating a stay at Madeline Island into a longer multi-day camping trip to other islands can be done using the Big Bay camping facilities or even by mixing in an upscale night at one of the island's hotel, bed and breakfast, or condominium accommodations. For example, consider launching from Bayfield, camping on Long Island for the first night, camping at Big Bay on nights two and four, and taking a side trip to Michigan Island on day three.

A circumnavigation of the island is also a possibility. Since the paddling distance is over 30 miles, for most paddlers the circumnavigation will take about two days. Start from Schoolhouse Beach and spend the night in La Pointe, either proceeding clockwise or counterclockwise around the island, depending upon the weather conditions anticipated from the two-day forecast. By staying overnight in one of the La Pointe accommodations, the circumnavigation can be completed while leaving the tent and other camping equipment at home.

Schoolhouse Beach on Madeline (photo by author).

A shady paddle break in a Madeline Island sea cave (photo by author).

Ice road to Madeline, looking back toward Bayfield (photo by author).

I CAN'T SWIM

In the early and mid-1990s the city of Bayfield hosted the Inland Sea Symposium, a four-day gathering of sea kayakers who came to listen to speakers at a variety of "how to" programs and to kayak in organized group paddle trips led by local outfitters.

The symposium's easier paddle options might involve a trip from Red Cliff over to Basswood Island and back or a trip up the coast from Bayfield to Roy's Point—3 to 4 miles total. An intermediate trip might be a paddle to Madeline, then on to Long Island with a return trip and stop on Madeline for ice cream, ultimately returning to Bayfield—an 8 to 9-mile paddle. Then there were the advanced trips. An advanced paddle might leave Bayfield early in the morning and make the long trip to the Outer Island sandspit, returning to Bayfield in the afternoon—almost 50 miles.

In the early 1990s I was a beginner who wanted to move up to the intermediate level. I never even met any of the advanced paddlers who went to Outer Island and back at any of the symposiums. Apparently if those advanced paddlers did exist, they got up earlier, went to bed later, and didn't enjoy sipping an evening beer as much as I did.

So seeking some reassurance that I was ready for the intermediate level, I tried to quiz the group leader who was soliciting paddlers for the Madeline/Long Island trip in front of the municipal swimming pool to determine whether I was qualified. My wife joined in the conversation with the group leader but did not plan to join in making the paddle to Madeline and Long Islands.

"How many paddlers are signed up for this trip?" I asked tentatively.

"Beside me, you will be number six," he replied. He was obviously presuming that he would build my confidence to the point that I would make the paddle trip with the group.

"And are the other six all experienced paddlers?" I continued.

"Well, two of them paddled with us for the first time last week, another has been paddling for a couple of years, and there is also a couple from Chicago. I don't remember how experienced they are, but they must have enough experience to be able to make this trip."

"Well, I have paddled six or seven miles in one day, but I never have gone quite this far," I said. "I just want to make sure that I won't be holding the group back."

"How fast do you usually paddle," he asked, giving me a one-question qualifier.

"About three miles per hour," I said, hedging a bit on the low side.

"You'll be fine," he reassured. "By the way, my name is Carl. Are both of you going?"

"No, just John," my wife replied for me. We all shook hands and discussed the details of the planned launch from the Broad Street Beach.

There, I felt committed to try the next level of paddling. We went to a Bayfield restaurant to get something light to eat before the one o'clock launch. If the paddling became intense, I did not want to have a heavy lunch slowing me down and making me sick. And after all, the trip included a stop at Madeline for a mid-afternoon snack of ice cream.

After we introduced ourselves to each other and launched, three paddlers—two men and a woman—paddled together engaged in a lively conversation. While the nature of their conversation was just beyond my hearing range, it was apparent that they knew each other and probably had paddled together before. I matched speed with the couple from Chicago, Robert (Bob) and Sarah. Carl, as a good group leader should, paddled with the other threesome some of the time and with the Chicagoans and me some of the time.

"Soon we will be at Grant's Point. We will stop there for a rest and a water break," Carl encouraged. "And remember, on the way back from Long Island we will stop at LaPointe for ice cream."

Carl made the stop for ice cream into a kind of reward for paddling hard. It was a relatively warm day and the reward of cold ice cream worked. Carl could have said, "Don't even think about the ice cream." But we could not keep it off our minds even though we were still in our first crossing to Madeline Island and that would be followed by the crossing to Long Island and the return to Madeline before the ice cream in our heads could become ice cream in our mouths and stomachs.

But as good as the ice cream might be, the most lasting memory of the trip was a small part of my conversation with Bob.

"So you and Sarah are from Chicago?" I half asked and half stated as I pulled my kayak parallel with Bob's and started matching his strokes. "Do you do any paddling around home?"

"We've done some paddling in the downtown area, but it is a bit of a hassle," Bob said. "Mostly we paddle outside the city. We try to get to Bayfield at least once a year for a few days, but we are not into camping very much. We have camped a few times at Big Bay and then done day trips in our kayaks. How about you, where do you kayak?"

"Well, I do get out on the Madison lakes several times a month, but I enjoy paddling on Lake Superior the most. And I do enjoy overnight camping out of a kayak. I have a great deal of respect and fear for the big lake. Conditions can change so quickly. I've been lucky up here—I have never tipped over."

"We have never tipped either," Sarah added from the other side of Bob's boat. "We try to avoid getting caught in weather changes and big waves."

"Do you practice rescues?" I asked.

"Yeah, but we like to practice in water that is warmer than Lake Superior," Bob responded. "And we don't practice too often because I can't swim."

"Wow." It was all I could think of saying. I became silent, thinking about the implications of not being able to swim and experience at least some degree of confidence in the water if you capsized. Here we were more than a mile from any shoreline somewhere between Bayfield and Madeline Island, and Bob doesn't know how to swim. Bob obviously was a decent paddler, and he and Sarah had been paddling for a while, including trips like this one on Lake Superior. "Well, I sure admire your courage," I finally added. Then I fell silent again contemplating Bob's paddling without being able to swim. For a time the whisper of the very slight breeze and the cadenced sound of our paddles in the water were the only sounds.

Bob noticed my silence and read my thoughts. He had probably experienced my reaction to his announcement before.

"You know," he said, "we always wear wetsuits on Lake Superior. I never go out without a PFD. It keeps me afloat. If you capsize, you are supposed to stay with your kayak and attempt reentry. You're not supposed to try to swim to shore anyway. Knowing how to swim really makes little difference."

Bob's reasoning was correct, I had to admit. If I capsized, I would never try to swim ashore unless it was only a couple of hundred yards away. Even then I would probably try to stay with my kayak and perhaps even try to tow it to shore with me.

"I guess you're right," I said, after another prolonged silence. "But I still admire your courage." I decided to stop there. Any further comment could easily be misinterpreted. But before we resumed our conversation, I resolved to treat Bob and Sarah to ice cream when we eventually made it back to Madeline. I still admired Bob's courage. Ice Cream? Such courage probably deserved a tribute of a beer or a shot of rum.

MANITOU ISLAND

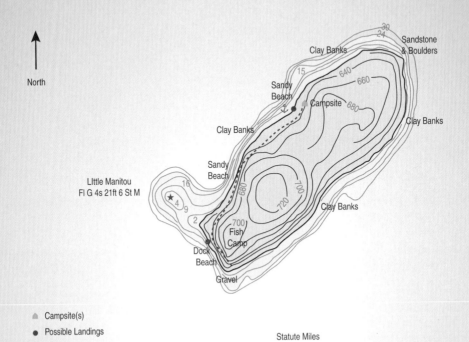

Sandstone
& Boulders

Clay Banks

30
24

640

660

680

Clay Banks

Sandy
Beach

Campsite

15

Clay Banks

Sandy
Beach

700

720

Clay Banks

LIttle Manitou
FI G 4s 21ft 6 St M

16

680

9

4

2

700

Fish
Camp

Dock
Beach

Gravel

⌂ Campsite(s)

● Possible Landings

⚓ Anchorages

- - - Trail

Statute Miles

1   ½   0   1   2

Manitou fish camp and dock (photo by author).

Location

Manitou Island is centrally located among the islands of the Apostle Islands National Lakeshore and is situated about half way out to the more remote islands from the launch sites on the mainland. Oak Island towers above Manitou about 1.5 miles to the southwest, and in the opposite direction to the northeast, the sandspit of Ironwood Island is about 1 mile from Manitou's northern shore. Otter Island lies about 1.75 miles northwest of Manitou and a sandy point on the western third of Stockton Island's northern shoreline is about 1.5 miles east of Manitou's southern tip.

Geography and History

The highest elevation on Manitou Island is about 128 feet above the lake surface. The island is shaped like a sausage, uniformly 0.75 to 1 mile wide and nearly 3 miles long. The long axis of the oblong sausage is oriented northeast to southwest. The profile of the Manitou sausage covers 1,363 acres.

Twentieth-century Manitou Island history merges into more current times at the well-preserved fish camp located by the dock on the southwestern tip of the island. Before its demise as a fish camp in the 1970s, the longest occupant of the cabins and outbuildings was Hjalmer Olson, who bought the island site with his brother in 1938 after logging operations ceased on the island. Olson and his fellow fishermen not only fished the waters in summer, but he also ran a fishnet

under the ice in winter. The buildings are currently maintained as if they were still being used in Hjalmer Olson's time, and the park service may have a ranger or a volunteer at the site during the summer months to provide a tour of the buildings. The detail of the volunteer's descriptions in the tour, together with the vintage equipment remaining in the buildings, make the fisherman's lonely existence, especially during the winter months, spring into life.

The modern dock serving the historic fish camp is about 165 feet long, was repaired in 2020, and has been improved and maintained to accommodate boats drawing 6 feet of water.

Shoreline and Landings

The dock at the southwestern corner of Manitou Island can be used by larger boats for temporary docking, but rises too high above the water to be usable by kayakers. However, kayakers should be able to land on the narrow gravel and sand beach next to the dock at the fish camp.

To the west and northwest of the dock, the waters around the island remain shallow out to a pile of rocks marked with a flashing green light. The rock pile is all that remains of an island named Little Manitou, which was eroding away when the Coast Guard speeded up the erosion process with power hoses. Although kayaks should be able to carefully cross the shallow area between Manitou and Little Manitou in good weather conditions,

Inside a shed at Manitou fish camp (photo by Paul Matteoni).

Little Manitou rock pile (photo courtesy National Park Service).

larger boats should skirt around outside of the rock pile.

The northwestern shoreline of Manitou, from the dock almost to the northern tip of the island, has intermittent clay banks with a mix of cobble and gravel shoreline and with occasional rocks and boulders to make any landing attempt more interesting. There are two sandy landings available to the kayaker on the northwestern shore—the first about 0.5 mile northeast of the dock and the second at the campsite about 2 miles northeast of the dock at the only designated campsite.

Sandstone and large boulders mark the shoreline for about 1.5 miles around the northern tip of the island and back to the southwest preventing any landing attempt. Perhaps a landing could be made in calm weather on a cobble "beach" along the southeastern shore southwest of the sandstone, but it would have to be done carefully to avoid the boulders. Farther to the southwest along the southeastern shoreline the shore again is lined with high clay banks or sandstone with boulders. At the most southerly corner of the island there is a gravel/cobble beach, separated from the dock area again by a clay bank with boulders at the waterline.

While there are three relatively good landing sites (the dock and the two sandy beaches along the northwestern shore), Manitou Island, more than most of the Apostles, has a number of marginal landing sites for the kayaker looking for a paddle break.

Camping

There is only one designated campsite on Manitou Island located about two-thirds of the way up the northwestern shore of the island from the dock. It is one of the more pleasant campsites in the archipelago, with a sand beach, bear proof food locker, picnic table, a stump privy, and fire ring. Making use of the food locker is important because Manitou lies between the two islands that have traditionally held the highest bear populations, and a problem bear has caused a closure of the island in recent years.

While larger boats could use the sandy bottom off the shore near the campsite for anchorage, the anchorage would offer no protection from westerly winds. Accordingly, the kayak camper may enjoy the solitude of this rustic campsite with a "private" beach.

There is a single primitive zone camping permit available for camping away from the designated campsite, the southerly corner of the island, and the fish camp.

Hiking

There is a 2-mile trail between the designated campsite and the fish camp, allowing kayak campers to walk to the fish camp, or day users or backpack campers to gain access to the campsite after arriving at the fish camp dock by water taxi. A second shorter trail leads from the fish camp 0.75 mile southeast to the southern tip of the island.

Kayak Trip Suggestions

With its central location among the islands, the Manitou campsite can serve as a way station for one night on a longer trip. It could also be considered for a two-night stay, since a leisurely visit to the fish camp, either by hiking or by paddling, can easily consume half a day, and a full day sunbathing on this secluded beach will make only the most restless feel like it was a waste of time.

MEETING HJALMER

As they paddled east toward the Manitou Island campsite, the kayakers noticed two moving figures, first appearing only as tiny dark silhouettes against the backdrop of the white sand beach and backlit by the blinding morning sun. When they approached closer to Manitou, the dark silhouettes turned into flesh-colored humans. The body shapes and movements indicated one male and one female. Adam and Eve were enjoying the morning skinny-dipping on the secluded beach.

The kayakers initially had some concern that perhaps the Manitou Island campsite was already occupied by Adam and Eve, even though they had a camping permit for the night ahead. The concern was unwarranted. Before the kayakers approached close enough to be able to distinguish facial and other features, the naked couple became aware of the brightly colored kayaks and clothing that were approaching them on the water. They quickly dressed and by the time the kayaks reached the beach, Adam and Eve had already left their Garden of Eden and disappeared down the path to the fish camp.

The kayakers were Signe and John, out on the third day of a planned five-day trip. Except for some wind on the first day of the trip, the early August weather had been perfect. After a night sharing the facilities of the Otter Island campsite with the people sleeping in their boats tied to the dock, the Manitou campsite seemed as remote and pristine as the Garden of Eden.

Although it was only about ten o'clock when they arrived at Manitou Island, the day was already hot and humid. It would be one of those rare days on Lake Superior that the temperature would easily top 80 degrees. After a couple of days of practice, the tent went up quickly and smoothly. The wetsuits were peeled off quickly, and while the lake was cold enough to shock, once their bodies adjusted to the change, the water was actually tolerable for a swim. After about half an hour, John and Signe emerged from the lake to dry off sitting in the sand. They had been in the water long enough to soak the sweat and grime from their bodies, and they were so clean they could make squeaking noises by rubbing a finger across their skin. Paradise had been reclaimed.

"How far is the fish camp from here," Signe asked.

"It's about two miles, walking or paddling. Which would you prefer?"

"After lunch, let's paddle down there and see what it looks like," Signe suggested. "But you know, I really don't want to put that hot sticky wetsuit on again."

"I don't blame you," John agreed. "Normally I would say that we should never go kayaking on Lake Superior without a wetsuit, but we won't be far from shore paddling down to the fish camp, and it isn't that long of a distance. It should be okay."

After lunch they paddled down the western shoreline of Manitou Island. Even without wetsuits, the exertion of the paddling soon had them sweating again. They beached their kayaks and walked over to the dock just as a tour boat was arriving. A volunteer park ranger greeted the passengers who had disembarked from the tour boat, offering a tour of the fish camp facility. John and Signe mingled with the group of tour boat passengers as they followed the ranger to the ramshackle buildings at the fish camp.

The cabin was arranged as if its main occupant, Hjalmer Olson, had left earlier in the day to check his fishnets and would be returning shortly. He apparently had washed the dishes and had carefully reset the rustic table before he left the cabin that morning. When he returned he might be drying and mending his fishnets on the rack outside the main outbuilding. Later he might smoke some of his catch in the smokehouse, preparing the fish both for his personal consumption and perhaps for commercial sale.

The stories the ranger told portrayed Hjalmer as an intelligent, independent single man who seemed to enjoy the simple, albeit sometimes dangerous, life in the fish camp. For example, Hjalmer was wise enough in winter to test the ice ahead with a long pole as he walked out on the lake to his set of winter fishnets. Blown snow could cover large

Hjalmer Olson's table set awaiting his return (photo by Paul Matteoni).

Manitou cabin (photo by Paul Matteoni).

cracks in the ice and Hjalmer did not want to end up slipping into a crack and dying of hypothermia in the cold water. In his cabin a boxy woodstove provided Hjalmer with a hot cooking surface as well as a minimum supply of heat to ward off the cold. If he had not been out checking his nets at the time, one could almost imagine Hjalmer's snores coming from the rough, wood frame bed.

Through the ranger's words and the furnishings and equipment around the fish camp, the image of Hjalmer grew in size to become a simple, somewhat rough-edged, larger than life authority on wilderness survival in the "early days" that ended just not that long ago. With his vast survival wisdom, Hjalmer became John and Signe's cited authority for wise advice for any plans they made on their first multi-day kayak trip to the Apostle Islands.

"Hjalmer says we should go back to our campsite now," Signe murmured as the tour group filed back to the dock to board the boat for their return trip to Bayfield. "He thinks that we should have another swim before dinner."

"Okay, whatever Hjalmer thinks is best," John said. "Hjalmer knows about these things."

They were headed back toward the shallow water between Manitou and Little Manitou, when they heard the tour boat captain addressing his passengers on the boat's public address system.

"Now off to the right of the boat you will see two kayakers. They really know how to enjoy the islands. Kayak camping has become very popular in recent years."

Both Signe and John thought to themselves: "If you only knew how inexperienced we are—so unlike the wise and confident Hjalmer." But it was true, they were enjoying this trip.

As the rudder on John's kayak dragged across some rocks in the shallow water near the shore, Signe, paddling farther out toward the Little Manitou rock pile, taunted,

"Hjalmer told me to paddle farther out from shore to avoid the rocks."

"I don't think Hjalmer ever paddled a kayak," John responded.

Signe: "I never claimed he had a kayak. But he did have enough sense not to take his boat into shallow water where he might scrape bottom."

After they returned to their campsite, Hjalmer became the tie-breaking vote on the choice for dinner, although his opinions seemed quite different and inconsistent when expressed through the mouths of each of the two campers. Hjalmer was becoming the cited authority for everything.

Since there was no vault toilet at the campsite at the time, Hjalmer later advised them to make two cat holes in the evening even though they would not likely be used until the next morning. "Hjalmer says, 'Make your cat hole in the evening, so that you don't have to dig a hole in the middle of the night if you have to go. You'll be happy that the hole is already waiting for you,'" John proposed. "Hjalmer also says, 'Leave the orange trowel stuck in the ground next to the cat hole so that it is easier to find with your light at night.'"

After watching the kind of sunset that might be expected in the Garden of Eden, the two tired campers were dozing off to sleep in the tent, hearing only the slightest whisper of a breeze and the repetitive slosh of small waves on the beach.

"You know, Hjalmer wasn't that smart," John mumbled.

"Hmm. Why not?" Signe mumbled back.

"Well, if he were really smart, he would have been born about thirty or thirty-five years later, and he would have searched around for you and asked you to become his beautiful and wonderful wife."

"Aww."

Sunset and Lupine (photo by Mark Weller)

MICHIGAN ISLAND

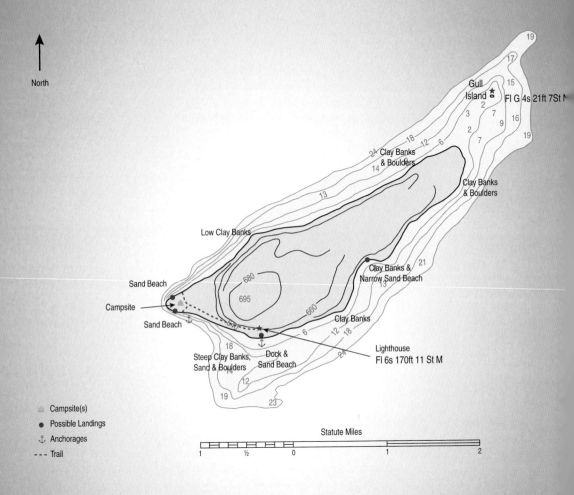

North

Gull Island Fl G 4s 21ft 7St M

Clay Banks & Boulders

Clay Banks & Boulders

Low Clay Banks

Clay Banks & Narrow Sand Beach

Sand Beach

Campsite

Sand Beach

Clay Banks

Steep Clay Banks, Sand & Boulders

Dock & Sand Beach

Lighthouse
Fl 6s 170ft 11 St M

Campsite(s)

Possible Landings

Anchorages

Trail

Statute Miles

1   ½   0   1   2

Location

Michigan Island stands alone as the south-easterly sentinel of the Apostle Islands. It is about 3 miles east-northeast of Madeline and just under 3 miles southeast of Presque Isle Point on Stockton Island. Small, rocky Gull Island lies about 0.5 mile northeast of the northerly tip of Michigan Island, but Michigan and Gull almost could be considered together as a single island, since they are separated by water only 2 to 3 feet deep, and except in very calm water, it can be difficult to negotiate the shallow gap between the two, even in a kayak.

Geography and History

Michigan Island's elevation rises less than 100 feet above the normal lake level with its highest point in the southwesterly third of the island. From southwest to northeast, Michigan measures about 3.75 miles. Its northwesterly shoreline is straighter than its southeasterly shoreline that irregularly bellies farther out into the lake, creating one larger bay. The width of the island from northwest to southeast is a bit over a 1 mile at its widest point. The southwesterly tip of the island has formed into a large, flat sandspit with a small lagoon closer to the north shore. Michigan Island has a surface area of 1,578 acres.

There are two lighthouses on the south-easterly shore about a mile from the sandspit. Michigan Island's first lighthouse (and the first in the Apostle Islands) was built in 1857 as a masonry building and tower. The money allocated for the construction of the first lighthouse was supposed to be used to erect a lighthouse on Long Island, to mark the entry to the channel between Long Island and Madeline Island into Chequamegon Bay. Initially, because it was erected in the "wrong" location, the first lighthouse operated for only a year, and then was shut down for a decade before it reopened.

The second lighthouse, a taller steel structure built in 1880, was dismantled at its original location on the Delaware River near Philadelphia (because the river changed course) and was moved to Michigan Island in 1919. The "new" lighthouse sat on the island for ten years before it was reassembled and put into operation at its new location in 1929.

The second lighthouse was automated in 1943 and still flashes at 6 second intervals, 170 feet above the surface of the lake, visible for 11 statute miles. Extensive restoration of the light station from 2014 to 2016 included

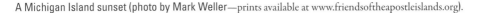

A Michigan Island sunset (photo by Mark Weller—prints available at www.friendsoftheapostleislands.org).

Michigan Island lights (photo by author).

concrete slab on the shoreline west of, and perpendicular to, the dock was added to reduce shoreline erosion and perhaps reduce the silting of the dock area.

Traveling northeasterly from the dock to the northeast corner of island, then back to the southwest along the northwesterly shore back to the western tip of the island, a shoreline explorer mostly will encounter high clay banks with boulders at the shoreline. Landings in calm weather at gaps between the boulders may be possible but not safe in higher seas. On the southerly shoreline of Michigan Island about two-thirds of the way from southwest to northeast, there is a bay with a sand beach and few boulders, which could serve as a landing for a short rest or a lunch break. The best landings are on either side of the sandspit extending for about 0.5 mile along the north shore from the westerly tip of the island and about 1 mile along the south shore nearly up to the dock area.

restoring the first floor of the original lighthouse and installation of exhibits explaining the history of the station. The station may be staffed by volunteers who maintain the grounds and, for a small fee, offer tours of the station during the summer months. A set of rails which straddles the stairs from the dock up the hill adjacent to the steps, is a remnant of a tram system. The tram allowed supplies to be winched up from the dock to the lighthouse grounds at the top of the steep hill.

Shoreline and Landings

It has been difficult to maintain a usable dock at the lighthouse site. Sand carried by the waves along the southeasterly shore tends to be deposited, especially on the east side of the dock, thereby effectively reducing the water depth at the end of the dock to 4 to 5 feet. For the kayaker, the sand deposits allow a soft landing in the dock area. A 150-foot

Michigan Island dock and stairway to lighthouse (photo by author).

Camping

There is a single designated campsite located on the sandspit on the south side of the island's westerly tip which can be accessed from the south side of the sandspit. There is a stump toilet at the campsite and a vault toilet is located at the lighthouse site. The campsite also has a fire ring, picnic table, and a food locker. Because of the relative remoteness of the Michigan Island campsite, the campsite on the beach feels like one of the more pristine areas in the islands.

Primitive camping is allowed in a single zone for the entire island, but is prohibited on the sandspit and close to the lighthouse grounds.

Hiking

There is a path between the lighthouses and the campsite leading through a heavily forested area of the island that includes some majestic hemlocks. It is a relaxing walk of about a mile, and the lighthouse site is well worth an afternoon or evening visit for campers after setting up camp on the sandspit. When the lake level is not too high, it may also be possible to hike the shoreline between the sandspit and the lighthouse grounds.

Kayak Trip Suggestions

While it is possible to integrate a trip to Michigan Island with a longer trip to other eastern islands, because of its remoteness, Michigan can also become a destination island, perhaps with a two-night stay in the campsite with a circumnavigation of the island, exploration of the lighthouses, and/ or simply relaxation on the beach during the intervening day.

Original Michigan lighthouse viewed from new lighthouse (photo by Paul Matteoni).

FOR MEN ONLY—IN BAD TASTE

Somehow it had become known as the "For Men Only—In Bad Taste" (FMO-IBT) paddle trip. While the paddle trip was intended to be a group trip for men only, the "in bad taste" portion of the name seemed to have been added a bit too automatically, perhaps by the opposite sex. The trip, organized through the Mad City Paddlers, a Madison, Wisconsin, paddle club, did not deserve the "in bad taste" label simply because it was an all-male event.

Most of the Apostle Islands trips organized through the paddle club were for a mixed group of both men and women. The four boys (men) who went on the FMO-IBT trip— Don, Paul, Jim, and me—believed that a testosterone-filled trip would allow us to have more aggressive paddling over longer distances. The exclusivity of the trip may have sounded sexist, but for the fact that on the same weekend the paddle club also sponsored a trip for women only to the Apostle Islands with no men allowed. Somehow the name of the women's group escaped any additional label referring to the tastefulness of their trip. The women's group included two wives of the men in the FMO-IBT group, and although advertised as a relaxing weekend without bothersome males, the women's paddling plans were just as aggressive as the men's group.

For several weeks prior to the July Fourth long weekend plus one day, the FMO-IBT group exchanged emails planning for the trip. The email message strings helped to extend the enjoyment of a four-day trip, allowing it to seem like a longer trip.

"So how do you want to work the food?"

"How about we do breakfast, lunch, and snacks on your own and each of us cooks an evening meal for the group? Two of us can combine for one of the evening meals since we have four paddlers and three nights. Some of the women think we are just going to eat hot dogs, beans, and potato chips for three straight nights anyway."

"Splitting the evening meals that way sounds great. And I have a twelve-cup coffee pot that I can use to heat water for breakfast. That way we can all have hot water for tea or coffee and oatmeal or some other hot cereal. Hot dogs and beans sound pretty good right now."

"That coffee pot would be great for the morning. It will help us get paddling earlier in the morning."

"I have a good friend who has come with me on several prior trips and would like to come along with us on this trip. He promises not to keep anyone up late into the night and to be on his best behavior and not cause any problems within the group. He especially enjoys relaxing with me in the evening at the campsite when the day's paddling is done. His name is Yukon Jack. Do any of you mind if he comes along?"

"I don't mind at all."

"I was wondering where you were going with that until you got to his name. I don't care."

"Is Jack a strong paddler?" What kind of kayak does he have?"

"Is each of us going to bring a tent? I have a tent that can easily accommodate two of us, but not all four."

"I have a two-person tent, too. Let's double up."

"That's a great idea. My wife is taking our tent on the women's trip. I will double up with John, and Jim can double with Don."

The emails continued through the Wednesday afternoon before the start of the trip. On

Thursday evening all of the paddle club taking the trip met and camped together at the campground in Red Cliff, and on Friday morning both the men's group and the women's group prepared to launch from the beach by the Buffalo Bay Marina. Some members of each sex group finished packing and launching their kayaks earlier than others. Those kayakers who had completed the launching cruised back and forth in the protected area inside the breakwater, testing equipment and exchanging advice and taunts, both with members of the group consisting of the opposite sex as well as with the members of each group who were still engaged in packing their boats along the shoreline, belittling their ineptitude and efficiency in packing their kayaks.

"So how do you like that new lightweight paddle?"

"It's great. I don't get nearly as tired as I used to. But sometimes in a headwind, it feels like the paddle will be blown right out of my hands."

"I didn't know that guys needed lighter paddles. I thought they just used a long two by four clenched in their teeth and paddled by shaking their heads back and forth."

"Let's test our radios. Try channel 27."

"Okay. You call me."

"This is a radio test on channel 27. Carol, do you read me?" (Paddling back closer to one another.)

"I could hear you fine, but did you hear my response?"

"No, my transmitter must be working, but not my receiver."

"That's probably better than the alternative. You can call for help if you need it, even if you won't know if anyone is coming."

"The men will be packed and in the water before the women. But why am I not surprised? The women are always slower."

"Well, I had to park the car while my husband simply had to pack his boat. This isn't a race, you know."

"Just sayin'. I kind of expect the women will still be packing on the shoreline when the men get back here on Monday afternoon."

As a group the four of us men did complete packing and launching before the women. We paddled beyond the breakwater into the open lake to the jeers of the female paddlers who informed us in no uncertain terms that men in general were not particularly useful to the human race and that the individual members of the FMO-IBT group would not be missed in the least for the next four days. The banter helped build the cohesiveness of each group.

The men paddled a variety of kayaks. Don, the group leader, paddled a new fiberglass Caribou by Current Designs. Paul was using his wife's new Current Designs Solstice while she used their double kayak on the women's trip. Jim had a new skin and frame collapsible boat, a relatively short boat compared to the others, and I paddled a Pisces, a model that Current Designs had not manufactured for over five years.

The male paddlers were in relatively good physical shape, ranging in age from mid-thirties to early fifties. Jim was diabetic but managed it well.

Our float plan included three nights of camping. Friday night would be spent on Michigan Island, Saturday night at the sandspit on Outer Island, and Sunday night would be at the sandspit on Cat Island. Monday morning we would paddle back to Red Cliff early enough to be able to drive back to our homes in the Madison area.

We paddled the initial crossing to Basswood Island uneventfully, testing ourselves and matching speed with one another, until we reached the northwest corner of Basswood. The mid-morning water was relatively calm and allowed us to land at the gravel-cobblestone shore for a snack and bathroom break.

Don shared some spicy deer sausage sticks he brought that were processed from the venison Jim harvested the year before. The salt and spiciness of the venison sticks replaced some of the salt lost through the sweating generated by the exercise of the initial paddle, and sharing the spicy "red" meat seemed to fit the "men only" theme.

After a pause for a few pictures at Honeymoon Rock, a very vertical, tiny and picturesque island just off the north shore of Basswood Island, we continued the 5 miles to the north tip of Madeline Island. Although the bay windows of a home stared down on us from a bluff above, we respectively answered the call of nature among the low willows on the beach and ate lunch before the last 4-mile push to Michigan Island.

Before leaving Madeline Island completely, Don, Jim and Paul posed for pictures while negotiating the low sea caves on the north corner of the island. The three of them advanced under the overhanging rock by abandoning their paddles and pushing with their hands against the rock above their heads.

"Avast, laddies," cried Don, mimicking a freshwater pirate returning to his treasure trove, "I know I left the treasure here somewhere." No treasure appeared.

As we paddled east and left the lee of Madeline Island, we encountered a significant southerly wind producing broadside waves of about 2 feet and requiring a constant correctional sweep stroke for the rudderless kayaks. While our testosterone level remained high after playing in the sea cave, all of us were tired and ready to reach our destination. Jim, without either a rudder or a skeg, needed a strong and tiring sweep stroke for the entire crossing, and we headed for a temporary stop on the calmer water on the north side of the Michigan Island sandspit.

After some refreshments, we were back on the water, paddling south around the tip of the sandspit to get closer to the Michigan Island campsite. The southerly wind was producing a narrow surf zone, but with a 2 to 3-foot dumping wave. While the beach itself, only a few feet away, provided a soft sand landing, all four of us knew that the existing surf conditions could turn a fully loaded kayak caught broadside in the waves into an injury machine.

"We'll go in one at a time. I'll go in first, then Paul, John, and Jim. Wait for my signal," yelled Don above the roar of the surf and wind.

The three of us maintained position just outside the surf zone as we watched Don slowly approach the breaking waves, catch the surge of a larger wave as it hit his kayak's stern, and paddle hard to ride the surge of the wave until it dropped him in the sand and started to recede. Still nimble after sitting in his kayak most of the day, Don broke the seal on his spray skirt, put his paddle perpendicular to his kayak behind his cockpit, leaned on it and—butt, left leg, right leg out—he was on his own two feet in the sand before the next wave reached him. He used the wash from the next wave to float his kayak as he pulled it up the sand beach to a point above the waterline. Well executed. The other three of us would have applauded if the waves had not required our constant attention to maintain our position just outside the surf.

Here is what the four of us did not discuss about the landing procedure: In landing a group in the surf, the best paddler goes in first, followed by the second best paddler, etc. If the group members vary greatly in ability, the second best paddler may defer landing and become the last one to land, thereby allowing him to help the less-experienced paddlers to maintain position and follow his landing orders and watchful suggestions. After landing in the surf, the best paddler indicates to the next person when to land. As the second lander nears the end of his ride on the wave surge, the best paddler will help bring the second's kayak a few feet farther up the shoreline and steady the second's kayak as he exits. Both paddlers pull the second's kayak out of the reach of the waves using the surge of the next wave. The third lander receives help from both the first and the second. The landings proceed until the entire group has landed.

Individually, each kayaker in the group removes his paddle leash before approaching the surf zone, stowing the leash in a manner that it will not become a hindrance to exiting the kayak. Then, edging toward the surf zone, the individual kayaker needs to feel the rhythm of the waves. As the "right" wave raises the kayak's stern, the paddler tries to accelerate and mount the wave using gravity to surf the wave for as far as it will take him. Ideally, each kayaker keeps his boat perpendicular to the shore as he rides the wave to the shore, always ready, however, to make a directional correction with his paddle or even to slide into a brace position, if the kayak goes broadside in the wave.

Because we had considerable experience among us, the four paddlers on the Michigan Island trip did not review the landing rules before executing the landing. While respecting the power of the waves and the potential for danger in making the landing, we all landed successfully, and soon we were sitting on the beach in the warm afternoon sunshine, tired but pleased with ourselves for having completed the 14-mile trip from Buffalo Bay.

While we gloated about the successful first leg of the trip in the sand on the beach, Don did an almost magical thing, pulling a cantaloupe from the bottom of his kayak where it had cooled during the trip exposed to the cold lake water. He cut slices and distributed them to Paul, Jim, and me as well as to himself. It may have been the best cantaloupe any of us had ever tasted. If Don had suggested paddling another 10 miles before sunset, we probably would have followed.

We transferred our equipment to the campsite, set up the two tents and fluffed up our tightly packed sleeping bags and pads. A quick splash in the surf refreshed us from the heat of the afternoon sun and freshened the odor of our wetsuits. In bad taste? Indeed not with such cleansing in the cold lake water.

Later in the afternoon, the wind diminished, the mosquitoes increased, and the quiet, muggy air started to grumble with distant thunder. Using two of our kayak paddles and a large nylon tarp with cords at the corners tied to nearby trees or staked to the ground, we put up a cooking shelter, anticipating a late afternoon or evening thunderstorm that might otherwise interrupt cooking the evening meal.

Jim and I took a late afternoon walk to the lighthouses. The newer steel structure towered over the much older block tower. We gladly accepted the volunteer lighthouse keeper's invitation to climb to the top of the steel lighthouse. From the top, gazing west we could see the dark blue clouds of a large thunderstorm somewhere in the vicinity of Oak Island. Inside the lighthouse we could not hear the distant rumble but could observe the thunderclouds casting bolts of electricity at one another. The lightning reminded us of the taunts hurled at one another by the men and women during the morning launch.

We paused to talk to the retired couple, temporarily quartered in the keeper's house, who were serving as volunteers. After a discussion of the history of the two lighthouses, the male volunteer asked, "Did you guys come in today?"

"Yeah, we paddled in from Buffalo Bay. We're camping at the campsite down at the sandspit with two other paddlers," I answered.

"Have you heard the weather warnings? We are likely to get a thunderstorm and possibly some high winds this evening and tonight."

"Yes," Jim responded. "We saw a pretty big storm brewing to the west when we were up in the lighthouse."

View of approaching storm clouds from Michigan light (photo by author).

"Well, be careful down there. If you need anything, let us know. We have a radio."

As we walked through the old hemlocks back to the campsite, Jim and I imagined the joys and seclusion associated with being a volunteer lighthouse keeper on Michigan Island. By the time we reached the campsite, Don and Paul were ready for the evening meal. We cooked steaks over an open fire, adding a bit of sandy grit to at least one of the steaks that resisted being flipped over.

Soon the thunder was louder and more insistent, complaining of the separation from its parent lightning roughly fifteen seconds after the flash. The length of the delay between the lightning and thunder indicated that the storm was still maybe 3 miles away, but it had advanced about 10 miles in half an hour and the wind, rain, lightning, thunder, and whatever else the storm had to offer would be seeking to flatten the cook shelter within eight or nine minutes. Moving at that speed, the storm, at least the first one of the evening, would be of relatively short duration.

The storm hit with thunder, sounding first like the crack of two paddlers whacking their paddles together high in the trees above but ending with a boom loud enough to shake the sandspit. As the wind began to gust, Jim and I each grasped one of the paddles supporting the shelter while Don and Paul finished tending to the cleaning of the cooking pots. The wind tried to upset the cooking shelter, but with the extra support it held fast to ward off the downpour and the pea-size hail that followed.

As the wind calmed and the rain diminished, I carefully collected some of the larger pieces of hail from the grass and sand around the campsite and enjoyed Yukon Jack on the ice provided by nature. Although the hail provided a unique opportunity of nature-made ice, only Don joined me and my friend for the evening cocktail party.

Having demonstrated its fury and capability, the storm slowed to a drizzle, allowing the four of us to finish cleaning up the cooking utensils, take down the tarp shelter, and check to make sure that our kayaks were still well secured. The storm continued to threaten us with a reengagement, as it seemed to circle the sandspit like a wolf, glaring at us with eyes of lightning and growling and grumbling with thunder as if it was demanding food scraps from our evening meal.

There was no good reason to remain awake trying to stay dry and free of mosquitoes outside the tents, so we all made an early decision to let the tents' nylon rain flys do their job and seek the relative dryness of our sleeping bags. Paul and I were secure and dry in our tent first when the rain started anew. I retain a sharp mental image of Jim caught with the top half of his body invisible inside the other tent door while Don, perhaps intentionally, seemed to take forever to rearrange the inside of the tent, leaving Jim's bottom half outside the tent getting drenched by the storm's second downpour.

While sleep initially came quickly to us tired paddlers, the storm continued its wolf-like threat, circling the campsite late into the night, intermittently disturbing our sleep with thunder and always reminding us it would be capable of more serious possibilities.

By early morning the weather had changed to grey skies, nearly calm winds, and waves of less than a foot. We experienced the closest thing to bad taste that the trip held for us, packing damp equipment into our kayaks, packing a damp breakfast into our stomachs, and wriggling into our damp, cold wetsuits. By 8:00 a.m. we launched and paddled briskly away from Michigan Island toward Stockton Island, using the warmth generated by the exercise to ward off the dampness and drive the grumbling weather wolf away for the rest of the trip.

(We made it to Stockton Island on Saturday morning, but while we were taking a lunch break at the north end of Julian Bay, the sky cleared and a strong northerly wind kicked up 5-foot waves, encouraging us to stay in a wilderness camp on Stockton Island on Saturday night instead of proceeding to Outer Island. We stopped at the Outer Island sandspit the next day before proceeding to Cat Island for the final night of the trip. We had a beautiful flat water paddle from Cat Island to Buffalo Bay on Monday morning, learning that the women's group had experienced an equipment-destroying storm on the first night of their trip, and had returned to the starting point early.)

NORTH TWIN ISLAND

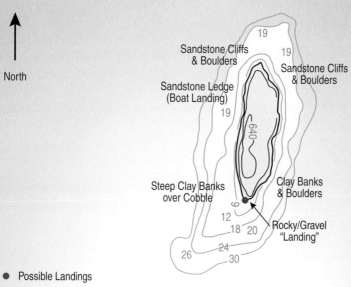

North

Sandstone Cliffs
& Boulders

Sandstone Cliffs
& Boulders

Sandstone Ledge
(Boat Landing)

19

19

19

640

Steep Clay Banks
over Cobble

Clay Banks
& Boulders

6

12

18 20

24

26

30

Rocky/Gravel
"Landing"

● Possible Landings

Statute Miles

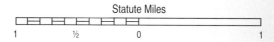

1   ½   0   1

North Twin "sandspit" (photo by author).

Location

North Twin Island is the middle island on the tier of the three most northern islands in the Apostle Islands Lakeshore. Devils Island, its neighbor to the west, is 6.5 miles away across open water and Outer Island, its other neighbor, is about 6.5 miles east. The southern point of North Twin is about 2.75 miles northeast of the northerly tip of Rocky Island and the north end of South Twin Island, about 1.5 miles north-northwest of Cat Island, and about 3.5 miles north-northeast of Ironwood Island. To the north of North Twin Island lie the open lake and ultimately the north shore of Minnesota.

Geography and History

This narrow island is just over a mile long north to south and only about a quarter mile wide. With about 175 acres, it is the smallest of the Apostles (except for Eagle and Gull Islands). On the south end of the island, in lieu of the usual sandspit, a flat, low-lying, stone and gravel tail breaks away from the high banks along most of the island's shoreline and continues out from its southern tip under the lake surface for several hundred yards to the southwest. The rocky tail off the southern tip of North Twin Island makes an approach to the island from the south hazardous except in calm seas.

While the shoreline rises steeply from the lakeshore around the entire circumference of North Twin, the island flattens after the initial rise from the inland sea to become a relatively level island 20 to 40 feet above the lake.

Probably because of its distance from the mainland and the stunted nature of its boreal forest exposed to the open lake, the island has never been logged. It has experienced only limited human habitation, with its last owner (other than the federal government) using a seasonal cottage located at the northwest "corner" of the island. Because of its inaccessibility, the island remains an isolated spiritual mystery filled with unique vegetation natural to more northern latitudes. Indeed, at least one level-headed local boater paying a short visit to the abandoned cottage before the park service removed it from the island experienced eerie, ghostlike sensations.

Shoreline and Landings

For the southern third of the shoreline of North Twin on both the eastern and western shores, steep clay banks rise above a narrow cobble "beach." On the northern two-thirds of the island, again both coasts are similar with red sandstone rising abruptly from the water to shelves 4 to 10 feet above the lake surface.

There are no easy landings for kayaks along the shoreline of the island. However, if there is little wave action, a careful kayak landing may be made on the gravel and rocky "spit" extending from the southern tip of the island. There are a few sandy "beaches" along the west shoreline of the southerly third of the island, however, once on shore, it will be difficult to penetrate the island's shoreline brush.

In calm weather a landing could be attempted on a flat rock shelf less than a foot above waterline located in a rocky cove about half way up the east shore of the island. A similar rock shelf landing could be attempted on another rock about 0.25 miles south of the northern tip of the island on the northeast shoreline. As with the sandy landings on the western shore in the southern third of the island, penetrating farther into the island after a successful landing on the rock shelves is questionable. There are boat moorings built into a rock shelf about 3 feet above the lake surface that served as access to the old seasonal cottage at the northwestern corner of the island, however, while useful to a sailboat or powerboat in calm weather, the rock shelf, because of its height above the water, will not provide a kayaker with an easy place to land.

Camping

There are no campsites on North Twin. One primitive zone camping permit is currently allowed for the entire island.

Hiking

There are no hiking trails on the island.

Kayak Trip Suggestions

On a relatively calm day, the unique flora and mysteries of North Twin Island could be explored as a day trip from Rocky, South Twin, Ironwood, or Cat Islands.

THE LAST ISLAND

I awoke before sunrise with a start, feeling somewhat disoriented. I sat up in my tent still encased in my sleeping bag and absorbed the silence, while mentally searching for the proper time and place to match my current limited awareness. My memory took over. Although unstimulated by sensations of sound, my brain, queued by the visual images on the inside of my tent, filled in the gaps left by the absence of sound. I was in the campsite on the southern tip of Ironwood Island.

Even the birds inhabiting the forest and shore around the campsite seemed to still be at rest, perhaps waiting for my lead before they also awakened to begin their early summer daily routine. A peak out of the door of the tent offered an additional reason for the silence. There was no wind and I had to strain to hear the faint sound of any waves on the shoreline only 50 feet away.

The adrenaline served as my body's alarm clock as I remembered that I was on a solo kayak trip that would complete a goal I had set for myself years before. In my quest to visit each of the Apostles in my kayak, now only North Twin remained as the last remaining unvisited island. I would complete that quest today.

From the sandspit at the south end of Ironwood Island I planned to paddle the eastern shore of Ironwood, then from the north end of the island I planned to paddle a bit east of north on a 3.5-mile crossing to North Twin Island, circumnavigate North Twin and return to Ironwood by way of South Twin Island. The total trip would be close to 14 miles. For about 8 miles in the middle of the day's trip—from the north shore of North Twin until I stopped for a rest on South Twin Island—I would be exposed to the mercies of the open waters of Lake Superior.

The anticipation of the potential dangers of the trip, the thought of completing the goal to visit all of the islands, and the desire to take advantage of the calm wind all increased my excitement and created an irresistible force ejecting me from the sleeping bag and the tent. I lit the camp stove to boil water for my morning coffee and oatmeal before venturing into the woods to visit a ready-made cat hole, since there was no privy at that time. Returning to camp with a couple of welts caused by mosquitoes taking advantage of my exposed cheeks, I struggled to don my wetsuit. The water was boiling and ready for making breakfast. The birds had awakened to serenade me with morning song and break the earlier silence.

The sun was up over the eastern horizon by the time I packed the things I needed for the day trip into the holds of my kayak. I went through the day trip in my mind checking off the equipment, water, and lunch that I would need. Everything had been packed in the holds of my kayak, in my deck bag, or under the bungee cords of the deck.

After a moment of meditation, I pushed off. About 50 yards out I tried to lower my rudder, not because I needed it in the calm water, but because I wanted to make sure that I would be able to deploy the rudder if I needed it later in the day. The rudder was stuck and would not go down. Reluctantly I returned to the sandspit, chastising myself for having caused myself a delay in the day's paddle even for five minutes. In my hurry to launch I had tightened the rear hatch cover over the rudder deployment cord. I freed the rudder cord from its restraint, thankful that I had remembered to test the rudder deployment before I had paddled too far from the vicinity of the launch area and launched again.

As I rounded Ironwood Island and looked north, I looked across the mirror-like lake to see the outline of North Twin illuminated by the early morning sunshine. The narrow southern exposure of the island was occluded by the low angle of the sun and the water vapor rising from the intervening expanse of open water. Spurred by the adrenaline of the morning wake up, the coffee, and the desire to beat any change in the weather, my paddle cadence and the power of my strokes pushed me to a top flat-water speed of just over 4 miles per hour. I would be at the south end of North Twin in about an hour.

About half way into the crossing I paused for a hydrating drink. The water remained calm with only a hint of a breeze from the southwest. The morning silence also remained. I could hear voices, although they were too faint to actually make out the conversation, from several fishing boats trolling almost 2 miles away near the north end of Cat Island. I resumed paddling, thinking about the voices, now no longer audible because of the sound of my paddle strokes. With the speed of sound across the water, the indistinct words I had heard from so far away had actually been uttered nine or ten seconds ago. I hadn't heard a conversation, I had heard recent history.

As I approached the southern end of the island, the lighter colored gravel on the exposed hillside on the tip of the island became my aiming point. The flat water allowed me to identify the rocks in the shallow water as I approached the island. Carefully I navigated the kayak through the clear water, always believing that the water was shallower than it was. I landed on the west side of the southern tip of the island, getting out of the kayak 25 feet from shore in just inches of water covering sharp rocks smaller than my fist.

After a quick snack and more water, I lined up my camera to focus on the bow of my kayak now resting in the small rocks and gravel along the shore. I took a delayed picture of myself squatting next to the bow. It proved to be a rather dull picture for everyone except me. I knew my beaming smile in the morning sun represented a celebration of the completion of a goal. I also photographed the end of the "spit" jutting south toward Ironwood Island.

North Twin selfie—The Last Island (photo by author).

After a brief rest, I launched again, paddling at least 100 yards south before crossing the shallow water covering the sharp stones extending out into the water from the southern tip of the island. I reversed my direction as I headed north along the east shoreline of North Twin. I paddled at a more leisurely cadence, making mental notes on the nature of the shoreline.

At the north end of the island, I glanced at the open lake to the north. Viewing the wide expanse across the open lake with only a hint of a distant line of land on the horizon always causes my mind to react with the uncertainty of a dilemma. It's not unlike the vertigo I feel when looking down at the edge of a high exposed cliff. I want to look long and hard to simply enjoy the view of an indefinite water horizon and explore my unreasonable apprehension about any danger potential, but I also want to avoid the view and the unreasonable feeling of foreboding without further analysis, turn around and refocus my gaze in the opposite direction toward perceived safety.

I paddled south past the iron "horns" securely fastened to a rock shelf about 3 feet above the waterline, contemplating what it would have been like for the former islander living on the north end of North Twin Island isolated from most human contact even for only one summer.

About two-thirds of the way down the western shore, a breeze out of the southwest started to ripple the surface of the water. I modified my course to face into the breeze and paddle toward the protection of South Twin Island lying about 2.5 miles away. The breeze initially was refreshing and cooled my sweaty forehead. However, the breeze quickly built to 15 miles per hour, producing 1-foot, then 2-foot waves and destroying the silence that I had experienced since the earlier disorienting end of my night's sleep and through the lesson in recent history. The wind and waves allied with the fatigue I was feeling from an aggressive morning paddle of about 8 miles and slowed my progress toward South Twin to less than 3 miles per hour.

Seemingly enjoying a bit of its own humor, the wind even reached under the bill of my cap and flipped it off my head into the water behind me. After turning the kayak around to retrieve the cap, I better understood the limited humor of the wind's joke. Paddling with the wind lead me back to the cap at twice the speed I had been paddling into the wind with cap in place. I told the wind a joke of my own. After retrieving my cap, I shook most of the water off but put it more tightly back on my head. I yelled to no one but the wind, "Hah! I defy you." The wind understood my humor no better than I had understood its joke on me, but the evaporation of the water from the cap left me more cool-headed.

My rudder occasionally dragged over rocks in the shallow water north of South Twin Island as I tried to hug the shoreline. The sand on the beach just south of the boat dock invited me to lunch and a rest free of any paddling obligation until the wind diminished and allowed me an easier crossing back to my campsite on Ironwood Island.

I snoozed in the sun on top of a picnic table and enjoyed the satisfying feeling of having visited the last major island, however briefly. Paddling back to Ironwood could wait till after my nap.

OAK ISLAND

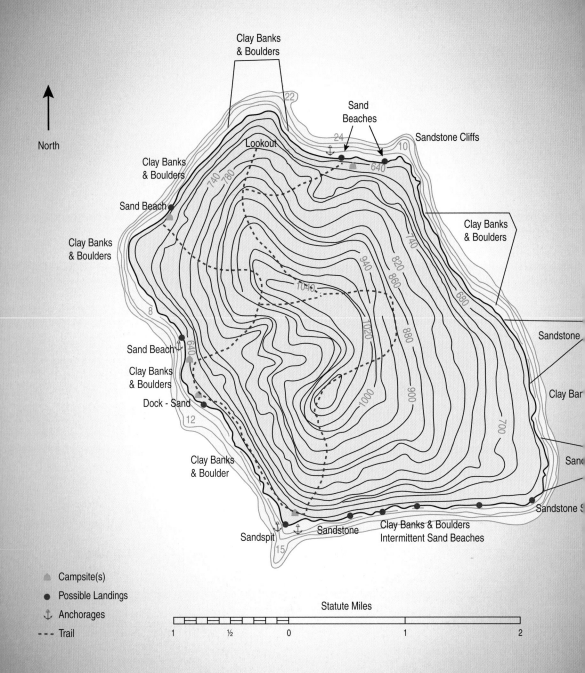

North

Clay Banks
& Boulders

Sand
Beaches

Sandstone Cliffs

22

24

10

Lookout

Clay Banks
& Boulders

Sand Beach

Clay Banks
& Boulders

Clay Banks
& Boulders

740 780

640

8

940 820
860
680

Sandstone

Sand Beach

Clay Banks
& Boulders

Dock - Sand

12

640

1040

1020

880

Clay Bar

1000

900

700

Sand

Clay Banks
& Boulder

Sandstone S

Sandspit

15

Sandstone

Clay Banks & Boulders
Intermittent Sand Beaches

Campsite(s)

Possible Landings

Anchorages

Trail

Statute Miles

1   ½   0   1   2

Location

Oak Island is located 1.25 to 1.5 miles northeast of the Bayfield Peninsula mainland and is nestled 2 miles southeast of Raspberry Island, 2.5 miles south-southeast of Bear Island, 1.5 miles southwest of Manitou Island, about 1.75 miles west of Stockton Island, and 1.5 miles northwest of Hermit Island.

Geography and History

Oak is the tallest island in the archipelago, rising about 480 feet above the lake level. The island's highest point is near the geographic center of the island, and while it is near a hiking trail, there is no vista of surrounding islands. A trained eye can locate cobble beaches high up from the current shoreline, a remnant of a time thousands of years ago when the lake level was much higher and Oak Island was one of only a few islands to peak above the prehistoric waterline.

Oak Island is about 3.5 miles long, north to south, and about 2.5 miles wide. The island covers 5,078 acres, making it the third largest island in the National Lakeshore after Stockton and Outer.

The Ojibwe used the island prior to Europeans for gathering maple syrup and other purposes, according to historical sources. Fishing and lumber attracted the European settlers in the mid-1800s, and a number of clearings on the island around the current campsites are what remains of their fishing and logging camps. In the second half of the nineteenth century Oak Island loggers provided cordwood for the boilers of passing steamers. The island was successively logged for pine, hemlock, and hardwoods from the 1880s to the 1920s. During the 1930s logging gave way to commercial fishing camps catching and marketing whitefish and lake trout. The National Park Service brochure

Oak Island overhang (photo by Robert E. Rolley).

Oak Island rock (photo by Don Hynek).

Crescent moon at sunset (photo by Mark Weller).

for Oak Island states that the sparks from the stove of one of the long-term resident fishermen, Martin Kane, started a fire in 1943 that burned about 80 percent of the island, but little trace of the fire remains today.

Shoreline and Landings

The south shore of Oak Island stretches west to east about 2.5 miles from the sandspit located at the southwest corner of the island to the sandstone rock shelf at the southeast corner. It is possible to land at the sandspit from a westerly approach or a southerly approach. Between the sandspit and the rock shelf there are at least four sandy beaches spaced .25 to .75 mile apart. The three westerly beaches may have some boulders to negotiate in making a landing. The most easterly beach perhaps offers the safest landing. The sandstone shelf at the southeast corner requires relatively calm water to use as a landing. Between the south shore beaches are clay banks with boulders at the waterline.

Along the west shore, landings can be made (carefully) at the dock about midway up the west side of the island and at a small sand beach about 0.5 miles (and around the shallow peninsula) north of the dock. The balance of the west shore typically has boulders at lake level backed by high clay banks.

Paddling northeast from the northwest corner of the island, there will be a smaller sand beach after about 0.25 miles of sandstone. For the next 1.5 miles and until the paddler has rounded the most northerly point on the island, there will be clay banks with boulders at the waterline. However, once past the northern point of the island, heading back to the southeast, the paddler will see a .75-mile protected beach with individual campsite #6 located in about the middle. A second smaller beach lies beyond a short stretch of boulders and clay banks separating it from the larger beach. The hole in the wall sea cave used to be located at the northeast

Unloading at Oak Island sandspit (photo by Robert E. Rolley).

Oak Island ranger station (photo courtesy National Park Service).

Rare wood flamingo at Oak Island sandspit (copyright & photo by Robert E. Rolley).

Oak Island Dock (photo courtesy National Park Service).

corner of the island until it collapsed sometime in the early spring of 2009.

The east shore of Oak offers intermittent sandstone cliffs and clay banks with boulders. However, there are several small beaches that can be used for landings for a rest break although large sandstone boulders or almost impenetrable foliage would make wilderness camping difficult.

The wooden dock on Oak Island can accommodate boats with a 4- to 5-foot draft.

Camping

There are currently two group campsites on Oak Island—Site A at the sandspit on the southwest corner and Site B near the dock halfway up the west shore. There are also five individual campsites, four spread along the westerly shore (sandspit, dock, small beach 0.5 mile north of the dock, and on the first beach north of the most westerly [northwesterly] point of the island at the end of the Northwest Beach Trail.) Campsite #6 (campsite #5 used to be located next to #4) is near the .75-mile beach on the north side of the island. Both campsites #4 and #6 offer secluded camping, however the bay by campsite #6 is shallow and depending upon the wind direction, the camper may have to share the bay with anchored powerboats and sailboats.

All of the Oak Island campsites have vault toilets, food lockers, and picnic tables. The individual campsite at the sandspit (#1), the site about 0.5 mile north of the dock (#3) and at the beach on the northwestern shore (#4) also have tent pads.

Besides the designated sites, Oak Island offers a single primitive camping zone outside the designated campsites. The island's size and the numerous places to land make Oak a good choice for primitive camping in spite of the increase in the bear population.

Hiking

There are over 11 miles of trails to hike on Oak Island. The Sandspit Trail is 1.5 miles long, running between the sandspit and the dock. Northeast from the sandspit, the 5.2-mile Loop Trail eventually turns west past the highest point on the island, then back southwest to Campsite #3 and south to the dock. The North-west Beach Trail branches off from the Loop Trail, about where the Loop Trail ventures southwesterly back toward the dock, and leads 1.6 miles up to campsite #4. The Overlook Trail also branches from the Loop Trail midway across the island, not far from the highest point on the island, and heads 1.8 miles to the most northerly point on Oak Island ending at an overlook more than 100 feet above the water. Finally, the North Bay Trail branches east about two-thirds of the way up the Overlook Trail and in a bit over a mile ends up on the north shore at campsite #6.

Kayak Trip Suggestions

Because it lies close to a number of islands, Oak offers an opportunity for establishing a base camp for more than one night while exploring the neighboring islands on day trips. As an island that's an easy one-day paddle from most of the launch points on the Bayfield Peninsula, its campsites also offer a variety of good choices for the first night out or the last night of a trip.

Park visitors without their own water transportation can enjoy camping and hiking on Oak Island by using the cruise boat service to the Oak Island dock if it is available or by using a water taxi for a drop off and pick up anywhere on the island (see the "Resources" section at the end of the book).

Oak Island Sandspit Trail (photo courtesy National Park Service).

Corpse plant or Indian pipe (*Monotropa uniflora*) (photo by Robert E. Rolley).

Oak Island American cancer root (*Conopholis americana*) (photo by Robert E. Rolley).

MEMORIAL DAY SNOW

Spring crept slowly and silently in winter's back door. You knew spring was there ready to take over the household, but winter was not yet ready to relinquish its control. On the Friday before Memorial Day, there were rumors of masses of ice lying out beyond Madeline Island. After setting up a tent for an overnight stay in Memorial Campground in Washburn, I stopped in at Patsy's Bar to check on the rumors. Perhaps the Mad City Paddlers trip to Oak Island would have to be called off or modified because of the lingering ice.

I told the female bartender, a woman in her fifties, about the kayak trip planned by the paddle club, and asked about the ice rumors. She confirmed that some of the early fishermen had reported ice.

"Some of the boats have reported ice out beyond Madeline Island," she said.

"Well, that shouldn't bother us then," I said, referring to the planned paddle trip. "We are only planning a trip out to Oak Island."

"Well no," she warned, "but if we get a strong wind out of the northeast, all of that ice could be pushed back among the islands and into Chequamegon Bay."

I returned to Memorial Campground half full of draft beer and half full of new concerns about a possible northeastern wind. The weather radio that I listened to before falling asleep mentioned only sunny weather with highs in the low seventies and little wind from any direction.

The paddle group met and launched at Schooner Bay Marina at 8:00 a.m. the next morning. There were eight of us altogether—two couples consisting of our group leaders Paul and Karen and Brian and Gina, and four singles—Sloan, a sixteen year old with an endless amount of paddling energy, his father, a laid back middle-aged man, Julie, a single mom in her late thirties, and me, with four years of paddling experience and having recently edged over the half-century mark. The couples both paddled tandem kayaks and the rest of us paddled singles. Every member of the group already knew a few of the other members, having paddled with them in other groups before the Memorial Day trip.

The group met at Schooner Bay where the town road meets the water. The marina does not cater to kayakers, but Memorial Day is relatively early in the season for kayakers as well as for the larger sailboats and powerboats usually found in the Schooner Bay Marina, and no one from the marina approached the kayak group to discourage us from launching at the small beach at the end of the road.

Getting ready for a group launch always involves a bit of chaos as boats and equipment are carried down to the water's edge and kayakers struggle into wetsuits and drysuits. Several members of the Oak Island group complained about the loss of elasticity in their neoprene wetsuits due to the lack of use of the wetsuit over the winter months. Other members wisely kept their silence, noting that the tightness of the wetsuit was more likely due to the slight change in the complainer's body shape over the same winter months. Sloan was not one of the complainers. His wetsuit slipped over his young, muscular body as if he was covering himself with a cotton sweatshirt and sweatpants.

A few of the paddlers finished packing their kayaks early, launched, and slowly paddled across Schooner Bay to examine the *H.D. Coffinberry* an old wooden shipwreck resting along the shoreline almost at water's edge. The ribs of the wreck's hull stuck up out of the water like the decaying ribs of a dinosaur that years ago had come to the lake for a drink, died, and rolled over on its back in the water. The other kayakers soon finished packing their kayaks and joined the early launchers by the shipwreck. The entire group now was ready to proceed to the Oak Island dock.

Keeping a kayak group paddling together in relatively close formation, heading in the same direction and at a somewhat uniform speed is always a challenge. Some paddlers prefer to paddle close to shore to preserve the illusion of safety or to examine the rock formations and sea cave indentations in the shoreline. Others range farther from shore, enjoying the solitude of the open lake air on a calm day. Some paddle fast as if the crossing is a race, while others lag to the rear of the group, oblivious to their course and pace while enjoying a trip filled with conversation with the other paddlers. In our group, Julie ranged out from the rest of the group, aiming directly toward the Oak Island dock rather than the Oak Island sandspit. Sloan alternated between paddling at a sprint speed, seemingly nearly fast enough to raise his boat to a hydroplane, and stopping completely to wait for the others to catch up. Paul and Karen, as group leaders, carefully put Julie on a corrected course to the sandspit and verbally pulled Sloan back to the rest of the group when he got too far ahead.

As the on-going conversation between the two couples in the double kayaks started to lag, I pulled my kayak alongside Karen and Paul.

"So what do you have planned for us on this trip?" I asked.

"Well, I thought that we would paddle north of the dock on Oak Island this afternoon, after we set up camp," Karen answered. "Then tomorrow, if the weather lets us, we will take a trip over to the Raspberry Lighthouse or up to Bear Island."

"That sounds great. The weather radio predicted good weather for the entire weekend. Maybe not as calm as it is this morning but only a slight westerly breeze tomorrow. I had heard there might still be ice on the lake."

"Yeah, I read about ice on the lake in the newspaper a few days ago," Paul added. "But if there is any ice left, it must be out in the open lake."

"The bartender at Patsy's Bar told me that some fishermen reported ice east of Madeline, but I guess that would only affect us if we got an east wind."

"Well, I doubt that there is much ice left. It's been in the sixties the last week or so."

We paddled on, chatting about recent trips. It would have been hard to match speed with Paul and Karen if they chose to paddle hard. Today, on their first longer trip of the season and with a group with mixed experience and stamina, they were paddling a leisurely pace. They always had an interesting story about a recent foreign vacation they had taken.

No one really needed a rest from paddling after the crossing to the Oak Island sandspit, except to obtain relief from the morning coffee. Coffee can be one of the strongest influences on the timing and location of morning paddle breaks. Without the influence of coffee, some of us might paddle until almost noon.

After the break, we continued the last mile or so up the Oak Island coast to the dock. Sloan was the first one at the dock, operating in his fast paddle mode. We all helped one another lift and slide the loaded kayaks up the shore onto the grassy clearing by the dock. As a healthy teenager, Sloan could handle lifting more of the weight of the kayaks than the rest of us.

We spent the rest of the morning setting up our tents, gathering firewood for the evening communal fire, and making arrangements for cooking the evening main meal.

At about one o'clock we met at the dock to return our kayaks, now lightened from their loads of equipment, to the water. We planned a leisurely couple of hours of paddling north along the westerly coast of Oak Island on a day trip of springtime exploration. Even without the time needed to pack food and equipment into the kayaks, it took awhile for everyone to get organized, get into their kayaks, and launch into the water. Family discussions occurred. Is the sun high enough to warrant the application of sunscreen? (Yes, of course.) Should we be taking along the binoculars? (Why not?) Should we get back into the wetsuits and drysuits? (Definitely.) Don't forget the camera. Julie and I mostly listened and adjusted our behavior to the emerging group standard.

Traveling north along the west shoreline of Oak, we ranged out a good distance from the island in calm water. Raspberry Island and its reflection seemed to hang suspended between earth and sky to our west, and Bear Island offered an open invitation for a visit to our north. We would visit each island tomorrow if the weather cooperated, but this afternoon we limited our exploration to the west and northwest coast of Oak Island.

After several miles we headed east toward the north end of Oak Island and to return south along the shoreline to the campsite by the dock. As we closed in on Oak Island we noticed streaks of white in several places just above the waterline.

"It's snow," Mike half shouted, his voice revealing the surprise felt by all of the paddlers.

"Or perhaps ice stacked up by wave action," Paul added.

Sloan accelerated toward the layer of white, broke the seal on his spray skirt, and secured his plastic kayak on the rocks. He was sitting on the 4-foot high snowdrift by the time that Karen and Paul approached the rocky shore next to him in their double. My kayak was the third to approach the remnant of winter and I held back to take a picture. Sloan responded to our requests for pictures by taking seat on the snowdrift. Warmed by the spring air, the drift was of a consistency perfect for snowballs and adequate to support a seated teenager.

In a late winter storm, the snow apparently had drifted along parts of the northwestern shore to a depth of several feet. Facing north and protected

Oak Island Memorial Day snow (photo by author).

from the bright May sunshine by the large overhanging trees and the island itself, the snow looked like it would not be gone at least for another week. Remnants of May snow along the northern shorelines of the Apostle Islands is not unusual, but I have never seen so much snow so late in May.

On group trips, Brian and Gina's cooler usually contained some special treat to eat or drink for the entire group. I suggested that he might want to harvest some of the snow for his cooler. Unfortunately, they had left the cooler in the bear box back at the campsite. And we really wouldn't need any snow or ice to maintain a cool temperature overnight.

We saw several more strips of snowdrift along the north-facing shore of Oak Island as we returned to the group campsite by the dock. Although the evening was not cold, the thought of the cold snowdrifts Oak Island shared with us made the hot evening spaghetti and garlic bread—with wine from Brian and Gina's cooler—taste that much better.

Sabrina's cousin on Oak Island (photo by Don Hynek).

OTTER ISLAND

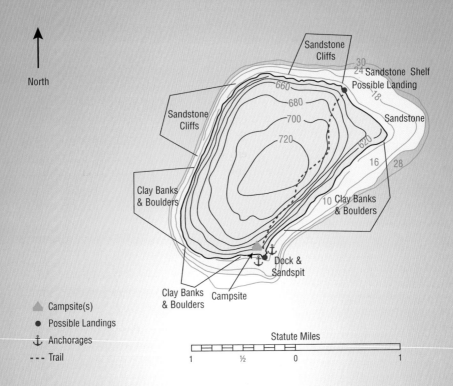

↑
North

Sandstone
Cliffs

30
24 Sandstone Shelf
Possible Landing
18

660

680

Sandstone

700

Sandstone
Cliffs

720

1320

16

28

Clay Banks
& Boulders

10 Clay Banks
& Boulders

Dock &
Sandspit

▲ Campsite(s)

● Possible Landings

⚓ Anchorages

- - - Trail

Clay Banks
& Boulders

Campsite

Statute Miles

1   ½   0   1

Otter Island dock (photo courtesy National Park Service).

Location

Otter Island's north coast lies just 0.75 mile south of the Rocky Island sandspit and a bit over 2 miles southwest from the South Twin dock. Bear Island is about 2 miles north-northwest of Otter, and Ironwood Island is about 2 miles north-northeast of Otter. The sandspit on the southeast corner of Otter Island is about 2 miles northeast of the north bay of Oak Island.

Geography and History

The east, northeast, and southwest shorelines of Otter Island rise gradually to an elevation of about 140 feet above the level of Lake Superior. The northwestern and northern shorelines initially rise more sharply from sandstone shelves along the lakeshore, and the southeastern shore rises steeply above a flatter, rocky shoreline.

The island is shaped like the head of a chicken without a comb and with its dull beak pointing east toward Ironwood Island. Without the beak Otter Island is almost 2 miles long and averages about 1.5 miles wide. The area of Otter Island is 1,333 acres.

The clearing around the dock area provides the easiest access to the island and probably served as a fish camp in earlier days. The island was last logged for hardwoods in the late 1950s. Shortly after the last logging, in 1960 the island served as a temporary home for about fifteen hundred Boy Scouts who held a Jamboree to commemorate the merger of the Gitchee-Gumme and North Star Councils into the Lake Superior Council.[18]

Shoreline and Landings

The southeast corner of Otter Island hosts a sandspit, a phenomenon common among the Apostle Islands. The sandspit is a result of the buildup of sand deposited by wave action generated by the prevailing and sometimes harsh north and west winds. Just north of the sandspit is the island's dock, which requires occasional repairs due to ice damage. The sandspit and dock area offer the best and perhaps the only location for landing a kayak or larger boat, although the island map shows a possible calm weather rock shelf landing just above the chicken's beak.

Traveling counterclockwise around the island, from the sandspit up to the tip of the beak on the chicken's head, after a few rocks and a sandstone cliff, there is over a mile of eroding clay banks with a rocky shoreline. From the tip of the beak all across the northern shore and to the middle of the back of the chicken's neck steep sandstone shelves inhibit any landing, except for the rock shelf landing at the top of the chicken's beak along the northeastern shore. Heading southwest along the lower half of the back of the chicken's neck and thence east along the southern shore back to the sandspit, the shoreline again features clay banks over 10 feet high with boulders and rocks strewn along the waterline.

The wooden U-shaped dock at the sandspit can accommodate boats with 5- to 6-foot draft.

Camping

The only designated campsite on the island is located at the sandspit on the southeastern corner of the island. It has a fire ring, vault toilet (shared with the dock users), and picnic table.

Outside the dock and campsite area there is a single primitive camping zone, perhaps difficult to use without a hike, because of the absence of landing sites outside the sandspit.

Otter Island campsite (photo courtesy National Park Service).

Hiking

A 1.9-mile trail, left over from the Boy Scout Jamboree days, still leads from the clearing at the sandspit to the north coast of the island.

Kayak Trip Suggestions

The designated campsite on Otter provides a convenient waystation for longer trips across the islands in the National Lakeshore, whether traveling either east-west or north-south. At about 12 miles from Red Cliff and 14 miles from Little Sand Bay respectively, the campsite at Otter might also serve as the stopover point for the first night out from, or last night on the way back to, the launch site for a trip.

THE DANNY SANDWICH

The Danny for whom this sandwich is named is now a man with all of the cares of middle age, including raising teenage children and trying to run a small school. However, when he invented the sandwich bearing his name, he was a young man in his early teens who was painting the trim on his uncle and aunt's house as a summer job. At that time in his life, he was in need of an almost unlimited number of calories to fuel his job and his teenage growth spurt.

The sandwich recipe is simple. Take two slices of bread, preferably white, and slather one liberally with peanut butter—smooth or chunky, according to your taste. On the other slice of bread lay out one or two slices of soft processed American cheese. Slap the two slices of bread together with the cheese and peanut butter facing one another. Squeeze the outer bread slices together to ensure adherence among the four layers and stuff in your mouth. Repeat as necessary. Barely serves one. Calories 455; for a daily 2,000 calorie diet it provides 42% fat (47% sat. fat), 23% fiber, 37% sodium, 20% calcium, 13% iron, 17 gr. protein.[19]

The Danny Sandwich is particularly well-suited for anyone on a high calorie, high fat, and relatively low fiber diet, or for a kayaker's high energy snack. Or breakfast. Or lunch. Or dinner. Or all four.

On an early kayak camping trip that included Otter Island, my wife, Signe, and I survived mostly on Danny Sandwiches. We not only survived, we actually began to crave them.

On our first day out we had paddled from Schooner Bay to the campsite on the north bay of Oak Island, with stops at the Oak Island sandspit, the Oak Island dock, and a rather uncomfortable clay bank above a rocky shoreline just south of the most westerly point of Oak Island. The last stop at the steep clay bank was made, in part, to allow the waves driven by a northerly wind to diminish before our final push around the northern tip of Oak Island to our campsite. With our kayaks resting above the waterline on rocks and driftwood while we waited for kinder winds, I precariously squatted 5 or 6 feet up the steep clay bank to boil water on our single-burner stove. If we ate our evening meal early during the time we couldn't paddle anyway, we could paddle to the campsite later when the wind and seas calmed down. Signe napped in a near upright position wedged into a gully in the steep clay bank about 15 feet above the shoreline.

The trip was only our second kayak trip on Lake Superior and the first one that included overnight camping. We were novices, and the 10-mile first day's paddle was simply too long, especially for Signe. After we reached the campsite and the tent was up, she was sleeping in minutes, albeit fitfully because of aching muscles. In the morning she questioned whether she could even paddle to our next reserved campsite on Otter Island. I noted that the second leg of our trip would take us only 2 miles, and indeed we could even see our destination, which seemed to be marked by an unidentifiable white spot across the water to the northeast. I compared the distance to Otter with paddling distances we had easily completed on outings closer to home.

"This really isn't that far," I offered. "It will be like paddling from home upstream on the Cherokee Marsh to the dock and storage building in Cherokee Park."

"Yeah, well that's still a pretty long way," Signe countered.

Although we probably had something more traditional along with us for breakfast, we opted simply for coffee and a Danny Sandwich or two. Whether it was the medicinal qualities of the Danny Sandwich or the stimulating sips of hot coffee, soon we both felt better and were able to pack up our tent and equipment and launch for our crossing to the Otter Island dock.

The exercise of the crossing and the bright sun made our muscles feel better and improved our dispositions. As we completed our crossing, the white spot materialized into a park service boat tied to the dock. A crew was cutting the grass and doing other maintenance. They finished soon after we arrived but stayed at the dock to take their lunch break before leaving in the boat.

It was a warm, sunny day. We removed our wetsuits, rinsed them off in the lake and took a refreshing dip in the shallow water at the sandspit. We draped our wetsuits on some of the shrubs around the campsite to dry, and we set up our tent.

Although we had paddled only a couple of miles, because of our late start it was already past noon. While I am quite sure we had brought along cheese and sausage for lunch, the nearly addictive combination of calories and fat in a Danny Sandwich prevailed again. As pasty as a Danny Sandwich may seem on other occasions, they certainly were very tasty and satisfying on this trip. I recall that we both had two Dannys for lunch. An inventory of our food supplies indicated that although the peanut butter and cheese supplies for the trip remained strong, the bread supply was dwindling. With the disappearance of eight more slices of bread during lunch, we started to contemplate the need to ration the white bread for the rest of the five-day trip.

After the long and tiresome paddle (for novices) the day before, we were content to bask and snooze in the summer sun after lunch. While pretending to read books we could alternatively doze off and startle awake again as a few other folks came and went at the dock. Shortly after assuming our reclining reading positions, two kayakers approached the dock from the east, crossing from Manitou Island. They rested for a while and then left on the next leg of their float plan. Later in the afternoon, a cabin cruiser slowly approached us from the north and tied up on the north side of the dock. A discussion with the friendly passengers gave us the indication that they would staying for the night. We would be sharing the vault toilet.

For many years the first evening meal on a camping trip has been steak. Frozen at home and packed into a small cooler in the bottom of the hold, the meat keeps well for twenty-four to thirty-six hours or more and also serves as an ice pack to cool other food items packed with it.

Because I wanted to keep cooking as simple as possible while perched on the clay bank during our wind delay the day before, I had prepared a prepackaged freeze-dried meal. We still had the steak to eat our second night out camped on Otter Island. Late in the afternoon I gathered wood for a fire and prepared to cook the steak directly on the sooty grill over the fire pit. Signe went for a walk on the trail leading off in a northerly direction from the dock.

We also had brought two russet potatoes, cleaned and individually double-wrapped in aluminum foil before we left home. The potatoes were placed into the fire pit, nudged directly up against the burning wood, now starting to turn into coals. The potatoes would be turned occasionally and would take about an hour to bake.

The final part of our dinner was a small can of peas. I opened the can halfway and set it on the fire pit grate a bit to the side and away from the hottest part of the fire. Like the potatoes, the can of peas could take some time to warm, but required far less heat than the potatoes.

Cooking the steak waited until Signe returned from her walk.

"So what did you find on your walk?" I asked, as she entered the campsite and sat down on the picnic table.

"Not much really. The woods are pretty much the same as down here," she said, nodding toward the trailhead.

"How far did you go?"

"The trail goes all the way up to the north shore of the island," she said. "The cliffs and rocks are pretty high off the water—easily twenty feet up. It looks a lot like some of the north end of Oak Island that we paddled past yesterday."

I added a few sticks to the fire and put the steak on the grate. It immediately sizzled and released an inviting aroma. I checked my watch. With one more turn the potatoes should be done, and the can of peas was starting to steam. We would take a break from the Danny Sandwiches tonight. It would conserve the white bread, and make the Dannys taste better again for breakfast in the morning.

OUTER ISLAND

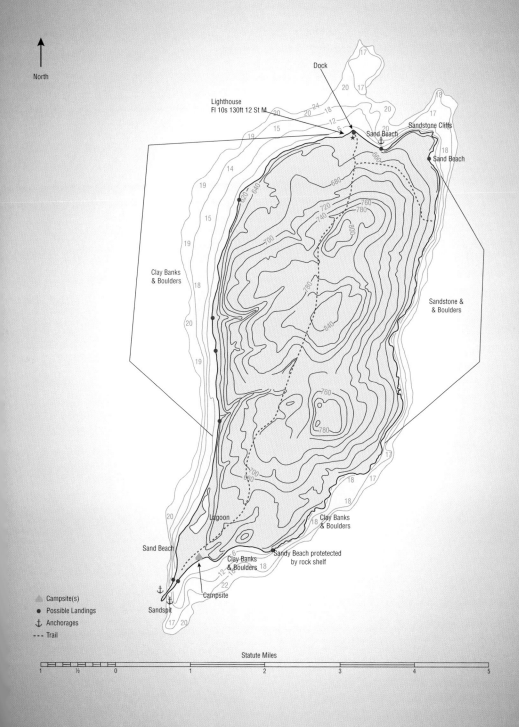

North

Dock

Lighthouse
Fl 10s 130ft 12 St M.

Sandstone Cliffs

Sand Beach

Sand Beach

Clay Banks
& Boulders

Sandstone &
& Boulders

Lagoon

Clay Banks
& Boulders

Sand Beach

Clay Banks
& Boulders

Sandy Beach protetected
by rock shelf

Campsite

Sandspit

🏕 Campsite(s)

● Possible Landings

⚓ Anchorages

- - - Trail

Statute Miles

Location

Outer Island's name is descriptive in that it simply is the island farthest away from the mainland—its sandspit is 24 miles out from Bayfield and 22 miles from Buffalo Bay and Little Sand Bay. It is even somewhat isolated from its neighbors, with Cat Island about 4 miles west of the Outer Island sandspit, Stockton about 3 miles southwest, and Michigan a distant 7.5 miles south. Its distant northern tier neighbor, North Twin Island, is 8 miles west of the Outer Island Lighthouse.

Geography and History

At 8,000 acres, Outer Island is the third largest island in the archipelago (after Madeline and Stockton). Outer also reaches a relatively high elevation at the center of the island rising about 270 feet above the surface of the surrounding lake. On the southwestern corner just north of the sandspit, the island hosts a large lagoon that connects to the lake itself in years of high water. Overall, the island is shaped a bit like a comma with a small notch at the top, being about 7.5 miles long and almost 3 miles wide.

The Outer Island Lighthouse was built in 1874, a 90-foot brick tower painted white and located at the northern tip of the comma. The lighthouse site had a tumultuous start. In the first year of operation, gale force winds created waves that destroyed the dock and

Lilacs backed by Outer Island light (photo by Mark Weller).

caused a collapse of the clay cliff taking the first foghorn building with it. As with the Raspberry Lighthouse, eroding clay banks below the lighthouse have been a continuing problem, and the National Park Service took steps to stabilize the bank below the Outer Lighthouse in 2004–2005. Repairs on the lighthouse site were also made during the summer of 2014.

The original steam fog whistle was housed in a second building in 1875 and another building was added in 1878. The two foghorn buildings were combined in 1900 and the steam whistle was converted to a diesel-powered air diaphone in the late 1920s. The two-story brick keeper's house remains on the lighthouse grounds.

Originally equipped with a Third Order Fresnel lens, the light station produced a flashing signal by using weighted mechanical clockworks to rotate the massive piece of glass. The Fresnel lens was removed in 1961 when the light was fully automated.[20] Today

Outer Island lighthouse grounds (photo by Mark Weller).

the light, elevated at 130 feet above the water, flashes every ten seconds and is visible for 12 miles.

On September 2, 1905, the same day that the *Sevona* ran aground and broke up near Sand Island, the 338-foot wooden schooner-barge, *Pretoria*, was being pushed broadside by heavy wind and waves, after losing its towline from the steamer, *Venezuela*. *Pretoria*'s dragging anchor caught ground in the shallower water north of Outer Island, but the heavy waves caused the *Pretoria* to start to break up and the crew took to a lifeboat to try to make it to Outer Island. When the lifeboat was upset by the waves, John Irvine, the only keeper at the Outer Lighthouse at the time, waded into the water to aid the stricken crew, helping to save the lives of five of the ten crew members. The *Pretoria* still lies about a mile northeast of the lighthouse at a depth of about 55 feet.[21]

Fish camps were maintained on Outer Island at two locations from the 1870s through the 1940s. The first location was the somewhat protected sandy bay just around the sandstone point east of the lighthouse, known locally as the Hans Austad Bay, named after one of the first fishermen to use the site. The second location was at the sandspit at the south end of the island.

The southern half of Outer Island was logged between 1924 and 1930 by the John Schroeder Lumber Company out of Ashland. It was a substantial logging operation that included a railroad with 40 miles of track.[22] As late as the 1950s the Lullabye Furniture Company, a manufacturer of infant's furniture from Stevens Point, continued a logging operation using a natural rock shelf on the northeastern shoreline of the island to load logs onto the converted World War II landing craft, the *Outer Island*, for shipment to the mainland.[23] The remnants of the Lullabye camp are still visible, and the *Outer Island* is still a working boat being used in construction projects to haul rocks and gravel in bulk around the Bayfield waters.

Outer Island Lullabye Logging Camp rock shelf landing (photo courtesy National Park Service).

The trees are winning—Outer Island logging camp (photo courtesy National Park Service).

Shoreline and Landings

In spite of the fact that Outer Island stands as an isolated sentinel at the north end of the archipelago, its western and northern shoreline is marked mostly by clay banks, not sandstone. The island claims perhaps the largest well-developed sandspit among the islands. Inside the western ridge of sand on the mile-long sandspit is a marshy area and substantial lagoon. The sand disappears about a mile up the western shore from the tip of the sandspit, and the predominant feature becomes high clay banks all the way north past the lighthouse at the northern tip of the island, well north and east of the point one would expect to see sandstone cliffs. The western clay banks are interrupted by four or five narrow sandy areas, where small streams drain the western half of the island. There is a small beach about two miles southwest of the lighthouse, and another beach guarded by some hazardous boulders east of the lighthouse dock. Kayakers will find an easier landing for visiting the lighthouse on the sandy beach rather than trying to use the dock.

Along Outer Island's eastern shoreline the sand does not extend as far north from the sandspit, and the shoreline again is marked by high clay banks for almost a mile. The clay becomes sandstone, then clay again in the next mile, finally becoming sandstone shelves and boulders for the next 4 miles to the bay east of the lighthouse. The eastern shore has two landing breaks, one is a sandy beach at a drainage break about 2 miles east and north of the sandspit, and the other is the sandy beach about a mile east of the lighthouse around the rocky sandstone point. Midway between the two eastern landing sites it may be possible to land for a paddle break on a

rock shelf unless an easterly wind makes such a landing impossible.

For larger boats, the concrete dock at the lighthouse is usable as a temporary mooring in relatively calm seas. The dock should be approached with caution because of the boulders in the area and the shallowness of the water around the dock (3–4 feet). Larger boats using the dock should keep a watchful eye on changing wind and weather, as well

Fishing tug *Faithful* marooned on Outer Island sandspit (photo by author).

Outer Island beach east of light (photo by Mark Weller).

as possible wakes from larger boats passing Outer Island on shipping lanes to the north.

Camping

There is one designated campsite on Outer Island at the north end of the east side of the sandspit. It has a stump privy, fire ring, food locker, and the tent area location is marked on the hill above the spit.

The island has a single primitive camping zone covering all of the large island outside of the sandspit/lagoon area and the area around and southwest of the lighthouse.

Outer Island trail (photo by Don Hynek).

Hiking

Outer has about 8.75 miles of trails. The main trail runs from the sandspit north to the lighthouse site. A crossing trail (the Lullabye Trail on some maps, named for the furniture company owner of Outer Island) departs from the main trail about .5 mile south of the lighthouse grounds and continues southeast for a bit over a mile to the old logging camp. The main trail through the center of the island has become exceedingly difficult to follow and hikers should come prepared for the hike with a compass, a topo map, and an extra dose of stamina.

Kayak Trip Suggestions

Since the sandspit camping area is about 22 miles from the launch points at Little Sand Bay or the Buffalo Bay Marina at Red Cliff, it is at the edge of the distance most paddlers are able to travel in one day. Accordingly, Outer Island is probably best integrated into a longer trip using one or more other island campsites as stopover points on the way to and from Outer Island. To fully explore Outer, it would be ideal to have a three-day window of good weather—one day to get to the island campsite and set up, a second day to circumnavigate the island with a visit to the lighthouse (14 to 15 miles) and a third day to break camp and return to the launch point or at least a campsite closer to the mainland. The exploration could easily be expanded to four days with the extra day used to explore the interior of the island for remnants of its logging and fishing past. Although pricey, paddlers could also hire a water taxi for the trip to Outer Island.

Beach landing two miles northeast of sandspit (photo by author).

STILL THE BOSS

"The lake is the boss" is a phrase that has been used by respectful boaters of all types in the Apostle Islands, even making its appearance on t-shirts sold in the area. For kayakers, sailors, and powerboaters alike, the phrase means lake conditions dictate the timing and direction of travel across the water, and even whether you travel at all. It's like dealing with the boss at work. The boss will tell you what to do and probably when to do it.

Now the lake isn't necessarily a bad boss. It allows you some discretion if you stay within its general rules. Boss Lake allows you to negotiate and make compromises with it just like you can with the boss at work. If the wind and waves are coming from the west, you still may be able to paddle and explore the eastern shore of a larger island even though Boss Lake will pound you if you violate its rule and venture over to the western side of the island. If you have confidence in the engines on your powerboat and the wind is not supposed to pick up velocity until the afternoon, you still might enjoy a morning cruise or fishing trip and make it back to your home dock safely before the weather changes. Boss Lake will allow you that kind of discretion.

In his book, *Apostle Islanders: The People and Culture,* Robert J. Nelson indicates that his father, Julian Nelson (for whom Stockton Island's Julian Bay is probably named) was using the phrase "The lake is the boss" as long as the author can remember, although Mr. Nelson speculates that his father may have heard the phrase from a prior generation of fishermen.

The use of the English word "boss" probably dates back further to the mid-nineteenth century, when it was borrowed from the Dutch word "baas" or "base," meaning master. It became less repugnant to use "boss" instead of "master," the English word associated with the master-servant or master-slave relationship.[24] But the lake has been the boss for an even longer time. Probably there was a similar concept expressed in French, in the Ojibwe language, and possibly even in earlier languages of people traveling among the Apostle Islands.

The lake became my boss for thirty-six hours on a four-day trip to Outer Island in 2014. They say that for every three to four days of paddling on Lake Superior you should plan on being weather-bound for one day. I had been lucky. In twenty-two years of paddling on the big lake, including some week-long trips, I had missed paddling for a whole day less than a dozen times. Maybe the lake was looking to even things out.

Although I had been retired for two years before making the Outer Island trip, I was slow to catch on to the realization that there are still obligations and schedules. To explore Outer Island, I wanted to spend two nights at the island's campsite near the sandspit. Spending two nights at the Outer campsite would allow me to circumnavigate the island on the intervening day. The day trip circumnavigating the island plus two days paddling out to the island and two days paddling back to the launch site made the total trip into a minimum of five days. And with a five-day trip the rule of the lake (one weather-bound day for every three or four paddling days) indicated I might need a sixth day for a weather layover.

Taking two days for paddling out to Outer and two days for paddling back to the launch site seemed to be a necessity for trip safety. Although I had paddled over 20 miles in a single day perhaps a dozen times in the last decade, mostly the long paddles had occurred somewhat spontaneously and were aided by flat seas or a moderate tailwind. Also, to be truthful, at age sixty-nine I was beginning to doubt my physical ability and stamina for a five to six day solo trip. Boss Lake would make no promises to provide me with ideal conditions on this trip and was not the least concerned about any decline in my stamina. "You do the job or you stay home," Boss Lake seemed to say.

Because of personal "obligations" at either end of the trip and the difficulty in scheduling two consecutive nights on the Outer campsite with the park service during the busy month of August, a paddle trip from Sunday through Wednesday would be the

Outer Island waves looking south to Stockton (photo by Mark Weller).

best I could do. So I added another complication to the mix by scheduling a water taxi for the trip out to Outer Island.

The use of a pricey water taxi was worth the cost. With the wind out of the east and northeast since Friday, the lake still displayed 2-foot waves even though the wind velocity had declined. The perfect conditions I would have needed to paddle to Outer in a single day were not there. In contrast, the water taxi trip took only about an hour.

The east wind continued into the afternoon, so as a compromise with Boss Lake, we lowered the kayak into the water from the bigger taxi boat while anchored off the western (lee) shore of the Outer Island sandspit and loaded some additional gear into my rear kayak hold while it was in the water. I then eased my dry-suited body over the side of the water taxi and down a foot or two into the cockpit of my kayak. While I had done such a transfer from a larger boat before, my back and legs did not bend as well as they did fifteen years ago. I was thankful for the strong young arms and shoulders of the water taxi captain who hung over the edge of his boat, reaching down to steady the bobbing kayak. I successfully lowered my center of gravity, affixed my spray skirt, and took my paddle from the taxi skipper. I was launched.

"So do you think you should give me your float plan?" The young skipper asked, as I drifted away.

He was right, of course. While my wife had some idea of my paddle plans, it would be wise that someone in the Bayfield area knew about the plans also. Although I had a hand-held marine and weather radio, probably only the Coast Guard or a boater in the vicinity of Outer Island would pick up any transmission. Outer Island is perhaps 15 miles from the mainland as the gull flies, and the taxi skipper and I had discussed that the weather forecast for the island would be an interpolation between the "near shore" (within 5 nautical miles) and the open lake weather forecast.

"Well, I will be at the Outer campsite tonight and tomorrow night," I said. "Tuesday night I have Manitou reserved, and I plan to paddle in on Wednesday."

"So if you are not back by Wednesday night, we should start to worry," he half asked and half stated.

"Yeah, subject to a possible weather delay."

While the taxi skipper pulled his anchor and readied his boat for the trip back, I paddled to the south end of the sandspit. The eastern wind still was producing breaking waves on the other side of the sandspit. Rather than risk a dumping trying to land in the surf at the campsite on the eastern side of the island, negotiations with Boss Lake made me turn around and head back to the north along the western shore of the Outer sandspit. The taxi captain gave me a quizzical look as he prepared his boat for the return to Roy's Point.

"I'll stay on this side of the island for now," I called. "Thanks for the ride." The captain gave me a thumbs up and I returned it. He started his engines, accelerated, and bounced off through the waves heading southwest. I would not see another human being for about the next fifty-two hours. Boss Lake, Outer Island, and I were alone.

Although I knew that the campsite on Outer had been moved up the eastern shore about a quarter mile, I did not know just where it was. Reminding myself that I was now on island time, I decided to land on the western shore of the sandspit and, taking two dry bags with me, I crossed the 200 to 300 yards of sandspit to the eastern shore in search of the campground. I walked past the old campsite, and just about the time that I started to question my decision to walk an unknown distance with a load of gear, there was the new campsite with a chainsaw-hewn stairway from the beach up to the level of the forest floor. I looked over the campsite and stowed my drybags in the bear locker, returning across the sandspit to my kayak on the western shore. [Author's note: Since 2014 the Outer Island campsite has again been moved further north on the east side of the sandspit.]

I had formulated a new plan for exploration of the island—another negotiation and compromise with Boss Lake. Today while the wind was from the east, I would paddle up the west side of the island as far as I felt comfortable on the first day out, then return to round the southern end of the sandspit in the late afternoon or early evening when the easterly wind and surf had died down. I would set up camp and enjoy a late meal. Tomorrow the wind was supposed to shift to the southwest, and it probably would be a good day to travel up the east coast, ideally as far as the lighthouse, although any exploration of the lighthouse grounds might be limited by the current construction by private contractors with the park service.

Paddling north I set a visual bearing toward a high clay bank shining red-brown in the afternoon sun about 2 miles up the western shore. The bearing took me about a quarter mile out from the concave shoreline and I noticed that the irregular ripple close to the shoreline changed to small waves that wrapped around the southern tip of Outer Island. On the way north I also noticed what appeared to be a shallow inlet to the lagoon— something to explore more fully on my return trip.

As I approached the clay bank, I could see that it was just north of the first significant ravine shown on the topographical map north of the sandspit. I paddled close to shore to explore the possibility of a soft landing and possible wilderness camping site on the ravine's "delta." There was a sandy area dotted with some boulders just below the waterline made narrower by the fact that the water level of the lake was about 16 inches above datum. The "beach" was simply too narrow to accommodate pitching a tent. Perhaps there was a flat spot for a tent beyond the brush line, but getting off the beach and beyond the alder brush could prove difficult. Because the lake level was higher than it had been for a few years, the last 50 yards or so of the ravine was at lake level and carried a strong promise of mosquitoes. I would happily return to the flat open area at the designated campsite to pitch my tent this afternoon.

On the trip back to the south, I stayed within 100 yards of the shore. The entryway to the lagoon that I had seen on the paddle north now appeared to be a passable entry, although there were some weeds and brush in the channel. I slid through the shallow water entry without even raising my rudder. With the high lake level, I could actually paddle into the lagoon in about a foot of weedy water.

The lagoon was calm, sheltered by spruce, pine, and birch on the east and south and by a sand dune ridge perhaps 15 to 20 feet high on the west. I paddled more than half a mile on the lagoon, enjoying the illusion of paddling a northern inland lake. As I approached the southern end of the lagoon, I chastised myself slightly for not thinking too far ahead. There was no exit from the lagoon to the lake on the south end of the lagoon. I would have to paddle back to the place I had entered the lagoon or pull the

Outer Island lagoon (photo by author).

kayak loaded down with all but two drybags over the 15-foot crest of the dune. "Should-have's" and "could-have's" entered my mind. I should have thought about an exit from the lagoon before I had paddled so far south on it. I could have carried more drybags and equipment on my walk across the sandspit from kayak to campsite earlier in the afternoon, making the contemplated dune crossing with the loaded kayak an easier alternative.

August blueberries on Outer Island (photo by author).

I dragged the kayak up the steep dune. Lilly pads, bulrushes, an unidentified low shrub, black-berry bushes, blueberry bushes, and ultimately Canadian yews, all assisted by gravity, took turns clutching at the stern of my kayak as I pulled and yanked its bow up-hill a few feet at a time. I collected berries as a small compensation for my toil. Both the blackberries and the blueberries were deli-cious. I even caught myself look-ing up and down the dune ridge to check for any bears that might also be enjoying the berry treats. Going down the west side of the ridge was easier. It was downhill, with little or no brush, but without any tasty treats.

There were still 2-foot waves breaking across the end of the sandspit when I paddled to the campsite. Again, I was bargaining with the boss.

"Okay, I will give the end of the sandspit a wide berth before I paddle east and north," I silently conceded to the boss. "But give me a break in the waves when I get to the beach by the campsite, Okay?" The boss didn't answer.

I thought that I had timed my approach to the beach perfectly, starting the fast paddle after the standard three large waves. The boss sent at least five big waves this time. When I was younger, I could break the seal on my spray skirt, get the paddle perpendicular to the kayak in back of me held tightly against the cockpit conning and be out of the cockpit standing next to my kayak ready to use the surge of the next wave to pull the boat farther up on the beach. Now the first wave after running aground turned my kayak broadside to the surf and my being half out of the kayak cockpit, the second wave rolled me into the water, filling the cockpit with sandy surf water. The water outside the drysuit quickly cooled my body, but the wrist and neck seals did their job. I was unhurt, but embarrassed by my very amateur landing. The boss only laughed at me.

As I rolled my kayak over to drain the water from the cockpit, I listened carefully to what the boss had to say.

"First of all, when you ride a water taxi out to an island, you do not have time to reach the height of your paddle skills and are at greater risk in landing in even the small surf I am throwing at you today," the boss started on me. "And who really said that large waves come in threes. Some human said that. I certainly did not say that."

"Yeah, Boss." The dip in the water had cooled me inside my drysuit but I still seethed at my incompetent landing.

"And another thing," the boss continued, "you are no longer fifty or even sixty years old anymore. How often have you practiced a fast exit from your kayak in the last two years? How often have you practiced a wet exit and reentry? I didn't think so. Around here, if you want to keep your job, you do the work."

Boss Lake left me alone for a while to set up camp, prepare a meal, and string a clothesline to hang up some wet things from the swamped cockpit to dry. Later, at dusk, distant lightning helped me find my way around the campsite without a headlamp, and thunder, one of the boss' foremen, grumbled about the general state of affairs from the southern horizon. I was asleep before 9:00 p.m., knowing that because I had the campsite for two nights, if I had to, I could avoid Boss Lake's ire completely on Monday by merely not going out on the water.

Boss Lake sent a west and southwest wind of 10 to 20 knots with gusts up to 25 and waves of 2 to 4 feet starting just before mid-day on Monday and lasting through early afternoon on Tuesday. While the boss allowed me to paddle a couple of miles up the eastern shore of Outer Island on Monday morning, it strongly suggested that I explore Outer Island from shore for most of the next two days.

Sitting on the shore next to the campsite on Monday afternoon and Tuesday morning I had time to study the lake northeast of Michigan Island where I had seen the flashing light the night before. The air was very clear despite the wind. Barely, I could make out the narrow line of the Gull Island light standing perpendicular to the horizon. With binoculars I also scanned the coast of Upper Michigan. The ski jump at Copper Peak materialized at the edge of the horizon. Once I had located the ski jump with the binoculars, I found I could even see it just with the naked eye. The map distance to the Gull Island light measured about 6.5 miles. A distance measuring app from the Internet told me later that Copper Peak ski jump is 32.75 miles from the Outer Island campsite. I silently hoped that there would be clear days in the distant future to allow my grandchildren to see the ski jump from Outer Island.

Later Tuesday afternoon, I broke camp on Outer as the wind shifted more to the south and calmed to 5 to 10 knots with waves of "two feet or less." In a final negotiation with the boss, I headed south to the lee side of Stockton Island rather than paddling west 9 miles into the remaining wind to Manitou. It was late enough when I started to paddle that I felt that I might not be able to make it to the Manitou Island campsite by dark against the wind. By doing 9 to 10 miles and camping on Stockton, I could easily make the final paddle of 13 to 14 miles back to Roy's point on Wednesday. Wednesday's paddle in from Stockton was easier than I expected after the two-day blow.

All I could say was, "Thanks, Boss, for the light and variable winds you sent me on Wednesday."

RASPBERRY ISLAND

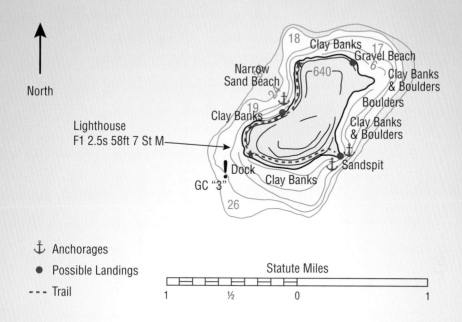

North

Lighthouse
F1 2.5s 58ft 7 St M

18
Clay Banks
17
Gravel Beach
Narrow
Sand Beach
640
6
Clay Banks
& Boulders
24
19
Boulders
Clay Banks
Clay Banks
& Boulders
Sandspit
Dock
GC "3"
Clay Banks
26

⚓ Anchorages

● Possible Landings

- - - Trail

Statute Miles

1   ½   0   1

Raspberry lighthouse grounds, with boathouse under renovation, 2014 (photo by author).

Location

Raspberry Island serves as the link to Sand and York Islands, more easily accessible from Little Sand Bay to the west and the dozen or so islands lying to the east of Raspberry, typically accessed from Bayfield or Red Cliff. It is 2.5 miles east of York Island, 2 miles southwest of Bear Island, and 2 miles northwest of Oak Island. The mainland lies about 2 miles south (Raspberry Point) and about 2 miles southwest (Point Detour), although these mainland points offer no usable launch points for boaters.

Geography and History

Raspberry Island is one of the smaller islands in the archipelago, only about 1 mile long from southwest to northeast and less than 0.5 mile wide. The highest point on Raspberry is 98 feet above the level of the lake. Raspberry Island is shaped like a fat-headed duckling swimming to the northeast with its bill pointed to the east and its tiny wing (a sandspit) pointing southeast. At the duckling's tail is the lighthouse area.

The history of Raspberry Island centers on the lighthouse. Construction on the first lighthouse built into the keeper's quarters was completed in 1863 and served to guide steamships through the "West Channel" between the lighthouse and the mainland. A foghorn building at the top of the stairs leading up from the dock was added in 1903.

The original lighthouse building was rebuilt in 1906 to accommodate three families, the keeper had the living unit on the east side of the lighthouse and two assistants each had a unit on the west half. The 1906 structure was renovated between 2005 and 2007 after completion of the shoreline stabilization project in 2003. Renovation and improvement of the dock in 2017 and renovation of the boathouse, with the help of the Friends of the Apostle Islands, a non-profit supportive organization, compliments the earlier renovation of the keeper's quarters and lighthouse.

The lighthouse grounds are restored and furnished in a style reminiscent of the 1920s. The grounds are tended by an employee of the National Park Service during the summer months, and visitors can tour the main keeper's quarters for a nominal fee. The electrical utilities now serving the grounds are supported by solar power.

The Raspberry Light, albeit now an automatic beacon operating from the top of a pole, still is in operation and is visible for 7 miles, flashing every 2.5 seconds at 58 feet above the lake.

Shoreline and Landings

Although sailboats and powerboats probably will be able to find dock space and adequate depth (5–6 feet on the west side dock) to land at the lighthouse dock, the dock is too high above the water to easily land a kayak. In calm weather it may be possible to land a kayak at the shallow rocky area on the east end of the reconstructed shoreline and scramble across the rocks to visit the lighthouse. If this rocky area is used for a kayak landing, the boat should be secured with rope and lifted to rest on driftwood or rocks well above the waterline so that the wake from passing powerboats does not grind the kayak's bottom against the rocks or worse yet, set the kayak adrift. For the kayaker, a safer way to visit the lighthouse would be to paddle about 0.75 mile east of the lighthouse dock along the clay bank and boulder-strewn

Raspberry Island lighthouse and keeper's quarters (photo by Mark Weller).

southern shoreline, landing at the sandspit on the southeast corner of the island (the duck's tiny wing) before walking back to the west on an easily followed trail to the lighthouse site.

Paddling northwest, north, and then northeast from the lighthouse, the kayaker will see the island's shoreline change from sandstone to high clay banks. As the shoreline turns north at the back of the duckling's enlarged head, there is a sand beach that can serve as an ideal rest stop for a break from paddling, but the steep clay banks in back of the beach and thick vegetation make it difficult to penetrate beyond the sandy shoreline. The north shore along the top of the duckling's head is mostly inaccessible with clay banks higher than 10 feet, although a gravel beach landing could be made in the shallow water just above the duckling's bill. The duckling's bill and the shoreline to the southwest down to the sandspit is a mixture of clay banks and boulders, making landing difficult until reaching the sandspit area.

The sandspit can be approached from either the northeast or the southwest and offers a beautiful setting for a picnic or a cool dip in the lake. Powerboats and sailboats are usually anchored overnight in the sandspit area.

Camping

There are no designated campsites on the heavily used Raspberry Island. There is one primitive camping zone for Raspberry Island, but primitive camping is limited to areas outside of the lighthouse grounds and sandspit area. The sand beach on the back of the duckling's head may provide the best spot to land, but finding a place to pitch a tent could prove difficult.

Hiking

There is a well-used trail just under 1 mile in length from the sandspit to the lighthouse area. While the trail provides an interesting nature hike, it is primarily used to provide access to the lighthouse buildings from a landing area available to kayakers as well as the larger

boats anchored around the sandspit. There is also a trail of about a mile in length from the lighthouse grounds to the northern tip of the island, but the trail is not well maintained. The trail to the north was used by the keepers of the Raspberry light to check the operation of the Sand Island light during a period of time that the Raspberry keepers were responsible for the automatic light on Sand Island.

Raspberry Island dock before replacement (photo courtesy National Park Service).

Approaching Raspberry lighthouse on Sandspit Trail (photo by Robert E. Rolley).

Kayak Trip Suggestions

Because of the absence of camping sites and the heavy use of the lighthouse area and dock, Raspberry Island has become a destination site for day trips or a stopover site for visiting the lighthouse or the sandspit on the way to or from camping on another island. Consider launching at Little Sand Bay and paddling to the sandspit in the morning, hiking to the lighthouse for a late morning tour, and re-turning to the sandspit for lunch and perhaps a noontime, midsummer swim before pad-dling back to Little Sand Bay in the afternoon and evening. For a longer trip launched from Little Sand Bay, Raspberry Island can be used for a break stop, either at the sandspit or the beach on the back of the duckling's head, before proceeding to Bear, Devils, or Rocky Islands.

Raspberry Island sandspit (photo courtesy National Park Service).

RENOVATIONS COMPLETE

Although the doors of the National Park Service office in Bayfield would remain locked until 8:00 o'clock, there already were half a dozen cars and two busloads of retired people waiting for the opening of business. The retirees looked like they would be heading for the casino at Red Cliff after getting basic information about the National Lakeshore in the park headquarters. The cars contained people with a variety of outdoor experience levels waiting to pick up their camping permits or at least be reassured by a friendly park ranger that their planned use of the National Lakeshore would be successful and enjoyable. Although I was already retired, I was not interested in getting information or an eventual trip to the casino. I was interested in picking up my camping permit for a three-day paddle trip. Having finally acquired some patience in retirement, I continued to wait outside after the initial "rush" of people when the doors opened.

I watched and listened as a ranger herded many of the retirees into the small the-
ater to view a video. Another ranger helped a couple in their late thirties with their first
trip using kayaks rented from one of the outfitters. A group of five enthusiastic college
students were seeking information for their day trips, using the Town of Russell campground at Little Sand Bay as their base camp. After waiting my turn, I found the ranger
at the main desk helpful but not overbearing as she checked my knowledge of leave-no-
trace wilderness camping, avoiding trouble with bears, and proper respect for weather
changes while paddling on the lake. Although my level of patience has increased in
retirement, it still is impossible not to become excited about facing the big lake for a
multi-day solo kayak trip. The trip to the launch site at Little Sand Bay seemed to take
longer than it should. I was as anxious as a bird dog waiting for the start of the hunt.

The five college students I had encountered at the NPS headquarters—three men
and two women—were preparing to launch at Little Sand Bay as I carried my kayak and
equipment to the beach launching area. Their group discussion indicated that they were
not well acquainted with one another, but it also revealed that each of them had respect
for the paddling abilities of the others in the group. What they lacked in equipment, they
made up in youthful energy. They were launched and paddling aggressively before I had
completed hauling my kayak and equipment to the beach. I envied their confidence and
youth, and wished I had approached them before they launched to hear more of their
story and perhaps tap into some of their emotional energy.

As I paddled out past the breakwater, I could just see the five young paddlers more
than a mile ahead of me, apparently heading for Raspberry Island or beyond. I settled
into a regular paddle stroke cadence on the relatively flat water. What little breeze there
was came from my back and helped me maintain a speed of about 4 miles per hour.

The kayak seems sluggish and the paddling boring for the first mile or so of the first
day of a trip. After planning a trip, assembling the equipment, and getting to the water's
edge, it is easy to forget that paddling is actually quite strenuous and progress across
the water in a kayak is relatively slow compared to traveling in a sailboat or a powerboat. The first mile encourages negative thoughts about the physical activity required
to move a kayak from one place to another and the relative discomfort of spending the
next several nights sleeping in a tent. It even raises troubling questions about the relative value of the trip itself. Later, after the first mile, the muscles become hardened to
the strains of paddling. The sights, sounds, and yes, even the smells of the open water
remind the brain of the reasons for making the trip, saying, "See, these are the things
you came here for. They are good and why would you question their value."

Still, my position relative to the shoreline and islands seemed to change too slowly as
I moved across Little Sand Bay aiming the bow of my kayak toward Point Detour. York Island mocked my progress and seemed to draw away from me instead of allowing me to
approach closer. I realized that Raspberry Island, my planned first stop, would again be
as far away from Point Detour as I was now from York Island.

But then an eagle stares down at me from its perch on the top branches of a white
pine high above the western edge of Point Detour. I search my memory for recollections
of the sandspit on the southerly corner of York Island now marked by my view of a thin
white strip of land just above the waterline a mile away. I reach the north point of Point
Detour and the Raspberry Lighthouse comes into view for the first time on the trip. Although it is still 3 miles away, it becomes the new heading for my bow and by now it just
doesn't seem that far away. Paddling toward the planned stop at the lighthouse, not just
arriving there, has become rewarding in itself.

I passed the buoy marking the Raspberry Island shoals and started to get a view of
the dock and boathouse area. It had been several years since I last visited the Raspberry
Light station, and the last time I looked up at the lighthouse grounds from the water
level, the work of shoring up the shoreline had just been completed and the renovation
of the buildings was still a work in progress. The dock remains too high off the water to
allow an easy landing for a kayak. The narrow rocky area that had a hint of sand east of

the boathouse is simply rocky now that the shore has been stabilized with riprap to dissipate the wave action.

I contemplated paddling over to the sandspit and walking back to the lighthouse. But wait, the shoreline beyond the large riprap installed for shoreline protection still has smaller rocks, mostly cobble without sharp edges and is strewn with the usual driftwood. The smaller rocks are backed by a substantial clay bank that would be difficult to climb, but perhaps I could secure my kayak on the rocky shore near the edge of the shoreline improvements and scramble across the larger rocks to the boathouse and dock.

As I passed the jagged boulders placed on the hillside of the lighthouse area, I kept an eye out for rocks just below the surface. Passing the rocks placed to prevent shoreline erosion near the dock, I rotated the kayak to be parallel to the shoreline. I edged toward the rocky shore sideways in relatively calm water. When I heard the first scrape of a rock on the bottom of my kayak, I saw that the bottom is rocky, but of fairly regular, shallow depth, allowing me to make a quick exit before the bottom of my fiberglass kayak lost too much gel coat to the rocks. While making sure my kayak did not drift into deeper water, I searched and found two hefty lengths of driftwood. I laid them at the water's edge perpendicular to the shoreline near the bow and stern of my kayak. I lifted first one end of the kayak, then the other to give the kayak a stable perch on top of the two chunks of driftwood and flatter cobble at the point where the water and land met. I stood back and briefly observed the light wave action on the cradled kayak. It rested high enough above the water to keep the waves from rocking the kayak and grinding it on the rocks. I rigged a line from the bow to some dogwood on the shore, reminding myself that even a couple miles from the mainland, the seiche of Lake Superior can raise the water level enough to float a kayak secured on rocks and driftwood. Finally I am satisfied that I can go to the lighthouse and return to my kayak without fear of having it mock me from a free-floating position a hundred yards off shore.

I stepped slowly from rock to rock across the shore-stabilizing boulders lying between me and the boathouse. My rock scrambling skills simply were not as good now as they were when I first visited the Raspberry Light. Twenty years before when I first visited Raspberry Island, parking my kayak in a similar manner on the rocks east of the boathouse, I could look up at exposed clay banks near the top of the bank and clumps of sod and bushes waiting to fall from the edge of the lighthouse site to the clay banks and rocks below. Now newly placed rock covered the clay banks all the way to the top of the incline.

Raspberries still grew among the rocks next to the boathouse even as I remembered them from earlier trips. I stopped to sample the fruit that provides the island with its name, choosing ripe red berries from vines bending over the boardwalk next to the boathouse 4 or 5 feet above the surface. There were lots of berries, and they were delicious. Maybe boaters stopping at the dock immediately went up the stairs to the lighthouse grounds without investigating the boathouse and finding the raspberries. The raspberries provided a perfect welcome to the island.

I plodded up the stairs from the dock to the lighthouse grounds. The buildings sparkled with new paint and maintenance. The grounds were well-kept and the vegetable gardens looked weeded and well-watered. Two members from the young paddling group that had left Little Sand Bay an hour or so before I launched were playing croquet on the lawn at the east end of the clearing. The other members watched the game or wandered around the grounds. I watched the croquet and started a conversation with one of the male members of the group who wasn't participating in the croquet match.

"I saw the five of you launch from Little Sand Bay this morning. You made good time paddling out here," I opened. "Where are you headed?"

"We're just heading back to Little Sand Bay this afternoon," he responded. "We have a base camp at the campground at Little Sand Bay and plan to do day trips from there."

"Well, the Raspberry Lighthouse is a good first-day stop," I said.

"Where did you land your kayak?" he asked. I explained that I had left it tied and propped above the waterline on the shoreline below.

"We landed at the sandspit and walked over here on the trail."

"That's a safer and much easier landing spot."

"So where are you headed?" he asked.

"I plan to paddle to Bear Island this afternoon. I have a backcountry zone camping permit for Bear Island for tonight."

"Oh wow. That sounds great," he said, with the enthusiasm of a twenty year old. "And you are paddling and camping all alone?"

"Yes," I said. "But I have a great deal of respect for this lake and I always paddle more conservatively when I am alone."

"Well you certainly have the equipment for paddling safely," he said, eyeing my drysuit.

I felt almost guilty as I noticed that the members of his group were wearing mostly knee-length neoprene. Some had long-sleeved tops of heavy nylon. Their equipment was adequate for warm weather, flat-water paddling on Lake Superior, but would not have been quite so adequate if the weather turned stormy. I told him I had acquired good equipment a few items each year over the twenty-one-year period I had been paddling. It was the best I could do to relieve the guilt. I realized then that I had just told him that I had been paddling as long as he had been alive, and my kayak was as old as he was. It made me feel very old.

The conversation continued with the usual "Where are you from?" The members of his group were all students from the University of Wisconsin at Madison. They were on a trip organized by the outdoor club of the university.

Our conversation stopped when we were approached by the resident park ranger, who introduced himself and asked if we wanted a tour of the lighthouse and keeper's quarters. I will call him Ranger Fred. Ranger Fred explained that there was a small charge for the tour, but when I said that I had left my wallet in my kayak, he offered to trust me to mail the fee or drop it off at the Ranger Station at Little Sand Bay when I returned from my trip. I thanked him for his trust and accepted an envelope to use for the fee, but he also wrote down my name and address. I doubted that his recording of my information would ever lead to a collection action by the park service if I did not fulfill my promise to pay when my wallet was more accessible; however, knowing that he kept the personal information of the persons taking the tour "on credit" probably resulted in a higher percentage of payment of the fee.

Ranger Fred started the tour in the kitchen of the keeper's quarters. A cooking stove and laundry tub with washboard dominated the kitchen entryway. Ranger Fred's stories of baking bread in the kitchen oven every day, doing the laundry by hand, and bathing in the laundry tub once a week brought to life the living conditions of the keeper's family. A wood-burning cooking stove in the kitchen, a bath once a week—for someone my age, they brought back "Oh Yeah" memories. For the children in the small tour group who had no memory of pre-web life, the stories bordered on incredible.

Keeper's quarters kitchen at Raspberry Island (photo by Mark Weller).

The dining and living rooms were furnished pretty consistently in the style of the 1920s. Ranger Fred even cranked up the old, but still operable, cylindrical phonograph, its strained tune sounding like it took great effort to push the sound from the needle dragging across the curved wax surface out the megaphone shaped "speaker." The tour group fell silent as each of us concentrated to hear the raspy sound. One of the younger children asked, just to make sure that he understood, that the early phonograph had no video.

Keeper's quarters dining room at Raspberry Island (photo by Don Hynek).

Writing desk at Raspberry keeper's quarters (photo by Mark Weller).

The lighthouse building, modified in 1906 to provide living spaces for the keeper and for the two assistants provided a contrast between life in the 1920s and life in a more modern setting. There was no electricity in the half of the "duplex" restored to the vintage 1920s style of living. The other half of the building where Ranger Fred and other park service employees stayed, was powered by solar power and storage batteries located in the shed that housed the foghorn signal. Ranger Fred enjoyed indoor plumbing from a well and had a flush toilet backed by a septic system and drain field in the backyard.

Upstairs the bedrooms came with quilt-covered beds and chamber pots that no doubt had saved a few people from falling down the steep stairs in the middle of the night. Ranger Fred divided the group into smaller segments for the last climb up another steep stairs to reach the lighthouse platform. The view from the lighthouse was terrific. The mainland, York, Sand, and Oak Islands all looked closer, yet quite far away.

While at the top of the lighthouse, I asked Ranger Fred about his past. He had been retired from teaching school for just about a year. He had heard of the job as a ranger at the Raspberry Light and applied for it. To his surprise, he was hired, and he now marveled that he was having a good time and was actually getting paid for his caretaker and tour guide role. His wife was still employed as a school teacher, at least during the school year. Clearly Ranger Fred enjoyed what he was doing, and his experience as a teacher helped him relate well to the younger members of the tour groups whom he amazed with his stories of primitive life. As we exchanged our brief summaries of our lives to date and recently our lives in retirement, I felt some envy for Ranger Fred. He seemed to enjoy his new "job," and his enthusiastic demeanor left the impression that he had not yet laid in bed after waking in the morning and stared at the ceiling with the least bit of dread for the coming day.

After reading several accounts of the life of a light keeper that were displayed on plaques on the walls and more daydreaming about what it would have been like to live on Raspberry Island a century ago, I stuffed the envelope Ranger Fred had given me into a safe place in my drysuit, trudged down the stairs to the dock and returned over the rocks to my kayak, now rocking slightly more than when I left it on its perch because of the wakes generated by the late morning powerboat traffic. I vowed that Ranger Fred's envelope would be returned with the proper amount of cash, as well as a note stating, "Enjoyed the tour."

Ranger Fred from the top of the Raspberry light with mainland in background (photo by author).

Master bedroom at Raspberry Island (photo by Mark Weller).

ROCKY ISLAND

North

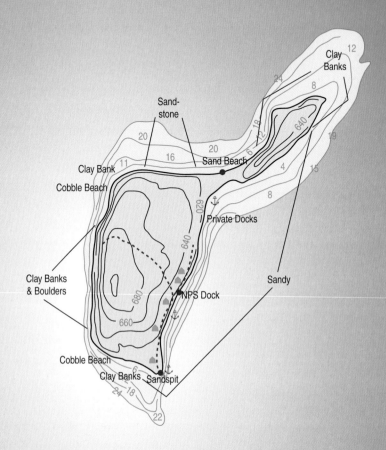

Clay
Banks

12

24

8

Sand-
stone

20

20

640

19

16

Sand Beach

6

18

12

Clay Bank

11

4

15

Cobble Beach

8

620

Private Docks

640

Clay Banks
& Boulders

Sandy

680

NPS Dock

660

Cobble Beach

Clay Banks

Sandspit

6

24

18

22

 Campsite(s)

● Possible Landings

⚓ Anchorages

- - - Trail

Statute Miles

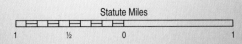

1   ½   0   1

Location

Rocky Island's facilities and location makes it a popular stop for a variety of boaters. Its northwestern shore is about 2 miles southeast of Devils Island and 2 miles east-northeast of Bear Island. The northern shoreline of Otter Island is less than 1 mile from Rocky's sandspit, and Rocky Island's long thin arm, extending to the northeast, offers protection from the northwesterly winds to its neighbor, South Twin Island, less than 1 mile to the east of Rocky.

Geography and History

Except for two physical features, Rocky Island is uniformly oblong on the north-south axis. The first variation from uniformity is a sandspit nipple extending into the lake at the island's southeast corner. The second anomaly is an arm-like extension from the island's northeast corner, initially at a lower elevation near the main portion of the island, but rising to a rocky 50 feet above the lake two-thirds of the way out the arm.

Rocky Island's highest elevation is located in the west-central part of the island and rises about 100 feet above the surface of the lake. With its long arm, Rocky covers 1,100 acres. The main oblong body of the island is 0.5 to 0.75 mile wide and about 1.5 miles long. The island's arm extends out to the northeast a bit over 1 mile.

Because of Rocky Island's shape and its long arm extending to the northeast, the "armpit" area provides protection from prevailing westerly winds and a relatively safe harbor. In the late 1800s, the protection of the island (referred to at the time as Rice's Island, named after its first white owner, Henry M. Rice, a U.S. senator from Minnesota) fostered a number of fish camps and cottages and, by the 1940s, even a resort.[25] However, even as early as the 1830s the island was investigated for use as a fishing base by the American Fur Company, and by the 1890s the Alfred Booth Packing Company had established Rocky as a regular fish pickup site.[26]

A string of individual and family fishermen based their summer operations on the protected Rocky Island eastern shore until commercial fishing lost economic viability to the sea lamprey in the 1950s. Eddie Boutin used the sandspit area for his fishing operation in the late 1890s. Hans Austad, a Norwegian-born immigrant, moved his operation from Outer Island's northeastern shore to the north end of Rocky Island's protective arm in 1899.[27] Other Rocky Island fishing families followed—the Hadland family, the Bernsten (Benson) family, the Nelson family, the Ericksons, and others. The Nourse family fishing operation, started in the 1930s, changed into a cabin rental operation and restaurant serving tourists that were brought to the island on the cruise boats from Bayfield until it finally closed in 1974. The National Park Service dock and ranger station now occupy the Nourse's "Air Haven" restaurant site.

There still are summer cottages and lands subject to life leases remaining along the eastern shore of Rocky Island north of the National Park Service dock, and Lakeshore visitors should respect the privacy of these families' leasehold rights. The cottages are remnants of Rocky Island's fishing history.

Shoreline and Landings

The easterly shoreline of Rocky Island is mostly sandy from the sandspit at the south (eastern) corner of the island up to the "hand" at the end of the long arm-like peninsula and can accommodate kayak landing (except avoid the areas subject to life leases marked by buildings and private docks nestled in the "armpit" area). Traveling counterclockwise around the end of the peninsula, the shoreline converts from sand to eroding clay banks. A half-mile of sand beach in the low elevation area where the arm rejoins the main body of the island again can serve as a landing area. To the west of the beach, the northern shore has the usual high sandstone converting to clay banks on the northwestern corner of the island. Turning south along the western shore, there is a cobble beach, and then the bulk of the western shore becomes high clay banks with boulders at the waterline. Going west to east along the southerly shoreline, there first appears a cobble beach, then a clay bank, before the shore again becomes sandy upon reaching the sandspit.

The National Park Service dock is about a quarter of the way up the eastern shore and can accommodate boats with a draft of 6 feet or more. Larger boats can also find plenty of space to anchor using the sandy bottom along the eastern shoreline, protected from most winds except a "nor'easter" or a strong wind from the south to the southeastern direction.

While it may be of little consequence to a kayaker or most powerboats and sailboats, there is some shallow water between Rocky's arm and South Twin Island, only 10 to 12 feet in depth.

Camping

There are five individual campsites and one group site on Rocky Island's eastern shore between the sandspit and a short distance north of the National Park Service dock. Campsites #1 to 3 are spread along the shoreline from the sandspit to the dock and are well separated and very private. Landing at Campsite #1 on the sandspit is easy, at Campsite #2, landing is nearly impossible, and landing at Campsite #3 may be possible on a cobble "beach". Campsites #4 and 5 are close together and adjacent to the ranger station. Their proximity to the dock makes them attractive to boaters. The group campsite is 0.25 mile north of the dock. Campsites 1-3 have stump privies, 4 and 5 share a vault toilet with boaters moored at the dock, and the group site has its own vault toilet.

No primitive camping is allowed along the eastern shoreline of Rocky Island from the sandspit to the end of the sand beach on the northeastern "arm". Only one primitive permit is allowed for rest of the island.

Rocky Island sandspit campsite (photo by author).

Hiking

Rocky offers 1.9 miles of trails—a short trail north of the ranger station to the campsites, a 0.5 mile trail down the eastern shoreline from the ranger station to the sandspit, and a longer trail heading northwest from the ranger station to the top of the clay banks above the western shore of the island.

Kayak Trip Suggestions

Rocky Island campsites can be used as a way station stop on a longer trip among the islands or as a base camp for a day or two allowing exploration of the Devils Island Lighthouse and sea caves and South Twin, Otter, and Bear Islands.

Ranger's cabin on Rocky Island (photo courtesy National Park Service).

IT HAPPENED IN AN INSTANT …

What units shall we use to mark the intelligible passage of time? Scientists working and imagining things at the subatomic level speak to us in units measured in fractions of a second, but the units tend to lose their meaning for most of us after we count more than a couple of zeroes to the right of the decimal point. Scientists discussing the concepts of a universe expanding since a time they patronizingly call the "big bang" usually use units of years to help us understand. But a time period measured by too large a number of years again becomes incomprehensible for most of us. Can we really understand a time period of a million years? A billion years?

A human lifetime—if we are lucky, say seventy-five years—lies somewhere between the shortest and longest units of time measurements and is easy to conceptualize. We are born; we die. Let the time in between be measured by one human lifetime unit, an "hl" for short. Although technically the length of a lifetime will vary from person to person, let's standardize the new unit of time at seventy-five years.

The beginning of Lake Superior was perhaps 150 hls ago, occurring over a period of perhaps 20 hls as the southern edge of the last glacier receded, initially leaving a deeper lake that drained south as well as east. The earliest Native Americans, themselves probably wanderers from Asia, traveling over many hls, followed the southern edge of the melting glacier north. The earliest modern Europeans explored western Lake Superior only about 4.75 hls ago. Congress created the Apostle Islands National Lakeshore about .6 of an hl ago. I have been kayaking for almost a third of an hl.

The following story describes a weather change on Rocky Island that occurred in .0000004 of an hl. Since time periods with more than a couple of zeroes to the right of the decimal are hard to understand, let's convert the fractional hl of the weather change back into more meaningful and familiar time units: the Rocky Island weather change occurred in about 15 minutes.

When John and Bob picked up the camping permit at the National Lakeshore office in Bayfield, the young woman who issued the permit said that the nicest campsite on Rocky Island was Campsite #1, located on the sandspit.

"Perhaps it is even the nicest campsite in the entire park," she stated. At the time, individual campsites on Rocky Island could not be reserved by number. The first camper to occupy a site got the first choice of sites, the next camper chose from the remaining unoccupied campsites, etc.

"So if the sandspit site is available when you get there, I suggest you choose that site," she added.

They thanked her for the advice. Neither Bob nor John had camped on Rocky before and were looking forward to a long weekend exploring Devils Island and South Twin on day trips paddling by kayak from their Rocky Island base camp.

The two had paddled together before, including a weekend trip camping near the rock shelf landing at the southeastern corner of Basswood Island. That was Bob's first trip on the big lake, and paddling the 1.5 to 2 miles from Buffalo Bay to Basswood seemed like a long exposed trip to him. Both campers were employed full time, and in order to get as many fractional hls as possible out of their holiday weekend trip, they had decided to load their kayaks on a water taxi for a faster ride to the Rocky Island dock.

When they arrived at Rocky Island, they noticed human activity in the dock area including a boat or two that seemed to be dropping off other campers. Remembering the highly recommended campsite at the sandspit, they left their kayaks at the dock and each grabbed a backpack and headed for the trail to the sandspit. There were no campers at the two campsites along the trail south of the dock and, finally arriving at the sandspit sweaty and out of breath, John and Bob realized no one had beaten them to the treasured sandspit either. Now, propped up against a log to regain their breath, they laughed and ridiculed the absurdity of their rush down the trail from the dock to the sandspit. Clearly, the choice of a fast water taxi for transportation to Rocky had prevented them from adjusting their mindsets to a more relaxed weekend mode, an adjustment that would have come easier if they had paddled out to Rocky. Sitting and panting at the sandspit, they were still suffering from a deadline-filled, workweek mentality associated with the more mundane existence in which they spent most of their fractional hls.

"What if there had been someone camping in one of the campsites on the way down here? What would they have thought when they saw two middle-aged men running down the trail with backpacks?" John mused.

"Well, if they had gotten a good enough look at my well-toned young body, they might think that we were Ironmen training for our next contest. At least they would have thought that until they saw your tired, middle-aged body pass by, then they would have thought that we were being chased by a bear," Bob puffed.

The jog had made both of them light-headed and giddy.

"You know the old saying about being chased by a bear, don't you?" John asked. Receiving only a grunt for a response, he continued, "You don't have to be able to run faster than the bear, only faster than the slowest member in the group the bear is chasing."

Bob's second grunt was louder and longer, more like a groan. Obviously, corny, heard-it-before humor would rule the banter of the weekend.

"Is your tired, middle-aged body ready to go back to the dock to pick up the rest of our stuff?" John followed.

"Just like the farmer said when his dog got its tail caught in the lawnmower," Bob responded, pausing to give appropriate timing to still another corny, old riddle-joke; "it won't be long now."

The ranger who issued the camping permit was right—the Rocky Island sandspit was the perfect setting for a base camp. For two mornings Bob and John packed lunch and supplies into their kayaks for day trips and spent the day exploring neighboring islands. Since the sandspit is at the end of the trail south from the Rocky Island dock, no one walked through the campsite after about five o'clock, and even daytime hiker traffic was almost nonexistent. Until the third night, the sandspit retained its pristine charm and, located well away from the activity of the Rocky Island dock, its quiet character. The third evening was humid and calm and warm enough to make the two campers happy that the sun was setting behind them. It was also the evening of the Fourth of July.

As John and Bob sweated over the preparation of the late afternoon meal, a sailboat, with sails trimmed, motored in toward the sandspit and set its anchors about 200 yards off shore. Initially the presence of the sailboat offered no disturbance to the campers. While they could hear the sailors' conversation across the water, most of their words became garbled and incomprehensible on their trip across the water from the boat to the sandspit.

As the darkness thickened, the sailors started their evening's entertainment—a potato cannon seemingly mounted right on the sailboat. About every fifteen minutes there would be a pop from the cannon, a cheer among the sailors, and a distant splash in the water where the potato hit. Perhaps the sailors were testing the cannon's range and accuracy in anticipation of a Canadian invasion on the patriotic holiday. The cannon firing seemed to be fueled by both hair spray and scotch.

John and Bob exchanged meaningful glances each time the cannon popped, maybe a little bit jealous of the scotch, but also unhappily resigned to the intrusion on "their" sandspit and the contamination of "their" lake, even if it was with biodegradable potatoes. They hatched a plan whereby they would muddy their faces, and after dark, disguised as Canadians, they would silently paddle out to the sailboat, creep aboard, and steal the ammunition—oh, and also the scotch. After two days of paddling and camping, the humor remained mostly absurd.

Apparently the threat of the Canadian invasion subsided at about 9:30 p.m. The sailboat conversation dwindled to mumbling, and the cannon firing and cheers stopped. As they dozed off, lying in their tents on top of their sleeping bags rather than in them because of the mugginess of the evening, they heard only a muffled mumble and an occasional ding from the boat's mast bell as the boat shifted with the crew retreating to their berths in the boat's cabin.

John and Bob were prodded awake by the sound of the wind, the crash of the waves on the sandy shore, the constant ringing of the sailboat's mast bell, and the groggy shouts of the sailboat crew as they awoke, scrambled to weigh their anchors and start their motor. The wind had gone from calm to about 15 knots out of the northeast in about the same number of minutes (.0000004 hls). By the time John peered out of his tent, the waves were already about 2 feet high. The lake was claiming revenge on the sailboat by regurgitating the potatoes and sending the projectiles on their way to a distant shore landing at Meyers Beach or Cornucopia and by chasing the sailboat itself from Rocky Island's sandspit to a new anchorage protected by South Twin. Over the sound of the wind and waves, the sailboat captain shouted orders to the scotch-soaked crew until the boat was safely underway.

In the initial blow, the temperature dropped from about 75 to 60 degrees Fahrenheit. Pushed by the wind, raindrops started in about another fifteen minutes (.0000004 hls), hitting hard enough to sting the bare face. The storm continued to intensify as John and Bob rushed to secure their tents better against the wind. Before long Bob's tent began to show where the seam sealer was old or had not been applied thickly enough. At John's invitation, he moved his sleeping bag and clothing into John's tent, which was still repelling water even though it was bowing to the northeastern wind.

Tent door view of "Red Sky in the Morning ..." (photo by author).

Before they dozed off to sleep again, this time huddled in their sleeping bags and not sleeping on top of them, Bob wondered out loud, "What if this storm had come up while we were paddling back from Devils Island yesterday?"

"Mmm. I was just thinking the same thing. I'm glad we weren't on the water when this thing hit. We would not have had time to beat the storm back to our sandspit."

Such a sudden weather change while out on the water also could have been a threat to end their personal hls.

Bob Mackreth posted the following on his "The Retread Ranger Blog," found at http://www.bobmackreth.com/blog/?p=5788 for August 11, 2011:

National Park Service Morning Report, August 11, 1995

Apostle Islands National Lakeshore, WI

On August 5th, volunteer lighthouse keepers on Devils Island reported that men on a sailboat anchored offshore were shooting at them with a "red and white rifle." Although the volunteers were forced to take cover, along with several park visitors, they were able to provide a full description of the vessel, including its name.

Rangers intercepted the boat, with backup assistance from the Coast Guard, and discovered that the rifle was in fact a homemade "potato cannon" — a device constructed from PVC pipe which employs combustible hair spray as a propellant to fire raw

Distant lightning (photo by Mark Weller)

potatoes with considerable force to a distance of up to 200 yards. Charles P___, 40, and Peter B___, 38, both from Minnesota, admitted firing toward the island, and were cited for disorderly conduct.

Initial research indicates that this may be the first naval bombardment of a shore installation on the Great Lakes since the War of 1812.

[Bob Mackreth, District Ranger, Apostle Islands NL]

A couple of days after I submitted this report, I [Ranger Mackreth] got a note back from the chief maritime historian of the National Park Service. He disputed my contention that this was a "naval bombardment" in that I failed to establish that the boat involved was a commissioned warship of any sovereign nation. Instead, he argued that this was clearly an unsanctioned operation by a private vessel, or by maritime law, an act of piracy.

He went on to add that considering that the traditional punishment for pirates was summary hanging, my staff and I had showed great mercy.

SAND ISLAND

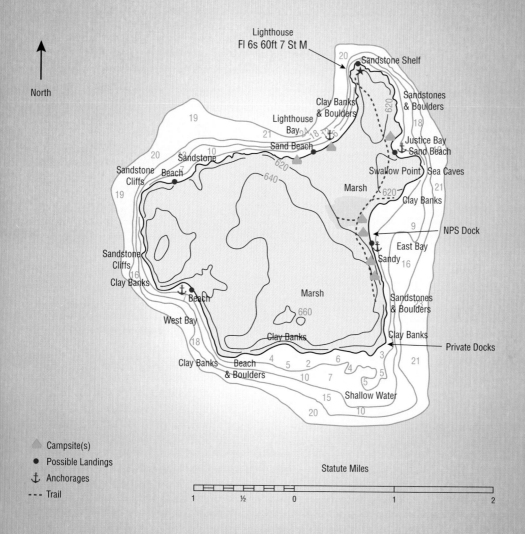

North

Lighthouse
Fl 6s 60ft 7 St M

Sandstone Shelf

20

Clay Banks
& Boulders

Sandstones
& Boulders

Lighthouse
Bay

18

Sand Beach

Justice Bay
Sand Beach

21

Sandstone
Beach

19

10

Swallow Point   Sea Caves

Sandstone
Cliffs

20

620

Marsh

21

Clay Banks

640

620

9   NPS Dock

Sandstone
Cliffs

16

East Bay

16

Clay Banks

Sandy

Beach

Marsh

Sandstones
& Boulders

West Bay

18

660

Clay Banks

Private Docks

Clay Banks

Beach
& Boulders

Clay Banks

4   5   2

6

3

21

4

10   7

5

15   Shallow Water

20   10

▲ Campsite(s)

● Possible Landings

⚓ Anchorages

--- Trail

Statute Miles

1   ½   0   1   2

Location

Sand Island is the most westerly usable island in the National Lakeshore. Although Eagle Island, lying 3.5 miles southwest of Sand Island, is technically the most western island, it serves as a bird sanctuary, and landing on Eagle Island is prohibited between May 15 and September 1. Sand Island lies about 2 miles west of York Island. The southeast corner of Sand Island is a bit over 2 miles northwest of the mainland launch site of Little Sand Bay, and the southwest tip of the island is about 1.25 miles from Sand Point on the mainland. Because of its somewhat remote location away from most of the other islands, sailboat and powerboat traffic may be somewhat lighter than one would expect in the busy months of July and August.

Geography and History

Imagine an elephant's head tilted counterclockwise 90 degrees so that the top of its head (ear) is on the west, its shortened trunk is pointing north, and its shortened tusk pointing east. The south side of the island, facing the mainland, forms the base of the elephant's head. On the tip of the shortened trunk is the lighthouse. Justice Bay lies between the trunk and the shortened tusk and there are some great sea caves at Swallow Point (the end of the tusk). Behind the elephant's ear at the southwest corner of the island is West Bay, the gap between the elephant's forehead and the tip of the trunk on the north side of the island forms Lighthouse Bay, and East Bay lies under the elephant's chin.

Sand Island has little elevation, with its highest point (58 feet above lake level) located along the base of the elephant's neck near the southern shore and on the "ear" of the elephant on its westerly shore. Because it is relatively flat, parts of the island drain slowly and provide a good breeding ground for mosquitoes.

The Sand Island Lighthouse is perhaps the most beautiful lighthouse in the Apostles. The keeper's house and the tower for the light were built in 1881 using local sandstone. Emmanuel Luick, accompanied by his surviving two (of four) children by his second wife, Oramill, served as the keeper of the light from 1892

Sand Island light (photo by author).

View from Sand Island light (photo by author).

until 1921 when the light was automated. The Sand Island light now flashes every six seconds from 60 feet above the water and is visible for 7 miles. Summer volunteers housed at East Bay may be available at the lighthouse during the daytime to answer visitor's questions and provide tours for a small fee.

The population on Sand Island, mostly Norwegian immigrant farmers and fishermen, reached one hundred permanent residents in 1918, and the village of Shaw, named after the island's first resident of European descent, Francis Shaw, was the center of activity. The residents maintained a school until 1928, had a post office between 1911 and 1916, and for a period after 1918, kept a cooperative store providing the residents with goods from the mainland. The population of permanent residents dwindled, and the last permanent resident left the island in 1944. Now only summer residents continue to occupy the remaining lands subject to life lease around the southeast corner of the island and along the southern shore.

Shoreline and Landings

The Sand Island shoreline has it all—rock shelves, clay banks, sea caves, and long sand beaches. Commencing a trip counterclockwise around the island from its southwestern corner, the 1.5- mile south shoreline offers places to land, but the landing sites should be avoided until the life leases expire. Paddling east from the southwest corner, the kayaker will encounter about 0.25 mile of beach with boulders, then about 0.5 mile of high clay banks. The second half of the south shoreline is sandy beach until reaching the shallow gravel sandspit at the southeastern corner of the island.

Heading north along the elephant's neck on the eastern shore, the beach turns rocky and develops sandstone shelves and pockets.

There is a new dock near the National Park Service cabin towards the north end of East Bay with a boardwalk connecting the dock to an accessible group campsite and an accessible individual campsite. Most of East Bay provides a soft, sandy landing for kayakers.

Paddling northeast along the elephant's tusk to Swallow Point, the sand beach gives way to clay banks and at Swallow Point (the flattened tip of the elephant's tusk) there is 0.25 mile of interesting sea caves to explore. Rounding Swallow Point, the sandy beach of Justice Bay comes into view. Unless the sea is relatively calm, allowing a landing on the rock shelves near the lighthouse, Justice Bay is the last landing site available on the easterly shore for access to the lighthouse. A trail along the clay bank above sandy Justice Bay leads about 1 mile north to the lighthouse.

Rock shelf at Sand Island lighthouse (photo by author).

Sand Island sea arch (now fallen) in summer (photo by Robert E. Rolley).

Sand Island peek-a-boo in 2008 (photo by Don Hynek).

Sand Island sea arch (now fallen) in winter, 2008 (photo by Don Hynek).

Sand Island glitter in 2008 (photo by Don Hynek).

From Justice Bay to the tip of Lighthouse Point there are sandstone shelves, boulders, and minor sea caves. If the winds are out of the southwest to southeast or very light from a northerly direction, it is possible to land a kayak or moor a small boat on the rock shelves below the lighthouse. But too much wave action at the rock shelves will give the rocks a great opportunity to grind the hull of a kayak when landing or launching, and the stairway from the rock shelf up to the lighthouse, frequently destroyed by winter ice, may not be in place to allow access to the lighthouse grounds..

Heading south and southwesterly along the top of the elephant's trunk across Lighthouse Bay, clay banks become boulders and ultimately there is about 0.5 mile of sand beach providing friendly landings for two campsites. The Lighthouse Bay beach is long enough to allow a lunch break landing away from the individual campsites.

Heading west from Lighthouse Bay along

the northern shoreline, after about 1 mile of sandstone shelves and rocks, there are two possible landing areas in the last 0.5 mile or so of the north shore. The first is a small sand beach and the second at the northwest corner of the island is a rock shelf. Landing on the shelf will be difficult if there is any wave action resulting from a northerly wind.

Turning south, along the entire western shoreline of the island there are sandstone cliffs, some sea caves, and high clay banks making landing difficult or impossible. There is a good landing in the sand/gravel beach in West Bay, but the dock and buildings at the north end of the beach, although stabilized, should be avoided.

Three features of the lake beyond the Sand Island shoreline can affect navigation around the island. The first feature is the Sand Island Shoals, which lie about 1.5 miles northeast of Lighthouse Point and is marked by a red nun buoy marked with a "2." The water depth over the shoal is about 15 feet and accordingly will not affect a kayaker or most small boats, but the shallow water over the shoal did claim the lives of the captain and most of the crew of the *Sevona* in a storm in September 1905. Information about the loss of the *Sevona* and the anchor of the ship are on display at the Little Sand Bay ranger station.

The second feature affecting navigation around Sand Island is the shallow sandbar extending from the southeast corner of the island south to the mouth of the Sand River on the mainland. Although some late nineteenth-century charts apparently show the water depth of over 40 feet in this area, current charts show the depth as shallow as 4 feet. The shallow water means that some large powerboats and sailboats will avoid passage between the mainland and Sand Island. While the depth remains more than adequate for a kayak, the kayaker should be aware that rolling waves produced by a strong westerly wind can turn into breaking waves as they approach the shallow sandbar.

The third feature is the current that fol-lows the mainland shore past York and Sand Islands. Even a slight current when combined with the wind can result in confused seas or enhanced waves seemingly coming from different directions. The crossing from Little Sand Bay to Sand Island can be more hazardous than the map would indicate and has been the location of kayaker fatalities in recent years.

Camping

There are two group camping sites and one individual campsite south of the National Park Service cabin at East Bay. North of the cabin there is another individual campsite and an accessible group and an accessible individual campsite. Both accessible campsites feature raised wooden platforms with metal cleats available for use as tent anchors.

The campsites near the East Bay dock have food lockers, picnic tables, fire rings and shared vault toilets; and well water usually is available near the ranger's cabin.

Individual campsites are also located in Justice Bay and (two) in Lighthouse Bay. Each of these sites has a fire ring, picnic table, bear-proof food locker, and stump toilet.

All of Sand Island is in a single primitive camping zone, but no primitive camping is allowed on or near the remaining leased land, within view of any trail, or within a quarter mile of any building or designated campsite.

Hiking

There are more than 3 miles of trails on the island, and the trails are becoming increasingly accessible with the installation of boardwalks. From the dock on East Bay, one can walk north almost 2 miles past Justice Bay, through some old growth pine forest and past an overlook above Lighthouse Bay to the Sand Island lighthouse. From the dock you can also walk south about .6 mile towards the remaining private property. Near the NPS cabin there is an unmarked and unmaintained trail heading west to the abandoned Noring family farm site, now with only clearings and the remnants of an orchard. On the trail north to the lighthouse there is a stub trail leading to the Hansen family fishery and farm, a site that will be undergoing some continuing preservation. Two abandoned cars are "parked" along the trail – one probably was owned by the Noring family or the Moe family, and the second car, a Chevrolet, was brought to the island by Gertrude Wellisch, who rented the lighthouse in the 1920's and 1930's and acted as a summer tutor for the island's children.

Kayak Trip Suggestions

Sand Island offers a variety of options for a day trip, an overnight camping trip, or as the first or last stop of a multi-day trip.

For a somewhat aggressive day trip, consider a crossing from Little Sand Bay to the island, a circumnavigation of the island, possibly with a lunch stop at the lighthouse or at Lighthouse Bay, and a return to Little Sand Bay before evening (15 to 16 miles).

Another more leisurely option would include one or two nights of destination camping at one of the campsites with hiking the trails, a visit to the lighthouse, some sunbathing on the beach or the dock, and a refreshing swim in the lake in the afternoon.

Finally a night or two of camping on Sand Island could be combined with a longer trip including visits or camping on York Island and a visit to the beaches and lighthouse on Raspberry Island.

MEMORIES OF SAND ISLAND

Sand Island lies close to a mainland launch site and has much to offer a visitor—a beautiful lighthouse, sea caves, two very different camping choices, and the physical remains from a more active human history. I believe I have visited Sand Island more often than any of the islands in the National Lakeshore and have many happy memories of the island. The first trip I made to Sand Island perhaps remains the most memorable. Although the crossing from Little Sand Bay to Sand Island described in the following story helped boost confidence and may sound exciting, hindsight now tells me that I should have had more patience and waited with my crossing. The crossing to Sand Island seems short and easy, but it can be more dangerous than it looks.

My first trip to Sand Island started at Little Sand Bay on Saturday morning of Labor Day weekend in the mid-1990s. It was only my second solo trip in the Apostles, and my love affair with the Islands was still in its courtship stage. The trip helped permanently seal the love affair and increased my confidence in my paddling abilities and in making solo kayak camping trips.

Because it was a holiday weekend, I had reserved one of the individual campsites near the East Bay National Park Service north dock weeks in advance. I slept in the car at one of the Washburn campgrounds after a grueling trip north, threatened by other northbound holiday traffic and by ghostly images of deer haunting the highway ditches and warning me that with a few hops they could put themselves on a collision course with my car.

I arrived at Little Sand Bay at about 9:00 a.m., but there was no reason to rush to arrive early or to pack and launch the kayak. The wind gauge at the ranger station measured the steady northwest breeze at 18 knots, and waves of about 3 feet and displaying whitecaps seemingly reached all the way out to Sand Island. The wind and waves were beyond my comfort range for a solo paddle trip.

I had not yet purchased a handheld marine/weather radio so I checked the weather and wave forecast at the ranger station. The wind was supposed to continue for most of the day, calm down a bit in the evening and return a bit lighter on Sunday. I sat on the beach and in my car until noon, hoping to wait out the wind.

Group leaders for a Bayfield outfitter took turns teaching beginner paddlers dry land paddling and rescue techniques in the grass above the beach. Their demonstrations and group practice seemed to drag along slowly as they struggled to keep the interest of the group on what promised to be a long delay for their paddle trip, if they would be able to paddle at all. My paddling self-confidence increased a bit as I watched the group lesson, realizing that I was already aware of most of what was in the lesson plan.

During one of the lesson breaks, I asked one of the group leaders where they were headed and learned that their destination was one of the group campsites on Sand Island and that they still hoped to paddle that day, albeit in the evening hours. I mentioned that I had one of the individual campsites reserved and asked if I could paddle with the group to Sand Island. While I could understand his concern for the safety of the members of his own group, I was surprised at the strength of his negative reaction. So much for the camaraderie of kayak paddling. I wondered to myself whether the group leader would even stop to provide assistance to a capsized paddler if he and his group happened upon one mid-crossing. I made a mental note that paddling solo means trusting only in your own ability.

In contrast to the group leader's reaction, I experienced a friendlier encounter with a female paddler at least ten years my junior. She arrived in a car with a Minnesota license plate and began to unload a beautiful wood strip kayak. Hoping that she might share my Sand Island destination and provide us with a mutual feeling of safety for the crossing, I approached her car to admire her kayak. She was not intimidated by my approach and exchanged information freely. I offered to help her carry her beautiful kayak to the beach, half expecting a "Don't touch my kayak" reaction that I had encountered in the past, particularly with some female paddlers treasuring their independence. I was pleasantly surprised at her genuinely thankful acceptance of the offer.

"Are you headed for Sand Island?" I asked hopefully.

"No. I haven't been to Raspberry Island for some time, and I really want to see the lighthouse and grounds," she replied. "Would you like to paddle there with me?"

I did, but the thought of making my way 6 miles back to Sand Island in the evening with uncertain weather and less than full confidence in my own paddling skills made me respond, "No, I have a campsite on Sand for tonight, and I probably am not ready for an eleven or twelve mile day." My ego did not like my admission of being such a novice in the presence of her self-confidence.

After she loaded her kayak and donned her wetsuit, I helped her launch into the strong surf, again with her appreciative consent. I watched her paddle off, traveling broadside to the wind in a shorter, less stable kayak than my own, with no rudder to assist her control in the waves. She struggled a bit in the waves, having to make constant corrections in her direction with sweep strokes and even some ruddering with her paddle, but her bearing north and east toward Raspberry Island did not waver significantly. I felt almost ashamed to still be on the beach waiting for calmer winds.

Rebuffed by the group leader and shamed by the female paddler so ready for adventure, I carried my own kayak to the beach and slowly started to load my camping gear and equipment. At least I would be ready to paddle when (and if) the wind calmed down. With the infusion of courage from the Minnesota paddler, I even talked myself into launching from the beach under the partial protection of the breakwater. My idea was to paddle about a hundred yards beyond the breakwater to determine whether I could handle the waves in unprotected water. My courage built to a higher level as I edged out farther and farther.

Bobbing in the waves, I calculated that at 4 miles per hour, the crossing would take about forty-five minutes, and it would be about thirty-five to forty minutes before I received any protection offered by Sand Island from the wind and waves. As usual when my fears of a crossing have been overcome, I started paddling hard with the thought that strong paddling will minimize the length of time of exposure to danger. Once the decision to paddle is made, it is more difficult to turn back. I was committed to the crossing.

My pace crawled along at about 2 miles per hour, something that I did not realize until I had done thirty minutes of hard paddling and still seemed to be less than half way to the island. Paddling required my constant attention with directional correction from my rudder as well as sweep strokes to keep me headed directly into the northwest blow. I tried to anticipate the larger waves that were likely to turn me broadside to the wind. The bow of my kayak would penetrate the larger waves as they swept my front deck and audibly slapped into my chest. Each such larger wave fouled my vision with beads of water splashed on my glasses and sent a trickle of water through my neoprene spray skirt as a cold reminder that I was allowed no rest from paddling, nor could I lose my concentration during this solo crossing.

Several times I prematurely thought that I had covered enough distance from Little Sand Bay to achieve some protection from the wind and waves from Sand Island itself. Several times I found that I was wrong as another wave would sweep the length of my deck and enlighten me with a cold slap in the face and chest. The trip became like a hellishly repetitive fever dream as I strived endlessly and unsuccessfully to resolve an ill-defined conflict with the wind and waves. Finally the fever broke and the dream disappeared as the protection of the island became real.

Pink lady slipper (*Cypripedium acaule Ait.*) on July 4 (photo by author).

I continued to paddle close to the island's southeastern shoreline, enjoying the protection from the wind and the shoreline scenery that was dotted with ledges of sandstone overhanging the lake.

I set up camp in the designated individual campsite and prepared my dinner earlier than I had planned, hoping to go back on the water to explore the sea caves and lighthouse in the evening if the wind and waves mellowed.

About an hour and a half before sunset, the wind calmed considerably, and I launched again in an unloaded, more buoyant kayak. As I rounded the first point north of the campsites, I heard the deep, thunderous complaint bellowing from the sea caves, their seemingly vocal response to air trapped between water and rock by the leftover waves. The rollers were no longer breaking waves although they were still 2 feet high. The waves, having lost some of their intensity wrapping around Lighthouse Point, served as a reminder of the afternoon's difficult crossing.

I landed in Justice Bay and walked to the lighthouse on an exploratory hike. The lighthouse was unoccupied when I reached it. Perhaps the volunteer's occupancy had already reached the end of the season. I retraced my path to my kayak and paddled an even calmer sea back to the campground.

Devils paintbrush (*Pilosella aurantiaca*) at Sand Island lighthouse grounds (photo by Paul Matteoni).

Sand Island Star Trails (photo by Mark Weller).

It was almost dark by the time I reached the National Park Service northern dock. The outfitter-led paddle group was straggling with carrying their equipment into the group camping area, at that time located next to the individual sites near the northern dock. They had delayed their crossing as long as possible to still arrive before dark. The outfitter's clients seemed tired and somewhat beaten. Evidently the open water between Little Sand Bay and Sand Island had still been capable of instilling fear and respect for the big lake.

I went to bed early, dreaming of my wrestling match with the lake. The group leaders in the outfitter's group lit lanterns as they worked into the darkness to set up the campsite and to prepare the evening meal for the group.

In the morning I awoke early and had struck my tent and prepared breakfast before the group was stirring. I was already packing equipment into my kayak as one of the outfitter group leaders carried his first load of equipment to the kayaks resting in the sand in the dock area.

"Good morning, kayaker," the group leader offered respectfully. I realized that the respect was a result of watching my solo crossing facing the wind and waves the afternoon before.

"Morning," I responded carefully, secretly hoping that perhaps the next time someone asked to make a crossing with the group, the leader's response might be more measured and friendly.

I pushed off and started the next leg of my paddle trip, my kayak fully loaded with my camping equipment and a kayaker filled with new confidence.

SOUTH TWIN ISLAND

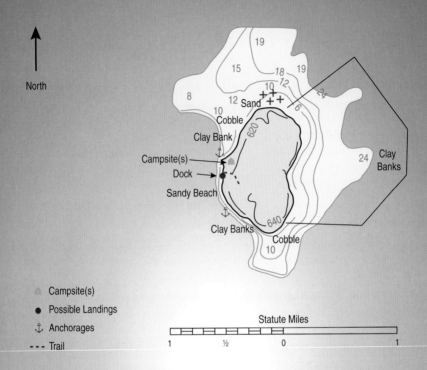

North

19
15   18   19
10   12
8   12   Sand
10   Cobble
Clay Bank
620
Campsite(s)
Dock
Sandy Beach
640
Clay Banks
Cobble
10
24
Clay Banks
24
6

△ Campsite(s)
● Possible Landings
⚓ Anchorages
- - - Trail

Statute Miles

1   ½   0   1

Clearing by dock at South Twin (photo courtesy National Park Service).

Location

Rocky Island is South Twin's closest neighbor, with its dock lying about 1 mile west of South Twin's dock and its "arm" protecting South Twin's northwest coast 0.5 to 0.75 mile away. North Twin Island lies about 2.5 miles northeast of South Twin, and Otter Island lies about 2 miles to the southwest. Ironwood Island is 1.5 miles to the southeast.

Geography and History

South Twin is shaped like a lima bean, standing on end north and south and concave to the east and convex to the west with a hump on its back. The "bean" is about 1 mile long and a bit over 0.5 mile wide east to west across the middle. The land area at 360 acres makes South Twin one of the smaller islands in the National Lakeshore.

Topographical maps show South Twin Island to be relatively flat, its highest elevation rising only about 48 feet above the level of the lake. Indeed, the island is flat enough that one of its prior private owners cleared a rough airplane landing strip toward the south end of the island running southwest to northeast. Before the island became part of the National Lakeshore, it was used for a fishing resort and earlier, for commercial fish camps. Most of the buildings used by former owners, including the one that housed the NPS ranger station mentioned in the "Raising the Flag" side story in this chapter, have now been removed from the island. Second growth forest is reclaiming the island in all but the dock area.

Shoreline and Landings

Starting at the northern tip of the lima bean, the shoreline at the tip is sandy but difficult to approach because of a number of boulders just above and below the lake's surface. Proceeding counterclockwise southwesterly down the northwestern shore there is a narrow cobble beach. The cobble extends out into the shallow water, making it difficult to hug the shoreline even in a kayak. Indeed, the "channel" between the arm of Rocky Island

South Twin dock (photo courtesy National Park Service).

and the northwestern shore of South Twin is no more than 10 to 12 feet deep even in the center of the channel. After the cobble and before the small hump in the back of the bean there is a low clay bank.

Below the sandy western hump on the back of the bean there is an L-shaped dock rebuilt in 2011 using a walkway between the shore and the dock. The walkway prevents coastal sediment from building up around the dock causing a reduction in the available depth. Use of the dock is available to the public, and the dock can accommodate boats with a 4- to 6-foot draft.

Although the water depth drops off quite quickly, there usually are sailboats anchored on the west side of the island, where they are protected from all but a direct westerly wind.

Kayaks can land in the sand/cobble adjacent to the dock.

The southern part of the bean displays high clay banks with cobble just east of the southerly tip of the island. The entire eastern shoreline consists of high clay banks.

Camping

There are four campsites around the edge of the dock clearing with fire rings, picnic tables, tent pads, and a shared vault toilet. Camping on South Twin is less primitive than on some of the other islands, with campers sharing the cleared area with day-use picnickers from the anchored and docked boats.

Hiking

There is a hiking trail about .5 mile in length leading from the dock clearing to the southwestern end of the former airstrip. Longer trails have been reclaimed by second growth forest.

Kayak Trip Suggestions

South Twin can be a destination site for a family camping trip that includes children or grown-ups interested in a less primitive experience. Getting to the island as a kayaking destination, however, means a good day's paddle of about 18 miles from Bayfield or Little Sand Bay and 15 miles from Buffalo Bay at Red Cliff.

The camping facilities on South Twin can also provide a more civilized base camp for an exploratory trip to the islands farthest away from the mainland.

Campsites on South Twin Island (photo courtesy National Park Service).

RAISING THE FLAG

It was a Fourth of July sometime after the first Gulf War and before the invasion of Iraq. Bob and I were base camped on the sandspit on the south tip of Rocky Island. On the second morning of our long weekend trip, we decided to paddle over to South Twin to explore the island.

It was a beautiful, sunny morning, and the wind would not be a factor on our paddle across the mile-plus channel between the two islands. We even slept later than we usually do when camping, tired from the previous day's paddle to Devils Island and the excitement of viewing the sea caves, the lighthouse, and walking the full length of the Devil's Island trail. The mid-summer sun heated our tents to a wake-up, get-up temperature. At breakfast the strong coffee in our cups already seemed too hot for a holiday morning, and we considered how nice an ice cold beer or soft drink would taste as an alternative to the coffee.

The crossing to South Twin itself was uneventful, and we landed in the late morning on the sand south of the dock. We marveled at the relative opulence of the dock area and the former owner's house that then served as a ranger station (but since has been removed). The lawn was mowed. There were vault toilets. Within the main park service building there were interesting displays and soft chairs. Although he did not make any comment at the time, Bob also noticed that the flagpole in the picnic area was bare of any flag.

Now let me digress and tell you about Bob. We met while we were still struggling in our early college years, seeking our way to a lifetime profession by experimenting with different majors. Bob's struggle led him to a Master's degree in social work and after a few years as a clinical social worker, to several long-term engagements as the executive director of nonprofit corporations. Funding the nonprofits was always a problem and Bob developed a keen ability to "schmooze," as we termed it. Bob's social skills helped keep the gifts to the nonprofits flowing in. A few years before his retirement, Bob's daughter aptly described his professional career to other family members, saying, "Just think. For thirty-five years all Dad has been doing is simply helping people."

In an alternative life Bob also became an officer in the Army Reserve while in graduate school. Although many of us were happy to walk away from the military after fulfilling our Vietnam-era military obligation of six years of service in the reserves, Bob sought ways to avoid being mustered out of the Army Reserve. He ultimately reached the rank of full Colonel after actively serving in a hospital unit in the Mideast during the First Gulf War. At the time that he received orders for active duty, Bob was forty-eight years old, and although he was in good physical shape, he could no longer run and jump with the twenty-something soldiers.

Bob and I share a sense of humor that can suddenly turn dark. It recognizes the irony in almost any set of circumstances and can expand the irony into such absurdity that the original theme of the humor becomes unrecognizable. Early in our friendship, the rigors of basic training in the military and the jargon of the drill sergeants were some of the favorite targets of our humor. For example, we would recall the drill sergeants calling cadence while marching new "recruits" in basic training.

"Ain't no reason for lookin' back; Jodie's got your Cadillac." And further, "Ain't no reason for lookin' down; Jodie's got your girl and gone." We claimed we simply could not understand the drill sergeant's words. Neither of us had ever owned a Cadillac, especially before basic training. And who was this Jodie guy? Neither of us knew a Jodie. Now according to the drill sergeant's cadence call, Jodie apparently owned our nonexistent Cadillac and had run off with our girlfriends. That cadence call obviously could not be meant for us, since we were both married while we were in basic training. Although the drill sergeants always seemed to know so much more than the recruits, how could their information be trusted if they got those Cadillac and Jodie things so mixed up.

Later in our friendship, our country's somewhat inconsistent foreign policies received our ironic criticism. Almost nothing, including ourselves, was too sacred to avoid our analytical irony.

Back on South Twin Island, after landing, Bob and I found the doors of the converted ranger station unlocked and entered to review the exhibits. A young, uniformed park ranger entered the building soon after we arrived, and Bob immediately greeted him with a compliment.

"Wow, this is a great facility you have here," he said. "And I bet the exhibits are really interesting to any families camped on the island."

"Thanks," the ranger beamed. "We do have some evening programs around the community campfire for the campers and boaters in July and August. Perhaps you guys would like to attend the one this next week. Are you camped here on South Twin?"

"No, we're camped on the sandspit over on Rocky, and just paddled our kayaks over for the day," Bob answered. "They say the sandspit is one of the most beautiful campsites in the Apostles. We would like to stay for the program, but we plan to head back to Bayfield on Monday."

"That sandspit is a beautiful campsite."

"Ya know," Bob ventured, "I see you have a flagpole outside. Do you have a flag for it?"

"Why yes, yes we do," the ranger responded. "I guess I just hadn't gotten around to putting it up yet."

"I would be happy to put it up for you," Bob offered. "After all it is the Fourth of July."

"Thanks. That would be great. The flag should be up on the Fourth."

The ranger gave the flag to Bob. He carried it outside to the flagpole, and draping the flag over his shoulder so it would not touch the ground, attached the flag to the flagpole chain and raised it to the top of the flagpole. Bob's respectful treatment of the flag was obvious. I felt as if I should be wearing my old army uniform and listening for a bugler sounding Reveille as he raised the flag. I made a mental note to make some part of military life the target of our ironic humor back at camp that evening.

From inside the building, the ranger also had noticed the respect that Bob had shown in the flag raising. When we returned to the building, he said, "You raised that flag as if you have done that before."

"Yes. I have done it a few times. I've been in the Army Reserves for over twenty years. Got back from Kuwait just a few years ago after serving as a Lieutenant Colonel in Operation Desert Storm."

There was a perceptable change in the gaze of the young ranger toward the older Bob. Instead of a somewhat disheveled graying paddler, the ranger saw a confident military veteran. I felt it too, and I made another mental note not to expose the flag raising experience to our evening irony attack.

Things change. Absence from family and friends and exposure to danger and the unknown can change personal values and elevate some subject matter to a level above any humorous assault. Perhaps there should be some limitations on the subject matter exposed to our ridicule. Back at camp that evening, I would not joke about raising the flag. I would make jokes only about whether the young ranger on South Twin Island would remember to take the flag down on the Fourth of July at sunset after we had paddled back to our campsite.

STOCKTON ISLAND

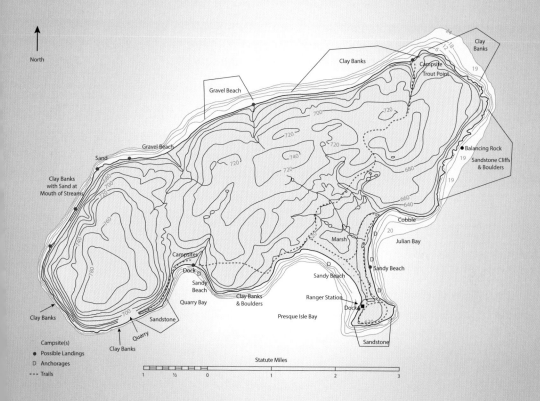

North

Clay Banks
Gravel Beach
Campsite
Trout Point
Clay Banks
19
700
720
720
740
720
Balancing Rock
19
Sandstone Cliffs
& Boulders
19
Gravel Beach
680
Sand
720
Clay Banks
with Sand at
Mouth of Streams
680
700
640
660
720
640
Cobble
760
Julian Bay
20
Marsh
Campsite
Sandy Beach
Dock
Sandy
Beach
Sandy Beach
780
Quarry Bay
Clay Banks
& Boulders
Ranger Station
700
Dock
Clay Banks
Sandstone
680
Quarry
Presque Isle Bay
Clay Banks
Sandstone

Campsite(s)
• Possible Landings
D Anchorages
- - - Trails

Statute Miles

| 1 | ½ | 0 | 1 | 2 | 3 |

Balancing Rock off eastern shore of Stockton Island (photo by author).

Location

Because of its size, the distances between Stockton Island and its neighbors need to be described with reference to the closest part of the island, rather than the entire island. The Presque Isle dock on Stockton is 14+ miles from Bayfield and 12+ miles from the Buffalo Bay marina in Red Cliff. Stockton's southwestern tip is about 1.5 miles east of the southeastern tip of Oak Island and the same distance northeast of Hermit Island. Stockton is Michigan Island's closest neighbor—it is a bit over 3 miles from the Stockton dock to the Michigan Island sandspit. Steamboat Point, the closest point to Stockton located on Madeline Island's northern coastline is about 2.5 miles south of Quarry Point and about 3.5 miles from Stockton's Presque Isle dock. The tip of Outer Island's sandspit is 2.75 miles from Stockton's northeastern tip.

Geography and History

It may take a sizeable imagination, but Stockton Island can be pictured as a croaking spring frog with its head facing northeast and its vocal sac expanded and ready to let out a loud mating call. Unfortunately, the image becomes marred at the frog's rear with too big of a tail and a bite taken out of the underside of its leg (Quarry Bay). The frog's front leg stretches out just east of south to reach the frog's foot at the part of Stockton called Presque Isle Point.

The highest part of Stockton Island is at the center of the frog's misshapen tail, about 200 feet above the lake level. At 10,054 acres, Stockton is the second largest island (after Madeline) in the Apostles. It is about 7.25 miles long and 2 to 2.5 miles wide. Its terrain includes a sandy lake level lagoon and bog along the tombolo forming the frog's forelegs, as well as higher elevation wooded bogs drained by small streams eroding their way down to Lake Superior. There is also sandstone on the island producing sea caves and majestic rock ledges and towers under the frog's chin, and an abandoned quarry where the frog's rear foot should be.

The earliest of the island's history should include a reference to the probability that Stockton was once two islands, the main island without the frog's front legs and an islet (Presque Isle) now forming the frog's front feet. Over more than a millennium, falling lake levels and wave action created the sandy tombolo that now joins Presque Isle to its larger neighbor and produces the beautiful sand beaches along both sides of the frog's forelegs.

Stockton Island's Native American archeological sites are traceable to the Late Woodland tradition probably around 800 A.D., although some earlier artifacts may go back around five thousand years.[28] These early seasonal occupants probably were not the Ojibwe, who were living in the area when the French explorers, fur traders, and missionaries arrived in the mid to late seventeenth century.

Evidence of Stockton's more recent use as a base for fishing operations can be found as clearings and remnants of buildings at the north end of Julian Bay (under the frog's expanded vocal sac), near the Presque Isle dock, and at Quarry Bay. Indeed, Julian Bay probably acquired its name from Julian B. Nelson, a fisherman who fished the area with his father in the 1930s and '40s from a base camp at the north end of the bay.[29]

The largest sandstone quarry in the Apostle Islands, located about a mile south of the Quarry Bay dock on the south side of the frog's misshapen tail, gave Quarry Bay its name. John and William Knight opened the Stockton quarry in 1886, but in 1890 sold the operation to a group of investors from Chicago. The sandstone from the quarry site was shipped out for use as building material until the market for stone declined, and operations at the quarry site ceased in 1897.[30]

By the 1880s, much of Stockton Island was owned by John H. Knight (one of the brothers who opened the quarry) and William F. Vilas, who acquired the land for speculation. They did some logging with their own company and leased some land in the northwestern part of the island to William King for white pine logging in the 1880s, but most of the logging of the island's virgin timber was done after the Knight-Vilas lands were sold or leased to the John Schroeder Lumber Company in 1905. The Schroeder operation reached a large scale with three hundred men working in three different logging camps in the winter of 1914–1915.[31] Logging on Stockton largely ceased by 1920 when few marketable trees remained.

Throughout the 1990s and the first decade in the new millennium, Stockton Island has been known as the island with the highest density of black bears. In 2013, Oak Island took over the bear density title, but there still are many black bears on Stockton.

Shoreline and Landings

Except for the rocky northeastern shore of the island (the top of the frog's head at Trout Point, down around the frog's vocal sac to Julian Bay) the shoreline of Stockton Island offers a soft landing every mile or two.

The best shore landing sites for kayakers is on either side of the frog's front leg at Julian Bay (the east side) or at Presque Isle Bay (the west side). The 1.5-mile long beaches are separated by sandstone rock shelves at the frog's foot. In calm weather it would even be possible to land on the low rock shelves at Presque Isle Point (the frog's foot).

The shoreline west of the multiple campsites in Presque Isle Bay becomes sandstone boulders at the end of the beach, then clay banks with boulders at the waterline until it again becomes a half mile sandy beach in Quarry Bay. West, southwest, and finally northwest from Quarry Bay the shoreline is sandstone for the first mile and then high clay banks for 1.5 miles to the tip of the frog's rear.

North and northeast around the rear of the frog the clay bank/boulder shoreline is marked by at least four sandy landing sites, formed by the sandy deltas of small creeks draining the interior of the island. The last sandy landing

Stockton Island ranger station (photo courtesy National Park Service).

Stockton Island's Presque Isle dock (photo courtesy National Park Service).

before heading north and east up the frog's back is a fairly flat stretch of beach with alders and willows on the shore and a shallow sandy bottom shelf reaching out into the lake. The frog's lower back sports 1.5 miles of gravel and cobble beach where a calm weather landing could be made. In the middle of the frog's back is another drainage area resulting in a sandy delta for a soft landing.

From the frog's upper back to the tip of its nose there are clay banks with some boulders at the waterline, making a landing difficult, except for the small beach at Trout Point. From the tip of the frog's nose southwest past "Balancing Rock" and south to the middle of the frog's vocal sac, there are sandstone cliffs and caves and only one landing site in a cove about half a mile south of Balancing Rock. While the cove could be used as a break from paddling, the sandy beach is backed by a high cliff face, making travel inland impossible. The balance of the frog's vocal sac down to the Julian Bay Beach is cobble and a clay bank.

For larger boats there is transient docking available at the dual Presque Isle docks and at the Quarry Bay dock, although the spaces fill up quickly in high season, especially on weekends. The west side of the west dock at Presque Isle may be silted in and not usable,

but the ends of all the Stockton docks can accommodate drafts of 6 to 7 feet.

If dock space is not available, larger boats can find anchorage in both Presque Isle Bay and Quarry Bay unless there is a strong wind out of the south. Julian Bay also is available for anchorage protected from a southwest to north wind. If the Julian Bay anchorage is used, boaters should be careful of fouling their anchor on the *Noquebay,* a lumber barge that caught fire and sank on October 9, 1905, and now rests in about 15 feet of water toward the north end of Julian Bay. If it becomes necessary for the boater to relocate anchorage from Julian Bay to Presque Isle Bay or vice versa, it will be wise to keep well away from the shoreline around Presque Isle Point, since shallow water rock shelves make the passage dangerous.

Camping

Up to nineteen campsites are strung along Presque Isle Bay northwest from the dock and ranger station. These campsites are popular, particularly for family camping, because they each front on the beach. In addition to the beautiful beach, each site offers a bear locker, fire ring, picnic table, and tent pad. Vault toilets are available for campers and there is potable water at the ranger station. The campsites may be reached by the cruise boat that makes stops at the Presque Isle dock, if available, or by water taxi. Accordingly, a

Quarry Bay Group Campsite B (photo courtesy National Park Service).

family can have a first-time, near wilderness National Lakeshore camping experience at a relatively low cost (perhaps complete with a bear sighting), spending two to four days or more camping, swimming, hiking, and perhaps attending an evening lecture at the new outdoor amphitheater completed in 2021 with the help of the Friends of the Apostle Islands and a grant from the Outdoor Foundation. Campsite #1 at Presque Isle also offers accessibility and is connected to the Presque Isle dock by a boardwalk.

There is an individual campsite as well as two group campsites at Quarry Bay and an individual hike-in campsite at Trout Point (the top of the frog's head). The Quarry Bay sites have fire rings, bear lockers and picnic tables, and share a vault toilet. The two group sites at Quarry Bay are accessible wooden platform sites with metal cleats provided to anchor tents, and they can be reached by boardwalk from the Quarry Bay dock. The individual site at Trout Point is located in the clearing for an old logging camp, a strenuous 6.25-mile hike from the

Tour boat off Stockton Island (photo courtesy National Park Service).

Presque Isle dock, and provides a more primitive wilderness experience with only a fire ring, food locker, and tent pad.

The western and northwestern shore provide landing sites that might be used for primitive camping. No primitive camping is allowed within .25 mile of the designated campsites or in any part of the Presque Isle lagoon and peninsula (frog's front foot).

Hiking

With 14.5 miles of trails, Stockton provides hiking opportunities through the most diverse ecological backdrops in the National Lakeshore.

There are two out-and-back trails—one to Quarry Bay (3.6 miles from the Presque Isle dock) and extending beyond the bay to the quarry itself (Quarry Trail, an additional 1.5 miles) and the other to Trout Point (1.6 miles on the Quarry Bay Trail, then an additional 4.7 miles through the island's central forest and upland swamps). A trip to the end of either trail with a same day return will be taxing for all but well-conditioned hikers, however, each trail also offers the opportunity of backpacking minimal camping equipment to Quarry Bay or to Trout Point, spending the night, and returning to the dock area the next day. The trail to Trout Point is not always well maintained and hikers should take at least a compass and a topographical map.

There also are two shorter loop trails that can provide a less strenuous half-day hiking experience. The first loop goes from the Presque Isle dock along the rocky shoreline of the frog's feet to the Julian Bay beach (Anderson Point Trail, 1.4 miles) then back to the dock on the Julian Bay Trail (0.4 mile). The second loop follows the Quarry Bay Trail past the string of bayside campsites for 0.6 mile, then follows the Tombolo Trail through bog and forest to the north end of Julian Bay, then back along the Julian Bay beach to the Julian Bay Trail (2.8 miles), and finally back to the dock on the Julian Bay Trail (0.4 mile) for a total of 3.8 miles. The second loop may require fording the shallow outlet stream draining the lagoon to the lake. Both loops could include

a break for sunbathing, a cooling swim, and perhaps a picnic on the Julian Bay beach.

Kayak Trip Suggestions

Stockton Island can be used as a base camp for farther day trips to Michigan Island, the Outer Island sandspit, or just exploring the coastline of Stockton itself. In case of bad weather, the island offers an alternative of a day of hiking the trails to investigate the island's history and diverse terrain, or in good weather, merely relaxing on the beaches.

For most paddlers the trip from launch to the Presque Isle dock is a strenuous full day trip. If a paddler is uncomfortable with the length or risk of the 12 to 14 mile initial and final day trips to Stockton, there is an easier, albeit pricey, alternative of taking a commercial cruise boat or water taxi to the island with a kayak, and spending the extra time and energy on the island itself.

Stockton Island rockshelf on a gloomy day (photo by author).

Herring gull resting on dock at Stockton Island (photo by Robert E. Rolley).

BEDTIME FOR LITTLE BEARS

"Your mom and dad say that Grampy can tell you a story to help you get to sleep. So this is a story about bears. This story happened at a time before either of you were even born yet back when your mother was just a teenager and Lala and Grampy went camping on Stockton Island while your mother was at camp. Stockton is an island in Lake Superior not far from Bayfield where you and your mom and dad have been on vacation. Remember when you stayed by the beach with that big chain in the ground, and you and your mom went for a paddle in the kayak?"

"I remember. I couldn't get to sleep at night. I was too excited."

"Yes, you had trouble going to sleep then too, just like tonight. Now, after I finish this story, you both will have to go to sleep. Okay?"

"Okay, okay."

"All right, well, this was so long ago that Grampy did not even have a kayak yet. Lala got one first as a Mother's Day and birthday present. Kayaking was just getting popular and not very many people had a kayak.

"It was also back in the day when there were more black bears per square mile living on Stockton Island than in any other place in Wisconsin, maybe even any other place in the whole United States."

"Grampy, what is bears per mile?"

"More bears per square mile? That just means that if you were to walk around on Stockton Island, it would be more likely that you would see a bear there than if you walked in the woods any other place.

"So Lala and Grampy took a big boat from Bayfield out to Stockton Island. We took along our tent and sleeping bags and swimming suits and Lala's kayak."

"But Grampy, where did they put Lala's kayak on the boat?"

"Wow, you have lots of questions tonight. It's no wonder you are having trouble getting to sleep. Lala's kayak fit on top of the big boat. So did our camping equipment. There were even other people on the big boat beside Lala and Grampy. It was a very big boat.

"When the big boat arrived at Stockton Island, Lala and Grampy took our camping equipment down a long path along the beach to a beautiful campsite. Then Lala went back to the dock where the big boat had stopped and let us off to get her kayak and paddled it across the bay to the place where we were going to set up our tent."

"Is that when you and Lala saw the bears?"

"No, we didn't see any bears yet. Even though there were lots of bears on Stockton Island, the bears didn't necessarily walk right into your camp to say hello. Black bears are usually pretty shy around humans and stay away from them. But if they smell food and find some in a campsite or if humans feed them, the bears become less shy and walk right into your campsite looking for a free meal. Also, if a mama bear has babies—they're called cubs—the mama bear can be very protective of her cubs, just like your mom tries to protect you. For example, your mother makes sure that you look both ways and hold her hand when you cross the street."

"Do baby bears hold the mama bear's hand when they cross the street?"

"Well no, mama bears don't really have to worry about crossing streets with their cubs on Stockton Island. There aren't even any roads on Stockton Island, only trails. But the mama bears want to make sure that no humans or anything else harm their cubs. So you do have to be careful not to get between a mama bear and her cubs.

"Your mom just called from downstairs and said that we should have a little bit less chit-chat and speed this story up a bit so that you can actually get to sleep. Also, she wants me to make sure to tell you both that black bears aren't so dangerous, so thinking about them after the story is done keeps you awake.

"So for two days, Lala and Grampy slept in our tent at night and went swimming and hiking during the day and we paddled around the bay in Lala's kayak but we didn't see any bears. And each night after we ate supper and were ready to go to sleep, we put our food and even our dishes into a special metal box where the bears could not get it."

"Why couldn't the bears open the box?"

"Well, the box for the food was made of strong steel, and it had a door with a latch on it. So people could open the door with their hands, but bears don't have hands, they just have paws with claws. So although the bears might be able to smell the food in the box, they would not be able to get it open."

"But if they can smell the food, why don't they just stay by the box until a human comes along to open up the box?"

"I think they would get hungry and bored waiting for the humans and they would go away to find something to eat in the forest.

"So getting back to the story—after two days of camping on Stockton Island, the big boat came again to the dock and Grampy and Lala packed up our tent and sleeping bags, our stove and cooking equipment and our clothes and took all of our stuff back to the dock. Lala carried some of it in her kayak across the bay and Grampy stuffed more of it into a backpack. Lala left the campsite first and paddled away. Grampy got the backpack on his shoulders and started down the trail back to the dock.

"Just as Grampy started down the trail, he heard a young woman call to him from behind. 'Hey, look over here, look over here,' she yelled. Grampy thought that she was trying to tease him so after she yelled again, I stopped walking, turned around slightly to glance back at her and gave her a little wave. Then I started walking faster down the trail back to the dock. Grampy thought, 'Some people go camping on Stockton Island to get away from other humans and especially from other humans who yell at them.'

"When Grampy made it back to the dock, Lala was already there with her kayak on the dock ready to load it onto the big boat. The young woman who had yelled, 'Hey, look over here,' to Grampy caught up with me at the dock. She was going to get on the big boat, too.

"'Didn't you see the bears?' she asked Grampy. 'No, what bears?' Grampy said. Grampy felt kind of dumb because I had missed something, and I now understood that the young woman hadn't been trying to tease me. She told Grampy that when she called to me on the trail, three bears were crossing the trail between her and Grampy, a mother bear and two little cubs. The young woman called to Grampy to make me turn around so I could see the three bears."

"Did the two little bears hold on to their mother's paw when they crossed the trail?"

"Well, I don't think so. It was only a trail out in the woods. And remember, even though Grampy turned around and waved to the young woman, I never looked down toward the ground to see the bears crossing the trail between me and the young woman. But after finding out that the woman really was trying to help Grampy see the bears, Grampy decided that I should do a better job of listening to people who are trying to tell him something.

"Now do you two know what those three bears do in winter?"

"They go to sleep. It's called hibernate."

"That's right. Those two little cub bears crawl under a tree stump and dig out a bit of dirt to make what is called a den. Then winter comes and it starts to snow, and the snow covers most of the den like a warm blanket. The two little bear cubs fall asleep in their warm den and they are so sleepy that they stay in the den and sleep for the entire winter. And now you two little bear cubs need to crawl into your beds as if they were dens and fall asleep just like the two little bear cubs in the story."

"Do we need to sleep all winter?"

"No, just sleep until tomorrow morning. Then we will get up again and play some more."

"Can we play camping?"

"We can play whatever you want. Now go to sleep. Mama Bear says no more chit-chat."

YORK ISLAND

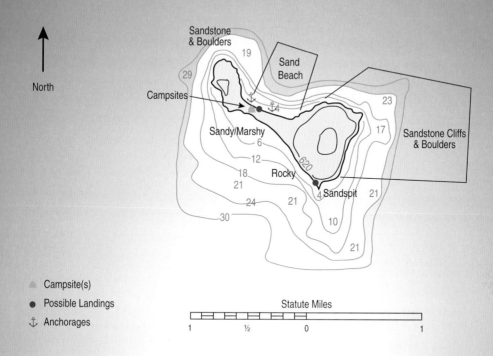

North

Sandstone & Boulders

Sand Beach

Campsites

Sandy/Marshy

Rocky

Sandspit

Sandstone Cliffs & Boulders

19
29
23
17
6
12
18
620
21
24
21
4
21
30
10
21

🏕 Campsite(s)

● Possible Landings

⚓ Anchorages

Statute Miles

1   ½   0   1

York Island campsite (photo courtesy National Park Service)

Location

York Island lies 2 miles east of Swallow Point on Sand Island, 2.5 miles west of Raspberry Island, and about 1 mile north of Point Detour on the mainland.

Geography and History

Think of the shape of York Island as a very unbalanced weight lifting barbell with only half of a smaller weight attached to the westerly end of the bar and a much larger weight attached to its easterly end. The "bar" between the two ends of the barbell is a sandy tombolo less than 0.25 mile wide. When Henry W. Bayfield, a British naval lieutenant, surveyed the islands in 1824, York Island may actually have been two rocky islands (the smaller and larger weights at the ends of the barbell) separated by shallow water over the developing sandy tombolo.[32]

The larger barbell on the east rises about 40 feet above the water—twice as high above the water compared to the smaller western weight of the barbell. Both ends of the island have enough sandstone and soil cover over their rocky surface to support a growth of deciduous as well as coniferous trees. The sandy isthmus between the two ends of the island is low and the vegetation is limited to alder shrubs with intermittent larger birches and conifers.

The entire island is about 1.25 miles long northwest to southeast and the larger eastern barbell is just under 0.75 mile in diameter. The smaller western end of the barbell is only a few hundred yards wide. At 321 acres, York is one of the smaller islands.

The island's "recent" history perhaps provides its most interesting segment. For over forty years prior to the 1970s when the federal government took ownership of most of York Island, it was owned by the Allen family. The family gave a two- to three-acre parcel to the local rural government (Town[ship] of Russell) in which the island is located. But a few years prior to the purchase of ownership by the U.S. government, the Allen family lost something even more dear than ownership

of the island. On June 30, 1967, then twenty-year-old Marine Lance Corporal Merlin Allen went missing in action in Vietnam. His remains were recovered in 2012 and were brought back home. After a memorial service in Bayfield on June 29, 2013, his ashes were interred next to the graves of his parents on the parcel now still owned by the Town of Russell. If you encounter the site of the memorial, pay your respect to L.Cpl. Allen and his family.

Shoreline and Landings

Two areas on the island offer great landing sites—the sandspit that points south toward the mainland on the south side of the easterly end of the barbell and the 0.5-mile long sandy beach located on the north side of the "bar" between the two "weights" on the ends of the barbell. The shoreline becomes increasingly rocky going north from the sandspit, turning to sandstone shelves on the north coast of the eastern portion of the island and maintaining the rocky banks as the shoreline curves back to the south and reaches the sandy beach. West of the sandy beach, the shoreline again becomes rocky with large sandstone boulders extending into the water as the western end of the island is rounded. The southern backside of the sandbar is somewhat marshy with vegetation close to the waterline. From the tombolo to the sandspit, the southwestern shoreline changes from a sandy to a rocky bottom before again becoming sandy at the sandspit. In calm weather, careful landings could be made along the southerly shoreline and perhaps on rock shelves on the northern and eastern shoreline of the larger weight of the barbell.

Camping

Primitive camping is not allowed on York Island, but there are three individual designated campsites located along the half mile beach on the north side. These campsites have a vault toilet, fire ring, and food locker, but no other amenities. In recent years, wind

York Island campsite beach (photo by author).

and waves, aided by higher water levels, have pushed sand into the campsites, limiting their use.

The three campsites located along York Island's long beach become a wonderful place to spend a sunny afternoon and evening. Much of the wooded area south of the beach is low and provides a wonderful nursery for mosquitoes and other insects. Their distinctive whine warns the camper to enter the tent early. A northerly breeze may keep most of the insects off the beach, but if the breeze develops into a northerly wind, launching a kayak from the beach will become more difficult.

Hiking

There are no hiking trails on the island, but hiking once back and forth along the beach provides an easy walk of a mile or more. More strenuous, but shorter, hikes on either end of the island are also a possibility.

Kayak Trip Suggestions

York Island can provide a steppingstone for the first or last day of a trip originating from Little Sand Bay. The campsites can also be used as a destination for a one- or two-day trip featuring some exploration and major relaxation on the beautiful beach. Using York Island as a base camp, a paddler could do 8-mile round trips to visit the sea caves and lighthouse on Sand Island or the lighthouse on Raspberry Island.

DON'T YOU EVER GET SEASICK?

When they find out that you kayak on Lake Superior, most people who have never been in a kayak ask two questions—"Aren't you afraid of tipping over?" and "Don't you get seasick?" To the first question I always answer, "Yes, but I have never tipped over unintentionally in my own kayak," and to the second question, I answer, "Yes, but only once."

The seasickness occurred on a solo trip to York Island.

Maybe it was the rush to leave work early on Friday afternoon and make it to Bayfield to get a camping permit before the park office closed for the day. I had made the drive from the Madison area north to Bayfield in the shortest time ever with no stops along the way. I beat closing time at the park office by only fifteen minutes. My early arrival allowed me to add a first night camping stop on York Island to my weekend itinerary. Armed with my camping permit, I jogged across the park headquarter's parking lot back to my car, and I continued with the rush mentality for the last leg of my drive to Little Sand Bay. It would be light till 8:30 or 9:00 p.m., and I had time to reach Little Sand Bay early enough to launch and paddle to York Island to set up camp before dark. Before launching I paused only briefly to make sure I had not forgotten to pack something major like a tent or a sleeping bag in my kayak.

Perhaps moving so quickly from workweek rules to Lake Superior rules did not allow my mind and body sufficient time to adjust. I launched and started paddling across Little Sand Bay with the same vigor I felt in the long drive north. But now my arms and shoulders were providing the energy for transportation previously provided by my car. In my mind I was still in the rushing mode when I approached the mainland at the west side of Point Detour and altered my heading toward the sandspit on York Island.

The water was neither flat nor heavy. The southwesterly breeze that had helped me in my rush across the bay now continued to try to push my stern to the east and make me head in a more northwesterly direction. But wait, as I started the crossing there was an irregular set of waves coming from the east causing a confusing chop of waves of 1 to 2 feet. Perhaps the size of the waves and the confusion of the seas were enhanced by the relatively shallow water between the mainland and York Island or perhaps it was caused by the currents that move along the western channel past York and Sand Islands. My gaze dropped from the York Island sandspit to the conflicting waves churning only a few feet in front of my kayak. My pace slowed as I tried to anticipate the irregular crests and valleys. A wave from the west would dampen my left elbow, then a wave from the right would splash high enough to pool water in my spray skirt. I could feel the cold dribble of water through my spray skirt onto my right hip.

Then there it was—a sudden gut-wrenching twist in my stomach together with a sort of dizziness in my head. Frightening. It was late in the day. I was alone half a mile from either York Island or the mainland. Nausea and dizziness could very quickly lead to a different answer to the first question, "Aren't you afraid of tipping over." That is, assuming I would have the opportunity of answering that question again.

"Arrrgh," I yelled like a pirate to no one but myself.

I needed to regain control of my body and mind. I raised the direction of my gaze above the water and back to the destination and consciously started a regular paddle cadence disregarding the confusing seas. My purpose in paddling no longer was to reach York Island quickly. Now the regular strokes were intended to provide physical and mental stability. There really was no rush. After all I still had at least two hours of daylight.

Thankfully it worked. I had regained control over my mind and body. While waves still cooled my elbows and occasionally pooled water on my spray skirt, the dizziness and nausea disappeared.

"Arrrgh," I yelled again, this time defiantly to the wind and waves and lake. I thought, "You are not going to make me tip over, at least not this time."

The last rays of sunset (photo by Mark Weller).

However, as a concession to the elements, I also counseled myself to adjust to the rules of the lake. "Pay attention. You are not sitting at your desk or in your car anymore. You are now on lake time."

The wind waves emanating from several directions seemed to calm as I paddled past the sandspit and the rock shelves, turned the corner, and headed west toward my camp-site on the lee side of York Island. The sun was setting over the western portion of the island on a beautiful summer evening, and the long sand beach beckoned me.

MAWIKWE BAY/ MEYERS BEACH

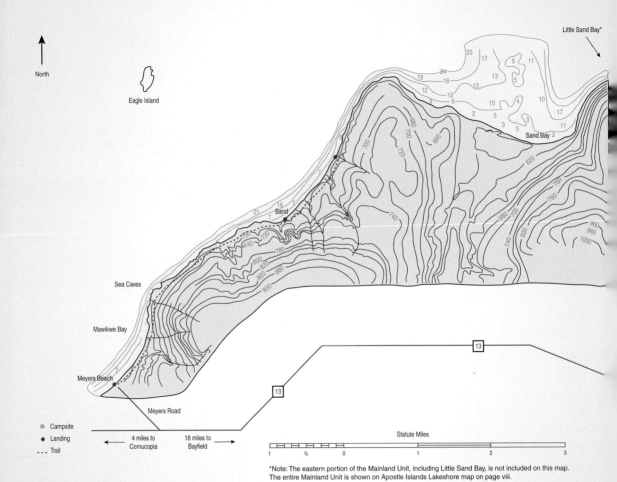

North

Eagle Island

Little Sand Bay*

Sand Bay

Sea Caves

Mawikwe Bay

Meyers Beach

Meyers Road

▲ Campsite
● Landing
--- Trail

← 4 miles to Cornucopia   18 miles to Bayfield →

Statute Miles

*Note: The eastern portion of the Mainland Unit, including Little Sand Bay, is not included on this map. The entire Mainland Unit is shown on Apostle Islands Lakeshore map on page viii.

Location

Meyers Beach and Mawikwe Bay are located at the western edge of the Mainland Unit of the Apostle Islands National Lakeshore. Meyers Road, providing access to Lake Superior and Meyers Beach, bridges the 0.3-mile distance between Highway 13 and the Lake Superior shore. To reach the Meyers Road intersection, follow Highway 13 about 4 miles northeast of Cornucopia or about 18 miles west of Bayfield and look for the National Park Service sign. There is a small parking lot at the end of Meyers Road on a clay bank above the sand beach. The stairway from the parking lot to the beach may be modified in the future to provide better accessibility.

Geography and History

Until its official name change in 2007, Mawikwe Bay was called Squaw Bay, but the former name was considered derogatory and crude, so the name change was requested by the National Park Service with the approval of the Red Cliff Band of Ojibwe and the local governments. "Mawikwe" (pronounced Mah' wee kway) means weeping woman and is a name that is perhaps closer in meaning to the original Ojibwe word used to name the bay.[33]

Unlike the locations described in the other chapters of this book, Meyers Beach is not an island at all, but rather a beautiful sand beach almost a mile long. At the northeastern end of the beach, the shoreline shifts to sandstone cliffs with sea caves carved out at the waterline by wave action driven by north and northwest winds.

Beside picnic and sunbather access to Meyers Beach in summertime, Meyers Road also provides a launch site for kayak trips to the mainland sea caves in summer and pedestrian access to the same sea caves encrusted in ice in winter. Increasingly, warmer weather has prevented "safe" ice from forming on Mawikwe Bay, and access to view the "ice caves" has become limited to nonexistent. In 2014, for the first time in five years, a substantially colder winter froze the bay and most of Lake Superior

Looking out from mainland sea cave, January, 2014 (photo by Author).

Venturing deep into the groove in 2008 (photo by Don Hynek).

from mid-January to mid-March and allowed over 138,000 people to make the cold 3-mile round trip to the ice caves on foot. To put the number of 2014 winter visitors in perspective, the number of winter visitors equaled over 90 percent of the number of visitors to all of the National Lakeshore during all of 2013. Since 2014, the ice was deemed safe in only one year (2015) for a period of about ten days.

Shoreline and Landings

Although crowded in late July and August, the kayaker can usually find room to stop and unload equipment at the top of the stairs above the beach before parking in the parking lot. Use of the parking lot requires a daily fee collected on a self-serve basis. It is possible to launch or land at any point on the long beach unless a strong wind from the north or northwest creates unmanageable surf on the beach. To the northeast of the beach, about a mile from the parking lot stairway, the shoreline becomes rocky and sandstone cliffs make a landing impossible. If the surf makes launching difficult, it will also make viewing the sea caves at the base of the cliffs too dangerous, and it will be wise to wait for better weather before launching.

After paddling northeast along about 3 miles of sandstone cliff shoreline, the shoreline explorer will find another long sand

Sea cave silhouette (photo by Don Hynek).

beach on the mainland shore (sometimes called "Lunch Beach" because sea cave visitors stop there) before the shoreline again becomes rocky around Sand Point.

The General Management Plan for the Apostle Islands National Lakeshore includes a possible future handicap ramp to make the beach accessible.

Camping

The only mainland camping in the Apostle Islands National Lakeshore is a walk-in (or paddle-to) campsite accessible from the trailhead at the Meyers Beach parking lot. It is a remote campsite requiring a 6-mile hike from the trailhead (or beach). The campsite has a fire ring, tent pad, bearproof food locker, a stump privy, and picnic table.

Hiking

The mainland trail to the campsite provides an opportunity for a 6-mile (one way) hike with a grand view of Eagle Island and a cliff-top view of sea caves (about 2 to 3 miles from the trailhead. A hiker can also walk along the beach for about a mile, crossing several small creeks that empty into the lake.

In winter, if ice conditions allow, there will be a packed snow trail along the shoreline or across the near shore ice. Initially, before the trail becomes packed by many visitors' feet, snowshoes or skis may be helpful, however, later, after visitors' boots have packed down the snow, good boots, perhaps supplemented with ice grippers, warm clothing, and possibly walking sticks, will be what is needed to make the mile-plus walk to the beginning of the ice formations. The Park Service monitors the ice conditions and will open and close the winter trail to the ice caves as conditions change, but any winter hiker should undertake the responsibility of being aware of dangerous conditions, including open water and large icicles that can fall on the unwary visitor from the roof of the caves. The National Park Service maintains a report of winter ice conditions online and on a recorded telephone message at (715) 779-3397.

Kayak Trip Suggestions

Because of its distance from the islands in the National Lakeshore, Meyers Beach does not provide a convenient launch site for multi-day trips. However, it is the perfect launch site to explore quality sea caves along the mainland shore. For many, a half-day or full-day trip with an outfitter is as much kayaking as they desire. For more avid paddlers, Meyers Beach may provide an alternative day trip if there is a southerly to southeasterly wind delaying a planned trip from the mainland. Always check the weather forecast and real time waves and visuals (http://go.nps.gov/ApostleWaves) before launching at Meyers Beach, and stay off the water if the wind is, or will become, too strong from the west to the northeast. A real time check of current conditions just before launch may be made by viewing the monitor in the small building at the top of the stairs above the beach or by checking online at http://wavesatseacaves.cee.wisc.edu. There have been kayaker fatalities at or near the sea caves.

Meyers Beach is also the ideal launch site for a day trip to Eagle Island, which is located about 2.5 miles northwest of the sea caves. Coming within 500 feet of Eagle Island is prohibited between May 15 and September 1

Meyers Beach in January (photo by Paul Matteoni).

to protect it as a nesting area for birds. If you paddle out to Eagle Island, check out the shallow water to the southwest of the island. In this shallow area Eagle Island used to have a smaller companion island named Steamboat Island, which disappeared completely as a result of a storm in late July of 1901.[34]

Meyers Beach on a warm summer day (photo courtesy National Park Service).

... SOME SAY IN ICE

The second line of Robert Frost's *"Fire and Ice"* may have been on the minds of at least some of the 138,292 people who visited Mawikwe Bay in the winter of 2014. With daytime temperatures in the teens or less and windchill rarely rising above 5 degrees F, it was hard for any visitor to imagine a world with enough desire to end in Frost's preferred fire. The parking lot was full and cars were lined up along most of Meyers Road. In spite of the cold, passengers donned snowmobile suits, parkas, and heavy boots to walk over a mile across the ice and along the shoreline to see the ice caves. The near record cold weather allowed winter visitors over two months to view the ice caves. Warmer winters causing treacherous ice conditions had kept most winter visitors away since 2009.

Winter sunset looking across Mawikwe Bay (photo by author).

To put the number of visitors to the sea caves in perspective, the average annual attendance for the entire Apostle Islands National Lakeshore in the previous five-year period was 163,032. The first three months of 2014 produced over 93 percent of the number of visitors for all of 2013.

The surge in numbers may have been due to the Internet coverage that the sea caves received. One would expect the beauty of the caves to be reported on websites with a Wisconsin and Minnesota base; but articles and pictures were also posted on a variety of national news and feature organizations, including Slate, CNN, Huffington Post, NBC, Smithsonian magazine, and Esquire.

Perhaps underlying the story of the ice caves is the story about how "news" is gathered in current times. A news agency trolls the Internet, hits an interesting storyline reported by a local news source or a competitor, and assigns a reporter to the story. Maybe the reporter actually makes a trip to the location or hires a local photographer and reporter/writer, but more likely the article is produced from the Internet sources and telephone or email interviews with someone close to the scene. Such coverage makes for economically sound news reporting. Such coverage also becomes widely read.

The people who read about the caves on the Internet and came to see them were not limited to Wisconsin, Minnesota, Iowa, and Illinois either. While no official polling was done (it requires pre-approval and there wasn't time), informal reviews of license plates and word of mouth would indicate that visitors came from all over the United States as well as from China, Japan, Australia, Hungary, and Chile, although some of the foreign

Fire and Ice—Sunset reflected on ice wall opposite sea arch (photo by Paul Matteoni).

visitors may already have been in the United States for other reasons.

The crowds coming to the caves required the National Park Service to gear up in a time when park activities are normally at a minimum. The National Lakeshore staff shrinks at the end of the summer season, and the park service was still adjusting to the sequester budget cuts that occurred earlier in 2013. As the ice cave viewing season progressed through February and into March, park rangers were summoned to the National Lakeshore from around the region, including special teams trained in crowd handling.

As you would expect, a percentage of the visitors slipped and fell on the ice and were taken to local medical facilities. The visitors also ate, drank, and sought overnight lodging. Cornucopia, Red Cliff, Bayfield, and Washburn, normally serving an occasional winter visitor interested in snowmobiling, skiing, and other winter sports, became thriving winter communities more comparable to summertime levels. Some stores, normally closed for the season, opened their doors at least on weekends, and skeleton wintertime staff worked overtime to ready lodging facilities for the next weekend rush. The Friends of the Apostle Islands National Lakeshore, Inc. support group served hot chocolate to many of the visitors.

Although written by Robert Frost over 100 years ago, long before most of us became aware of climate change, "Fire and Ice" provides us with a backdrop for reflecting on the differences between an icy winter visit to Mawikwe Bay and another very different visit on a warm summer afternoon. Experiencing nature in its extremes may even make us wonder about how the world will end.

Holding up the sea arch (photo by Paul Matteoni).

Notes

1 Busch, Jane C., Ph.D., *People and Places: A Human History of the Apostle Islands.* Prepared under contract to Midwest Regional Office, National Park Service, United States Department of the Interior, 2008, page 33; on line at www.nps.gov/apis/historyculture/upload/Historic%20Resource%20Study.pdf

2 Warren, William W., *History of the Ojibways, based upon traditions and oral statements.* Minnesota Historical Society, St. Paul, 1885.

3 Busch, Ibid, pp.244–265.

4 http://www.nps.gov/apis/upload/APIS-GMP-short-version.pdf.

5 http://www.coldwaterbootcamp.com

6 "Sand Island At Apostle Islands National Lakeshore Closed To All Visitors Due To Bears." National Parks Traveler, www.nationalparkstraveler.com. Submitted by NPT Staff on July 7, 2013.

7 Strzok, Dave; *A Visitor's Guide to the Apostle Islands National Lakeshore.* Superior Printing and Specialties, 1988,

8 *The Milwaukee Journal,* October 1, 1939. p.1.

9 Mackreth, Bob, "Rescuing the Keeper's Daughter," Apostle Island Scrapbook, http://www.bobmackreth.com.

10 http://www.bobmackreth.com/Scrapbook/hermit.htm.

11 Warren, William W., *History of the Ojibway Nation.* Collections of the Minnesota Historical Society, Vol. V, published 1885, reprinted 1897, pp. 102–4.

12 Noble, Vergil E., "The 1992 Archeological Survey of Long Island, Lake Superior, Apostle Islands National Lakeshore." Technical Report No. 47, U.S. Department of the Interior, National Park Service, Midwest Archeological Center, Lincoln, Nebraska, 1996.

13 Noble, p. 22.

14 Warren, William, *History of the Ojibway People.* Minnesota Historical Society Press, 1984.

15 Dahl, Bonnie, *Superior Way, Third Edition, The Cruising Guide to Lake Superior.* Lake Superior Port Cities Inc., 2001, p. 110.

16 Nute, Grace Lee, *Lake Superior.* University of Minnesota Press, 2000.

17 Dahl, op cit., p.134.

18 Strzok, Dave, *Visitor's Guide to the Apostle Islands,* p. 57.

19 Constructed from information at www.nutritiondata.com.

20 http://www.nps.gov/apis/historyculture/outer-light.htm

21 Wisconsin's Maritime Trails, Wisconsin State Historical Society, http://www.maritimetrails.org/

22 Sasse, Timothy, http://sassmaster.tripod.com/

23 Mackreth, Bob, http://www.bobmackreth.com/blog/?p=3717

24 www.cbsnews.com/news/what-is-the-origin-of-the-word-boss

25 Nelson, Robert J., *Apostle Islanders: The People & Culture.* Blue Box Press, 2011.

26 Nelson, ibid, p.95

27 Nelson, ibid, pp.32–3.

28 Jones, Meg, "Clock is Ticking for last Apostle Island Lifers." *Milwaukee Journal Sentinel,* August 17, 2013, www.jsonline.com

29 Nelson, Robert J., *Apostle Islanders,* p.57.

30 Busch, "People and Places," pp. 245, 251.

31 Busch, "People and Places," p. 226.

32 Strzok, Dave, *A Visitor's Guide to the Apostle Islands National Lakeshore.* Superior Printing and Specialties, 1988.

33 "It's Finally Official—Squaw Bay Renamed Mawikwe Bay." Apostle Islands news release, National Park Service, June 14, 2007, http://www.nps.gov/apis/parknews/upload/Mawikwe%20name%20change.pdf

34 *The New York Times,* August 2, 1901.

Resources

Camping

See the "Camping" section in each chapter. There is also a listing of campgrounds outside the National Lakeshore at the end of the "Camping" chapter.

Chambers of Commerce

(Accommodations, Restaurants, Points of Interest)

Bayfield Chamber and Visitor Bureau
42 South Broad St | P.O. Box 138
Bayfield, WI 54814
715-779-3335
http://bayfield.org

Cornucopia Business Association
P.O. Box 224
Cornucopia, WI 54827
715-742-3232 (Ehler's Store)
https://visitcornucopia.com/

Madeline Island Chamber of Commerce
P.O. Box 274
La Pointe, WI 54850
(715) 747-2801
https://www.madelineisland.com/

Washburn Area Chamber of Commerce
100 W. Bayfield St. | P.O. Box 74
Washburn, WI 54891
715-373-5017
https://washburnchamber.com/

Cruise Boats, Ferries, Water Taxis, Charters

(Visit https://go.nps.gov/Outfitters for information on current authorized services)

Apostle Islands Cruises
2 Front Street
Bayfield, WI 54814
800-323-7619
http://www.apostleisland.com

Dreamcatcher Sailing
P.O. Box 159 100 Rittenhouse Ave
Bayfield, Wisconsin 54814
715-779-5561
https://www.dreamcatcher-sailing.com/

Escape Excursions
37600 Onigamiing Dr
Red Cliff, WI 54814
612-805-7454
https://www.escapeexcursion.com/

Good Earth Outfitters, LLC
22670 Siskiwit Bay Parkway
Cornucopia, WI 54827
715-742-3910
www.good-earth-outfitters.com

Nourse Charters
78390 Washington Avenue
Washburn, WI 54891
715-292-9115
www.noursecharters.com

PMG Charters
P.O. Box 1519
Bayfield, WI 54814
262-337-3078 & 641-757-2796
www.pmgcharters.com

Superior Charters Inc.
34475 Port Superior Road
Bayfield, WI 54814
715-779-5124
www.superiorcharters.com

Willigan's Adventures
Mail: 110 Main St S., Cambridge, MN 55008
Local: 37735 Roy's Point Boulevard, Bayfield, WI 54814
763-381-7076
www.willigans.com

National Park Service

(Current information on Camping, Closures, Authorized Services, Water Taxis, etc.)

Apostle Islands National Lakeshore
415 Washington Avenue
Bayfield, WI 54814
(715)779-3397
http://www.nps.gov/apis

Outfitters

(Kayak instruction, daytrips overnight kayak camping)

Adventure Vacations
P.O. Box 476 | 104 Middle Rd
La Pointe, Wisconsin 54850
715-747-2100
www.adv-vac.com

Apostle Island Kayaking, LLC
2 Front Street & 88260 State Highway 13
Bayfield, WI 54814
715-779-9503
https://aikayaking.com/

Apostle Islands Kayaks
690 Main Street
LaPointe, Wisconsin 54850-0498
715-747-3636
www.apostleislandskayaks.com

Lost Creek Adventures
22475 Highway 13
Cornucopia, Wisconsin 54827
715-953-2223
www.lostcreekadventures.org

Rustic Makwa Den
37600 Onigamiing Dr
Red Cliff, WI 54814
715-209-3216
https://rusticmakwaden.com/

Trek and Trail
P.O. Box 832
7 Washington Ave
Bayfield, Wisconsin 54814
800-354-8735
www.trek-trail.com

Whitecap Kayak
31375 Wannebo Rd
Washburn, WI 54891
715-513-6196
www.whitecapkayak.com

Wilderness Inquiry
1611 County Rd B West, Suite 315
St. Paul, MN 55113

33095 Little Sand Bay Rd
Bayfield, WI 54814 (local address)
612-676-9400
www.wildernessinquiry.org

Nonprofits

(NGOs supporting the Apostle Islands National Lakeshore)

Apostle Islands Historic Preservation Conservancy
P.O. Box 88
Bayfield, WI 54814
www.aihpc.org

Bayfield Heritage Association
PO Box 137
30 North Broad Street
Bayfield, Wisconsin 54814
715-779-5958
www.bayfieldheritage.org

Friends of the Apostle Islands National Lakeshore
PO Box 1574
Bayfield, WI 54814
715-449-6900
http://www.friendsoftheapostleislands.org

National Parks Conservation Association
Minnesota Field Office
546 Rice Street, Ste. 100
St. Paul, MN 55103
612-270-8564
http://www.npca.org

National Parks of Lake Superior Foundation
420 Summit Avenue,
St Paul, MN 55102
651-681-1566
http://www.nplsf.org

About the Author

Before his retirement from the practice of law in 2012, the natural beauty and solitude of the Apostle Islands National Lakeshore provided John Frank with a series of wonderful escapes from the routines of work and everyday life. As he fell in love with the area in the early 1990s, he promised himself a kayak visit to each of the islands in the archipelago. Twenty years later that promise was fulfilled, and it seemed very natural to put some of the things he learned and experienced into a guidebook as a thank you gift to the National Lakeshore that he loves.

Some things have changed in the Apostle Islands National Lakeshore over the last thirty years, and they will continue to change in the future. While the Apostle Islands National Lakeshore will continue to be protected by governmental ownership, increasingly, in order to thrive, our public lands and parks will need greater support, both moral and financial, from the people who enjoy them.

The Apostle Islands National Lakeshore is lucky to have several nonprofit organizations dedicated to that support, and the author invites those who use this book to consider helping them—particularly the Friends of the Apostle Islands—as a means of preserving these island gems in Lake Superior. The nonprofits may well be the key to maintaining the National Lakeshore as a welcome destination for escaping from everyday routines in generations to come.

If you enjoy the beauty, the solitude, and the basic lessons of the natural world, take a water trip and start your own love affair with the Apostle Islands National Lakeshore.